A. PAUL MAHAFFY

BUSINESS SUCCESSION GUIDE
THIRD EDITION

CARSWELL®

A cataloguing record for this publication is available from Library and Archives Canada.

ISBN: 978-0-7798-5394-6

Composition: Computer Composition of Canada Inc.

Printed in Canada by Thomson Reuters

TELL US HOW WE'RE DOING

Scan the QR code to the right with your smartphone to send your comments regarding our products and services.
Free QR Code Readers are available from your mobile device app store.
You can also email us at carswell.feedback@thomsonreuters.com

 THOMSON REUTERS

CARSWELL, A DIVISION OF THOMSON REUTERS CANADA LIMITED

One Corporate Plaza	Customer Relations
2075 Kennedy Road	Toronto 1-416-609-3800
Toronto, Ontario	Elsewhere in Canada/U.S. 1-800-387-5164
M1T 3V4	Fax: 1-416-298-5082
	www.carswell.com
	E-mail www.carswell.com/email

To Cynthia

Acknowledgments

At the beginning of the first edition of this book, I mentioned that I had helped a number of clients to sell their companies during 2006 but that I didn't seem to have helped any clients in buying companies during that same year. I wondered why, since the odds of that occurring in any given year appeared to be fairly low. I felt that the number of purchases and number of sales over my years of business law practice had been roughly even. Perhaps I had arrived at a certain stage in my career when everyone I knew was selling and not buying. Maybe the looming retirement of the baby boom generation was closer than I thought.

Whatever might have been the reason that I advised a lot more sellers than buyers that year, I realized that my owner clients would have bene-fited at the time from a guidebook that walked them through the process of selling their companies, from start to finish. For almost all of them, it was the first time they had ever sold a company.

It was as if they were about to become travellers in a foreign land and they wanted a travel guide with enough information to give them the confidence and comfort to embark on the journey. Even though I and the other professional advisors involved may have helped those owners to better understand what was going on, the owners still appeared to want something that could give them a bit more control of the process, some-thing that might make sense of the perceived randomness of it all. Their desire for that something was the reason for this book.

Now years later, the desire of owners to understand the business suc-cession process remains strong, perhaps even stronger in light of the challenges created by the Great Recession. Finding willing buyers with adequate financing seems more difficult than before.

Although this third edition is dedicated to the overall purpose of the first two editions in attempting to describe the process owners go through when transferring ownership of their companies, it contains two new "overview" chapters, one dealing with the creation of a written business succession plan, and the other dealing with the plan's implementation. It also contains expanded versions of the chapters on *Valuation* and *Family Trust Agreements* which appeared in the second edition.

I am grateful to my clients for giving me the insights and inspiration I've needed to write all three editions of this book. I've become an observer and recorder of their experiences and am thankful that I can pass along the learning from those experiences to other owners about to embark on the same journey.

While some of my clients have considered passing ownership of their companies on to their children, and others have thought that their employees or fellow shareholders might have been possible buyers, most of them have ended up selling their companies to outsiders. For that reason, much of this book is devoted to doing a deal with an outside buyer.

One of the chapters, describing purchase and sale agreements, reflects the thoughts and experiences of four colleagues of the Ontario Bar with whom I was privileged to work in preparing annotated share purchase and asset purchase agreements for continuing professional development programs sponsored by the Law Society of Upper Canada. Frank Herbert and Paul Wickens, and later Jordan Dolgin and David Street, were great collaborators.

In preparing the different editions of this book, I have been fortunate to have received the advice and encouragement of Sarah Payne, Todd Pinsky and Lisa Gordon, all of Carswell.

Contents

Introduction

As the baby boom generation approaches retirement age, the ownership of many closely-held companies will need to be transferred. While many transfers will be made to family members of the current owners, other transfers will be made to employees, other shareholders or outside parties. Transfers to each of these groups can involve quite different business issues. For the owner who has done little succession planning, retirement from the company may not be easily achieved.

The numerous issues related to business succession can seem overwhelming to the owner, who is certainly tempted to deal with them at a later time. The day-to-day problems of the company always seem to be more important and demand immediate attention.

But dealing with business succession needn't evoke anxiety although it may take more time and require more thought and soul-searching than the owner might expect. Some of the questions aren't easily answered. How much is the company worth? How can the ownership of the company be transferred on a tax efficient basis? How can the owner's risk be reduced or eliminated in the transfer? Should the owner stay involved afterwards with the company?

This book sets out many of the steps which a current owner might take when attempting to transfer ownership of the company. It will look at how the company might be valued, put into saleable condition, and reorganized to help defer or reduce taxes arising upon the transfer. It will look at how ownership can be transferred to family members, employees, other shareholders, or to outside parties, along with the process to be followed and some of the main documents to be used.

Because the process is complicated and the outcome not always certain, this book is designed to manage the owner's expectations, and to let him know what he's getting himself into.

Since one of the owner's main goals should be to ensure the survival of the company as a going concern, he will try to engage in some management succession planning to leave the company in "good hands". And since he must consider his ability to pay any taxes which become due upon the transfer of his ownership and his ability to afford a comfortable lifestyle and provide for his family afterwards, he will try to engage in some estate planning. Consequently, this book will touch on both management succession planning and estate planning, but it will be primarily concerned with the legal and tax issues related to ownership succession.

Although this book is mainly intended to assist the current owner in transferring ownership of the company while he is still alive, it will also attempt to discuss some of the issues which arise should the owner prefer to pass ownership to his family members upon his death through a will.

While this book assumes that the company has been incorporated under the *Canada Business Corporations Act*[1], or CBCA, many of the ideas expressed in this book will apply to companies wherever incorporated in Canada because most provincial companies acts are modelled after the CBCA, However, the reader should be aware that minor differences do exist and should consult the provincial act which may govern a particular company.

This book also assumes that the company is a private company. Although a private company is not specifically defined in the CBCA, it is often taken to be a company which has not issued its securities to the public, or is not a "distributing corporation" as defined in the CBCA.[2] It is also often taken to be a company which has "private company restrictions" in its articles of incorporation or other charter documents as prescribed by provincial securities legislation. These restrictions generally limit the number of shareholders, prevent share transfers without, for example, approval by a majority of directors or shareholders, and prohibit solicitations to the public to subscribe for company securities.[3]

Accordingly, all references in this book to the issuance or sale of the company's equity or debt securities assume that such transactions are exempt from the prospectus and registration requirements under such provincial legislation. Furthermore, in its references to various income tax implications, this book assumes that the company is a Canadian-controlled private corporation.[4]

In its references to a successor being selected by the current owner, this book generally assumes that the successor is the party intended by the owner to acquire ownership of the company. Furthermore, to be gender neutral in its references to the owner and other parties, and in place of he/she, this book will alternate such references between genders by chapter.

PRELIMINARY QUESTIONS

Before contemplating any of the steps set out in this book, the current owner has to ask himself a number of basic questions. Is he personally ready to retire? Is he prepared to disengage from the business, to finally let go? Does he have financial resources apart from the business? Will there be enough income from the business to pay him during his retirement? Will he be comfortably able to pay any taxes owing? Is he looking to the ownership transfer as the main source of his retirement income? If he retires, who will take over? If his successor requires that he stay on as a consultant to the business after the ownership transfer, will he agree? In essence, what goals should he set for himself?

The owner may not need to sell out. The company may have already established a retirement compensation arrangement or an individual pension plan for him, or undertaken to provide him with a substantial retiring allowance. Or he may have built up a sizeable registered retirement savings plan or non-registered investment portfolio, or acquired substantial holdings of income producing real estate. With sufficient financial assets, he may have more choices and be able to set different goals.

But the owner will still have to seriously question the goals he has set. Not all of the goals can comfortably co-exist, and in order to reconcile the conflicts which appear among them, he may be faced with some awkward choices. Some goals will have to be sacrificed when setting priorities.

For example, he may wish that all of the employees of the company continue to be employed by his successor at the same compensation and with the same benefits as they were provided by the owner. Or that each member of his family receives an equivalent amount of money following the sale of the company. Or that he will pay the minimum amount of tax. Or that his successor will provide uninterrupted service to all of the customers he worked so hard to please over the years. Or that he will be able to walk away from the company without any residual risks or liabilities. Only an extremely optimistic owner would consider all of these goals to be achievable at the same time.

Nevertheless, an owner has to be motivated by certain goals in order to undertake the process described in this book. If his overriding goal is wealth preservation for future generations, or the opportunity to generously contribute to a charitable cause, or simply to have enough freedom from responsibilities to travel or play golf whenever the mood strikes, such a goal may well be achieved. However, the process demands trade-offs, and whatever goals are set, they must be realistic and not become an obstacle to arriving at the compromises which are invariably required.

Some goals may not be easily achieved because the owner will have insufficient control over the process to assure a particular outcome. For example, even though the owner may insist that the business should stay within his family, and hope that family harmony will prevail once his ownership is passed on to at least one of his children, conflict and jealousy amongst his children may render his goal unsustainable. He may not be able to avoid family fights once he leaves.

In setting his goals, it may be difficult for the owner to separate his own identity from the business and to figure out what he wants to do without the business. His transition away from the business can take many forms. He may become a business mentor, sit on advisory committees or boards of directors of other companies, devote himself to charitable causes, or perform volunteer work within his community. If he remains involved with the company, he may work on special projects on a contract basis, or may possibly stay on as chairman of the board.

ASSEMBLING THE TEAM

Only in the rarest of circumstance will an owner be prepared to embark on this process alone. Even when attempting to set his goals and determine priorities, he will generally want someone to bounce ideas off, preferably someone who is impartial and not timid about offering unpopular or contrary views. That person may be a long-time professional adviser, perhaps a stockbroker, lawyer, or accountant, who has become quite familiar over the years with the owner's personal and business interests, yet has remained independent and objective throughout.

But while such a person may play a key role in facilitating the various decisions which the owner has to make during the process, there is nonetheless a broader group of advisers which the owner will need to assemble in order to properly deal with all of the various issues that will arise. Many of those issues can be quite technical and become overwhelming to an owner struggling to resolve them. The owner will need some help in interpreting and simplifying them. Although this book may attempt to identify some of those issues, it cannot replace the insight and experience which such additional advisers will apply when considering the owner's particular circumstances.

The members of such an advisory team will vary from one business succession to another, but the team will usually consist of a lawyer, accountant, valuator and tax adviser. Of the different advisory roles required to be performed, some may be performed by the same individual depending upon the skills and experience each may possess when joining the team.

Creating a Business Succession Plan

The owner's initial objective should be the creation of a written business succession plan. While the plan needs to address how ownership of the business is to be transferred, it may also address how management of the business is to be transferred, particularly in connection with ownership transfers to family members. It essentially takes into consideration not only the needs of the owner and her family but also the needs of the business. It may cover a variety of issues affecting the company's survival, such as any skills gap in leadership, and provide a long-range business plan.

The plan should reflect the input the owner has received from her team of advisers, but may also take into account the views expressed not only by the members of her own family but also by any senior managers of the business who are outside her family.

For those business succession plans that attempt to address management succession as well as ownership succession, the owner and her team will look at how major business decisions will be made and at how family members, business managers, and other shareholders if any, will relate to each other while the owner continues to be involved in the business as well as after the owner retires from active management or ceases to have an ownership stake. Many plans also provide for certain contingencies, such as the disability or death of the owner before the full succession has been completed, and include a certain amount of legal, tax and insurance planning.

WHY A PLAN IS NEEDED

Whatever specific goals the owner may have set for herself, she will likely want to protect her personal legacy in the company in order to secure her own future as well as the future of those who depend upon her. She will likely also want to benefit her employees and her community by maximizing the chances that the company's business will survive.

In the absence of a business succession plan, she could be forced to sell the company at a significant discount, or hand it off to inappropriate successors, or perhaps close the business entirely. Should the question of business succession be postponed to her death, the company will be placed in the hands of her executors who may be unskilled or unprepared in running the business. The business may simply not survive the administration of the owner's estate. Even her disability (including mental disability) prior to her death could also threaten the survival of the business.

If the owner is depending upon a future dividend stream from the company, or the proceeds from an eventual sale of the company, in order to fund her retirement, the company will have to remain profitable. Creating a business succession plan for the company will help to ensure its profitability.

A successful plan should generally attempt to satisfy a number of basic requirements. It should provide for the future needs of the owner and her family, while maintaining family harmony. It should provide for the financial stability of the company, and preferably provide for the company's growth and increase in value. It should also provide some stability for the company's employees. Finally, it should reduce the potential tax liabilities which may arise upon the transfer of company ownership, and set a timeline for when the transfer should take place.

To meet these basic requirements, the business succession plan should be integrated with the owner's personal financial plan, as well as her estate plan reflected in her will, to avoid any conflicts among them.

While the business succession plan attempts to manage a change in company ownership, the owner will likely have to manage a change in company management, at least for those ownership transfers to her children. In such cases, any management succession plan will have to be integrated with the owner's business succession plan.

For the purposes of this chapter, management succession planning in the content of family businesses is included in the overall discussion of the creation of a business succession plan.

OBSTACLES TO CREATING A PLAN

In the *Introduction* chapter, it was suggested that the numerous issues related to business succession can seem overwhelming to the owner, who will be tempted to deal with them at a later time. After all, the day-to-day problems of the company will always seem to be more important and demand immediate attention. Many of the questions which the owner needs to ask at the start of her business succession planning are not easily answered.

But the owner's inclination to postpone the planning process may be influenced by more than just the amount of time required, although the time required is often cited as the main reason why the owner should start planning sooner rather than later. A business succession plan takes considerable time to create and implement, and it will fail if it is rushed, or is not properly thought out and executed. Business succession may take years, and the plan needs to introduce some formality and certainty into the process.

Yet succession planning is still an emotional process. It involves a major life change.

The owner's biggest obstacle to creating a plan may actually be her strong personal attachment to the business. It may have been her life's passion as well as her life's work. Her decision to step aside after years of commitment is not easily made.

Deciding what she will do after she severs her connection with the business can be problematic as well. She may have few interests outside the business that can sustain her after she leaves. This prospect of idleness can represent a significant deterrent to creating her succession plan.

The emotional side of the planning process can be complicated when family relationships are taken into consideration. The possible conflicts which exist, or may arise, amongst her family members can create a real obstacle. The owner may be unwilling to start planning if she feels that she must favour one of her children over the others, or that her choices will create envy and resentment among them.

Although her family's involvement as described below throughout the planning process will help to reduce the severity of family conflicts and encourage the "buy-in" of family members, the potential for such conflicts to become major obstacles in creating a business succession plan should not be minimized or overlooked.

WHAT'S IN A PLAN

A business succession plan usually comprises a number of somewhat technical components. Although it is intended to generally set out how ownership of the business is to be transferred, it often covers at lot more.

Many plans address the relevant legal and tax considerations governing the transfer, the various issues affecting the owner's retirement, the desired time line, the mechanics of the transfer, and even the division of future profits after the transfer.

Where ownership is intended to stay within the owner's family, the plan will also reflect some management succession planning. It will ordinarily address the selection process, the required qualifications of the successor, the training and preparation of the successor, the key management roles to be played, and perhaps the means for resolving disputes.

But there are other "soft" issues that a business succession plan should consider in addition to the technical issues.

Many plans identify the owner's long-term personal and family goals as well as the goals of each family member, each individual's anticipated role in the business after succession, and how the plan will be communicated, monitored and possibly revised.

Sometimes a business succession plan appears to be a combination of a number of related but separate plans, possibly created at different times. In devising the overall succession plan, there might first be prepared a strategic plan for the business to figure out where the business is going. Next, a contingency plan might be prepared to address what should be done in the event the owner dies or becomes disabled before the succession plan is finalized. The contingency plan can address what might otherwise be the owner's estate plan covering the administration of her estate upon her death. Then a family participation plan might be prepared to deal with the various roles and entitlements of family members. And finally a management development plan might be prepared to provide the eventual successor with sufficient training and experience to become ready to take over.

WHO'S INVOLVED IN THE PLANNING

While the owner may prefer to keep her succession planning private and confidential, and to share her thoughts on succession only with her outside advisers, her plan may be doomed to fail if it doesn't reflect the input of her family members. She should never assume that any of her children wants to be the successor. The owner must ask each of her children directly about whether they want to take over.

While the intended successor has to be consulted in the creation of the plan, all of the company's "stakeholders" should get together to discuss common objectives. This group might include anyone who is affected by the succession, but should at least include all of the owner's immediate family and the company's senior employees.

It's important for the owner to keep her family and the senior employees informed throughout the planning process and to avoid springing any dramatic surprises on them. The employees should all be advised of their continuing roles in the company and the possible timing of any succession transaction.

Sharing the plan with others may reinforce the financial and managerial stability of the business and foster harmony among its various stakeholders. The company's employees, suppliers, bankers and customers may be reassured by the existence of a succession plan and remain confident that their own interests will be protected despite the owner's retirement from the business.

When dealing with her children during the planning process, the owner should try to deter her children from competing with each other, and discourage them from lobbying the owner in order to obtain specific favours.

The owner needs a way to regularly communicate with her family about business succession issues. She may decide to establish a "family council" comprised of the adult members of her family. The family council may meet regularly to keep the family informed about the company's business and may discuss more than just succession issues. The topics for family council meetings might include policies for family involvement in the company and the business education of younger members.

In addition to, or perhaps instead of, a family council, the owner may appoint a family "facilitator" to co-ordinate any meetings of family members which are convened to discuss succession issues.

There can be an advantage to using a facilitator to address any conflicts among family members. With the help of a facilitator, family members can discuss both management and ownership succession, particularly their personal roles and objectives in connection with the business. Since selecting a particular family member just to avoid a family conflict is not the way to get the most qualified successor, a facilitator can assist in the selection of a qualified successor who is supported by all of the owner's family.

These meetings of the owner's family can lead to the creation of a family participation plan that, as mentioned above, can be integrated into the overall business succession plan. A family participation plan might identify the experience and education which a family member needs to be involved in the business, how family members will be supervised and evaluated, and whether spouses and other family "in-laws" will be welcome to work in the business. It may also address who can own shares in the company, how family members will be treated if their involvement with the company doesn't work out, and what happens to those family members who are working elsewhere.

THE PLANNING PROCESS

In preparing the business succession plan, the owner and her advisory team first embark on gathering as much of the relevant information as possible, including obtaining through confidential interviews the views of family members, senior employees and possibly the representatives of major suppliers and the company's bank.

It is at this initial stage that the ability and motivations of potential successors as managers and owners can be explored, along with the financial rewards expected or deserved by family members, the existence of any conflicts among them, the desire of the owner for continuing control, and the owner's need for financial security. Eliciting the views of family members at this stage helps to support the planning process going forward and increases the likelihood that the family will accept the succession plan when it is eventually finalized.

While the owner and her team may then wish to share the results of their preliminary interviews and information gathering with the owner's family members, they must be careful not to divulge any confidential information obtained from one family member to the others, nor engage in debating or negotiating the various alternatives that the family feel should be taken into consideration in devising the plan.

These preliminary efforts usually lead to more detailed planning sessions. The planning sessions attempt to generate a number of alternative actions and analyze the merits and likelihood of transferring ownership to the owner's family as well as transferring ownership to the company's employees or other shareholders, or to outside parties.

If transferring ownership to family members is being considered, how and when the shares are to be transferred, and whether they will be given away or sold, or whether they will be the subject of an "estate freeze" as described in the *Transfers to Family - Part 1* chapter, are likely to be examined in these planning sessions.

In addition to identifying the potential successor when ownership is expected to remain within the family, the planning sessions will likely address a number of other specific issues relating to management succession and corporate governance. For example, what roles, if any, will be played by the owner after her ownership is transferred, what management duties will be assumed by family members, and what involvement in the company will family members have if they are not active in management? Should non-active family members be entitled to attend meetings of the directors or shareholders of the company, or to own shares in the company, or to receive some form of compensation from the company?

After the detailed planning sessions have concluded, the owner and her advisory team can prepare the written plan which identifies the various actions to be taken and sets out an appropriate time line. The written plan will specify when ownership is to be transferred, whether to be transferred on a particular date or phased-in over time. Perhaps the ownership transfer will take place upon the satisfaction of certain conditions or the occurrence of certain events. If the plan addresses the transfer of management, it will state when the owner is to retire and assign various operational responsibilities to specific individuals, and may specify who might sit on the company's board of directors or advisory board.

SELECTING THE SUCCESSOR

Since management succession issues take on greater significance in the context of ownership transfers to family, the owner and her advisory team may spend a lot of time deliberating over the next "leader" of the company. Yet at the end of such deliberations, and whether or not a family participation plan has been created, the owner will eventually have to select her successor.

But just as she should not simply assume that a particular child wants to be her successor, she should not simply assume that the child is capable of being her successor. She should objectively assess the ability of the child as she would an outsider. She should try to determine whether the child has the same drive, ambition, intelligence or energy as the owner. While many qualities are needed to be a good successor, the child's motivation may be the most important.

The owner may select two or more of her children to be her successors in order to avoid having to decide upon only one. Yet she should never assume that her children can work together, or even want to share ownership. If her children cannot get along as successors, the business may not be able to function without the owner being around to mediate. Joint successors may not work if each child has a different or conflicting view about the business. Even if the children agree, they may not share the owner's plans for the business, and may see it going in an entirely different direction.

However, instead of appointing joint successors, the owner may consider separating the business into divisions each headed by a different child, although the ability to accomplish such a separation depends upon a number of factors, including the product lines and geographic markets involved.

This alternative approach is discussed in the *Transfers to Family – Part I* chapter in the context of trying to treat children equally. Treating all family members equally under the succession plan can prove to be a challenge for the owner and her team, and perhaps the most that can be achieved is fair treatment. Those children who are not chosen to be a successor or who are not part of management may nonetheless become entitled to receive non-company assets or income in the spirit of "equalization". This solution may depend upon the extent of the owner's outside investments, or upon the diversity of the company's asset base which may allow for certain assets to be transferred to another company which may, in turn, be owned by the non–active family members.

When attempting to select a successor, the owner should first prepare a successor job description and then identify the key attributes which the successor will need in order to perform that job. The requisite skills and experience should be specified. The owner should then look at each potential family successor and identify the respective strengths and weaknesses of each.

Since choosing among several qualified candidates can be the most difficult step in the selection process, the owner may try to evaluate each candidate according to certain criteria. She may ask herself which candidate has shown the greatest commitment to the task of preparing for succession and which candidate has best demonstrated the skills and capabilities necessary to lead the company, including who has the best decision-making ability.

She may also consider each candidate's vision for the future of the company and ask whose leadership style might be most appropriate given the company's current and future operating environment. When looking at candidates who are already involved in the business, she should determine who has earned the most respect of the company's employees and other business associates.

In short, the owner should assess which candidate best fits the successor job description.

Although the above criteria may be used by the owner when selecting a family member as a successor, they may also be used to select possible employee successors in the event that none of the owner's family is willing or able to become a successor.

PREPARING THE SUCCESSOR

As part of the owner's overall goal to ensure that the company remains in "good hands" and continues to prosper after the owner has retired from the company, there is a distinct advantage to the owner in preparing her successor to take over. While this need for preparation may seem to apply only when a family member has been selected to be the successor, it may equally apply when an employee, even an outside party, has been selected. A prepared successor will ensure a smooth transition.

How long it will take the owner to prepare her successor will depend upon a number of things, including the level of additional skill and education the successor will need, and the degree of urgency the owner may face in passing on the business.

Preparing the successor to take over often involves the creation of a management development plan, which may be incorporated into the owner's business succession plan. The development plan attempts to expose the successor to the key areas of company management and operations and determines the additional training which the successor needs. Such a plan should be reviewed and updated regularly.

In preparing the development plan, the owner may have to consider whether the successor should be brought into the business on a short-term, probationary basis, whether a formal mentoring period is necessary, or whether a series of managerial promotions with increasing responsibilities for the successor should be put into place. Specially tailored training programs, an apprenticeship, job shadowing, or outside business management education may all be considered by the owner as necessary preparation.

She may also provide in the development plan for comprehensive visits by the successor to all of the sites used in operating the business, and for the introduction of the successor to all of the company's support personnel, outside advisers, customers and suppliers. If appropriate, the plan might even suggest a seat on the company's board of directors for the successor. Alternatively, an advisory board consisting of experienced outsiders might be established to provide support to the successor in those areas where skill gaps exist.

The management development plan may require the intended successor to undertake a number of different activities within the company. The successor may have to work in various departments to understand the processes and products, and receive mentoring from a senior person in each department, including a stint in company sales to develop relationships with the company's customers. The plan may require that specific projects be assigned to the successor.

In some circumstances, it may be desirable for the plan to provide that the successor work outside of the company for a certain period of time in order to not only develop needed skills and gain personal confidence but also to achieve credibility with the company's non-family employees.

The owner should ensure that the management development plan sets time lines for the prescribed activities and provides objective means to measure the adequacy of the progress being made by the successor. It's important that the plan maintains a businesslike focus, so that the successor's failure to become properly prepared will allow the owner to reassess her succession decision. At the same time, the plan will give the successor a chance to try things out, even change her mind.

PLANNING FOR CONTINGENCIES

The business succession plan needs to include an emergency plan, or a contingency plan, to address how the business will carry on in the event of the owner's death or disability before the succession plan is fully implemented. As mentioned above, the contingency plan can address what might otherwise be the owner's estate plan.

An estate plan is designed to protect the owner's legacy and provide financially for those who depend upon her should she die or become incapacitated. It generally deals with the owner's assets, how they will be managed and distributed and whether or not they will be sufficient for her beneficiaries once they are distributed.

Because the contingency plan can serve as the owner's estate plan covering, amongst other things, the owner's shares in the company, it should include not only how the owner's shares will be dealt with upon the owner's death, but also how the company's business will be administered in the event the owner is incapacitated. The contingency plan, in other words, should look at both management and ownership succession.

The contingency plan for the owner's death ordinarily requires that the owner execute a will, a topic which is discussed in greater detail in the *Transfers to Family – Part II* chapter. The contingency plan for the owner's incapacity ordinarily requires that she execute a power of attorney.

To address her possible incapacity, the owner grants a "continuing" or "enduring" power of attorney[1] over all of her assets, including the business, to someone else. The power of attorney may state that it comes into effect when doctors sign a declaration that she is no longer competent to make decisions. Since her will doesn't come into effect when she is disabled or incapacitated, a power of attorney is needed before her death. In the absence of a power of attorney from the owner who becomes disabled while she is still alive, the owner's family will likely apply to a court for a family member to become a guardian[2] or trustee of the owner's property even though such a person may not be entirely suitable.

A power of attorney lets the owner provide for another person to trade her shares, or to attend shareholder meetings for the purpose of voting her shares, should she become incapacitated. While the owner's spouse may not be an appropriate attorney, a child of the owner who is involved in the business or a business partner may be a better choice as attorney, or perhaps a key employee acting jointly with the spouse.

The owner may consider having two powers of attorney governing her property, one for the business and the other for her remaining assets. Also, at the same time, she may grant a power of attorney for her personal care,[3] or prepare a health care directive regarding any decisions to be made in connection with her medical condition and treatment.

The contingency plan may also require that a buy-sell agreement, or a shareholder agreement if there are other company shareholders, be put into place which provides, among other things, what happens if the owner dies or is permanently disabled and who is entitled to buy the owner's shares. Sometimes the owner's shares may be purchased by the company. This share "buy-back" may be over time or at just one time, and may be enabled by a special fund, or paid for out of future company profits.

There may also be a need for life insurance to fund the company's purchase of such shares. Company-owned life insurance on the life of the owner can provide the proceeds to buy her shares on her death from her estate. The sale proceeds can then be used by the estate to pay any capital gains taxes owing. The company pays the premiums and is the beneficiary under the insurance policy.

Alternatively, the contingency plan could require the owner to buy and pay the premiums on an insurance policy payable to her estate. Her estate could then use the insurance proceeds received upon her death to pay for taxes and other estate liabilities so that her assets would not have to be sold.

FIXING A TIME LINE

In order for a business succession plan to achieve the owner's goals, it needs to have a clear time line. It should specify the due dates for the various action items it prescribes. At the very least, a time line should allow for the stakeholders in the company's succession to become prepared and help to avoid any anxiety of the owner's family about when things are about to happen.

Yet fixing such dates long in advance is not easily done and will depend upon a number of factors.

The initial timing will depend upon whether the owner enjoys her work and involvement with the company and doesn't really want to leave it. She has to ask herself if she is ready to move on, and if she's not ready when starting to create the succession plan, she must ask herself when she will be ready. She should question whether she will need to find other employment to replace the work she does at the company, or to replace the income she currently earns, or whether she is prepared to stay on as a consultant.

The time line will also be affected if the owner is in ill health and or in poor financial circumstances, or needs to sell in order to be able to buy another business quickly, or if an unexpected and unsolicited offer emerges for the business from a "suitor" who wants to buy right away. Financing questions or training issues will influence the time line, as will the presence of a family member who is ready, willing and able to buy soon.

Generally speaking, transferring ownership to family members can take a long time, especially if an estate freeze is involved or a successor has to be mentored. But transferring to an employee group can take a long time as well, not only to address possible financing issues but also to allow for mentoring and to provide transitional consulting by the owner. Even a sale to an outside party can take longer than expected, particularly when the owner is trying to obtain the best price.

Implementing a Business Succession Plan

Once the business succession plan has been written, the owner and his advisory team will attempt to initiate the various actions proposed in accordance with the plan's time line.

These might include preparing wills, trust documents, and shareholder agreements, arranging for insurance coverage, reallocating the owner's outside investments, enrolling a family member in a graduate business program, obtaining a valuation of the company, transferring existing company shares, creating new classes of shares, transferring company assets to a new corporation, disposing of an unprofitable company division or surplus company assets, or perhaps even retaining a business broker.

The rest of this book is essentially about implementing many of the actions often found in a written business succession plan.

But just as the creation of the plan can be a complicated and frustrating process, the implementation of the plan can be as well. Although the owner and his team may attempt to carry out the plan's various actions, they may not necessarily succeed, despite all the hard work put into creating the plan.

This chapter will attempt to address a few of the issues that may arise after the plan is committed into writing and is regarded by the owner to be in final form. In an effort to increase the likelihood of the plan being put into practice, the owner and his team will need to be quite flexible in their approach to the plan's implementation. They cannot assume that the circumstances prevailing when the plan was created will remain the same when the plan is implemented.

COMMUNICATING THE PLAN

The business succession plan should be communicated to the owner's family members, as well as to the company's employees, customers, suppliers and advisors. Implementing the plan generally requires further communication with the same stakeholders who were consulted during the plan's creation.

Such communication should demonstrate that the succession is a managed process, and should encourage a greater acceptance of the plan and the successor's leadership by the company's stakeholders. Meeting face-to-face again with the company's employees, suppliers and customers, as well as the owner's family, may be necessary to facilitate the various actions prescribed in the plan and reduce the likelihood of any resistance to them.

But the announcements should not be too early. The announcements of the formal succession plan should occur when the plan is finalized and the successor is prepared to assume the leadership role. The announcements generally include internal meetings and memos to employees, personal meetings with suppliers, lenders and key customers, and then formal announcements to the community if the company is large enough.

MONITORING AND CHANGING THE PLAN

While each succession plan has its own particular time line, with some plans covering many years and others stretching over only a few months, it's important for the owner and his team to monitor not only the implementation of the plan but also the continuing appropriateness of the various actions proposed by the plan.

A plan is not a one-time exercise but an ongoing process that requires updating and amendment as circumstances change. There is a need to revisit and revise the plan regularly.

In some cases, the company's financial performance may fall below expectations and may not justify or support certain actions. For example, the redemption or repurchase of shares or payment of dividends may not be sensible, and may even be illegal if the company is unable to satisfy certain statutory solvency tests.[1] The cash required by the company to perform these actions may be put to much better use elsewhere.

In other cases, the people may have changed. For example, the death, disability or divorce of a key family member may cause the owner to reconsider the plan and the various roles in the company he intended his family to play.

Or the owner may have changed his mind about his own retirement and the extent of his continuing participation in either the management or ownership of the company. If his personal financial situation has deteriorated since the plan was created, he may be forced to stop further implementation and even attempt to reverse certain actions that were taken under it.

Continually reviewing the succession plan's implementation can result in changes to the company's operations, to the plan itself, or to both. The longer the time lines prescribed for carrying out the plan, the greater the chances that the plan will need to be revised.

An ongoing review of the succession plan may become particularly crucial when the owner has preferred one of his children to become his successor, not only in terms of management succession but in terms of ownership succession as well. He may have underestimated, or perhaps ignored, certain rivalries among his children at the time the plan was created. During the plan's implementation, he may come to realize that having disgruntled children involved in the business can break down the mutual trust and respect among the owner's family members and threaten the company's continuing success.

While sibling rivalry may not be eliminated, it may be controlled to some extent by reducing the perceived arbitrariness of the owner's treatment of his children through the implementation of independent review processes within the company. An independent review of the performance of the children in the business is desirable, and their compensation should be at market rates as determined by outside experts. There is also an advantage to having job descriptions and organization charts like other businesses, in addition to performance reviews. With such an approach, the emotions can be removed from some of the company's decisions.

Therefore, as part of the implementation of a succession plan which selects one of the owner's children to be his successor, its ongoing monitoring and possible amendment may have to involve input from his family. Issues such as compensation and performance, outside family issues, and even issues in selling the business, can be considered by the family so that everyone in the family is kept current on where the business is going. By involving the family in a regular review of the plan's implementation, the risks of a failed implementation as described below might be reduced.

USING AN INTERIM MANAGER

Even though the plan has been finalized and the successor has been selected, the successor may not be ready to take over. Or the owner may become too disabled to effectively manage before the successor has been selected or is properly prepared.

The appointment of an interim manager of the company may then have to be considered. It may be necessary to replace what the business will need in the owner's absence, at least on a short-term basis.

Even though succession planning is mainly about transferring ownership, the interim manager acquires no ownership and is only paid temporarily until the intended transfer takes place. Such a manager is usually outside the ordinary company employee benefit and pension plans. The interim manager can replace the owner, or work alongside the owner, as a bridge between the owner and the successor, and may stay through the actual transfer of ownership.

The interim manager may overlap with the owner but must be able to get involved with the business immediately and not take the time the successor would take to "get up to speed". There should be no need to train the interim manager, who should already have the requisite skills and experience to be able to contribute to the business on the first day.

FINANCING THE OWNERSHIP TRANSFER

Depending upon the successor selected, the ownership transfer contemplated under the business succession plan may not take place unless suitable financing can be arranged. Regardless of how thorough the plan may appear to be, its implementation will be frustrated should financing be unavailable to complete the transfer.

After all, the whole point of the plan is to achieve an exit of the owner from the company, preferably on the owner's terms. It may turn out, however, that the tremendous efforts of the owner and his advisory team to craft a well thought out plan may have been expended for nothing if a succession transaction fails for lack of financing.

Financing is often the main obstacle to achieving a successful transition. Even if the owner is contemplating a sale of his ownership to an outside party, financing the sale is not strictly the buyer's problem. All too often, the owner is expected to assist the buyer in financing the purchase to some extent.

Financing issues include the calculation of the purchase price and the terms of payment, and likely involve a combination of financing arrangements. While many sales to company employees, other shareholders or outside parties may require the buyers to obtain purchase financing from external sources, the owner will usually play some financing role.

Even when ownership is to be transferred to members of the owner's family, perhaps through the implementation of an "estate freeze" as more comprehensively described in the *Transfers to Family – Part I* chapter, there are still financing issues to be resolved. An estate freeze, under which the owner is issued redeemable preferred shares, is essentially a financing scheme which allows the owner to be paid over time.

There are a number of financing schemes the owner may wish to consider. A scheduled share purchase program, as may occur following an estate freeze, can be used in a purchase from the owner that is completed in successive "tranches" and that causes the owner to have a gradually declining ownership in the company over time.

Alternatively, the purchase from the owner may entail the purchase price being paid in installments over time. Sometimes described as a "vendor take-back", this scheme is essentially a loan from the owner to the buyer for some or all of the purchase price, either on a secured or unsecured basis, with specific terms of repayment at either a fixed or variable rate of interest.

Other financing schemes to be considered may include a scheduled payment of dividends to the owner over a prescribed period of time, which may occur in connection with the preferred shares issued to the owner under an estate freeze. Or the owner may enjoy an "earn-out" arrangement after his ownership transfer, under which he receives an additional portion of the purchase price in the event the company meets certain financial goals after the transfer.

How a buyer is going to pay the purchase price to the owner will affect the actual amount to be paid, since the price should reflect the risk to the owner that he may not be paid on time, or perhaps not be paid at all. The owner's receipt of any purchase price installments will depend upon the future success of the business when it is in the buyer's hands.

Even if the owner does not intend to follow through with any of these financing schemes, and his business succession plan is based upon an "all cash" sale under which the purchase price is to be paid to the owner in one lump sum, his plan may well have to be amended later on to include one or more of the schemes to make a specific transaction workable.

Should an all cash deal become available, perhaps because a buyer appears able to tap into sufficient financing from external sources, the owner will still have to understand the buyer's financing structure and the buyer's ability to pay. The owner will need to assure himself that the buyer will be "in funds" on the day the purchase is to be completed. If it turns out that the buyer is unable to raise the necessary funds, the owner may then have to move on to another buyer, even if a lower purchase price may be the result.

In order to reduce the chances of this happening, the owner should assist the buyer and the buyer's financier by providing sufficient information about the company when asked. As discussed in much greater detail in the *Due Diligence* chapter, it's usually in the owner's best interest to co-operate with them since the financier's preparedness to fund the purchase price will depend upon whether the financier believes that the company's historical financial performance is sustainable. The financier will need to know the expected future income and cash flows of the business, and will ask for confirmation of the information presented to support the company's valuation.

RISK OF FAILED IMPLEMENTATION

While this book focuses on the current owner of the company and his transfer of company ownership to others in furtherance of his retirement goals, he may face quite difficult succession challenges if the company operates a "family business" which employs one or more of his family members, or has one or more of his family members as shareholders.

The particular dynamics of his family may create a number of issues for him to consider and obstacles for him to overcome in the implementation of his business succession plan.

Family businesses are different from other businesses in certain ways, and keeping them in the family is not easy. The owner will likely be mindful of the adage "shirtsleeves to shirtsleeves in three generations". Various studies have concluded that only 30 per cent of family businesses successfully carry on from the first generation to the second, and only a third of those succeed in making it to the third generation.² The likelihood of the business being carried on by the owner's grandchildren is only one in 10.

A variety of causes might be suggested to explain why family businesses don't make it to the third generation, or what the second generation often does wrong. Tired brands, antiquated technology, bigger and better cap- italized competitors, a family business too narrow and regionally focused to compete globally against multinationals, or the desire of the second generation to spare the third generation from the drudgery and stresses of carrying on in a tougher world, are all possible causes.

Even poor communication within and between the different genera- tions involved can be viewed as a cause. The inability of family members to have open, frank and frequent conversations about performance and compensation issues, let alone control, can jeopardize the family's chances of making money, managing risk and preserving capital. If the children always defer to their parents, the business may lack the kind of constructive criticism prevalent in non-family businesses.

While some may argue that family members work harder, and make more sacrifices, in a family business, others may argue that family busi- nesses are often killed with love, since children are promoted because of love, or are given too much money because of love. While some may argue that a line needs to be drawn between the family and the family business, and that family issues must be separated from business issues, others may argue that separation isn't possible, so don't try. Others still have forcefully argued that the current generation should always be trying to sell the business instead of trying to pass it along to the next genera- tion.[3]

BIAS TOWARDS A SALE OF A FAMILY BUSINESS

There is certainly some appeal to this last argument. Many family busi- nesses are inherently risky because personal net worth is often tied up in just one investment. There is often too little diversification. The goal should be about preserving wealth, not protecting a name or creating an enduring legacy. Longevity of the business destroys wealth, as the argu- ment goes, and the desire to have the business carry on as a legacy will result in bankruptcy and loss of family wealth.

A related argument is sometimes made against promising employment to family members, since the business exists to make money, not to provide family members with jobs. All of the family should know that the business is for sale and that there is no job for life.

If the current owner finds these latter arguments appealing, he may revisit his succession plan with a bias towards a sale of the company rather than an ownership transfer to the next generation. But while he may favour a sale, the sale may not necessarily be a sale to an outsider, but to his children instead. He may feel that his children need to have their own money at stake in the company or be liable on loans they take out when acquiring the company.

Alternatively, he may feel that he should at least give his children a chance to buy the company at market rate, so that they may then decline to do so with no regrets. If the children don't like this approach, they can always leave the company just as they could in any other business. This theme is explored later in the *Transfers to Family - Part I* chapter as it discuses how the owner may treat his children on an arm's length basis.

As a consequence, the company would therefore always be for sale to the highest bidder, whether the bidder is inside or outside the family. A sale to an outside party might be preferred, since an outside sale often results in payment of the purchase price more quickly, in contrast to the long installment payments frequently associated with an inside sale which can be very costly to the owner.

While economic conditions change, and the desires of the owner and his children over buying and selling company shares will change regularly, the owner shouldn't wait for the company to deteriorate. If he has no desire to risk additional personal capital, it's time for him to sell.

But if a sale to an outsider is favoured, the owner should nevertheless be aware that he or one or more of his children may be required to stay behind after the sale to assist the outside buyer in the transition.

Putting the Company in Saleable Condition

Before the current owner commences the actions suggested in this book in carrying out her business succession plan, she should concentrate her efforts on putting the company in a "saleable" condition, even if she intends for her immediate family to take over. Attempting to identify and fix any problems with the company early on will make running the company a lot easier later, and will certainly increase the value of the company which a prospective successor might be prepared to pay. It will also make the company look better in the eyes of the bank or other financier contemplating whether to lend the successor sufficient funds to buy the company.

Some problems can prevent a sale of the company unless they are fixed. For example, a potential successor may be deterred if the company's plant is situated on polluted land, or if a contract with the company's largest customer can be terminated by the customer if the company's ownership changes, or if the company's main product lacks patent protection, or if the company's key employees are free to work for a competitor if they leave the company.

Perhaps a shareholder agreement allows a minority shareholder to effectively veto a sale of the whole company by refusing to sell her own shares, or the company is carrying large amounts of obsolete inventory or uncollectible receivables, or is saddled with an excessive level of relatively expensive debt. Any of these conditions may encourage a potential successor to consider looking at other companies instead.

In addition to fixing the more glaring problems, getting the company ready for sale also means ensuring that the company's many relationships with its employees, customers and suppliers are well-documented, and its various records and government filings are up-to-date. Such actions should be regarded not just as good "housekeeping" but as good business. Having things well-documented and up-to-date will give a successor not only a better understanding of any risks arising from the company's past actions but also some certainty in determining the profitability of the company in the future.

Although some may argue that a company only reaches a saleable condition when it ceases to be dependent upon the owner for its profitability and continuing success, such an abstract notion provides little practical guidance for an owner trying to decide what steps might be useful to take. The remainder of this chapter will identify some of the matters on which an owner might wish to specifically focus in an effort to make the company more saleable.

LIMITING OR REMOVING LIABILITIES

Some of the problems which may need to be fixed relate to liabilities which a successor may not be prepared to assume when acquiring ownership. It may be necessary for the owner to carefully review all of the company's liabilities in anticipation of a successor's resistance to them and to determine whether such liabilities can be either limited or entirely removed.

Some of these liabilities may relate to the company's current financing arrangements. A successor may regard them as an unnecessary or imprudent burden, especially if the successor has access to financing which is less expensive or is on more favourable terms, or if the current financing has been provided by a party related to the owner. As the owner may likely be asked by the successor to pay off all amounts owing under such arrangements and to obtain a discharge of any security which may have been given, the owner should inquire of the bank or other financing party in advance if there are any obstacles to accomplishing this.

The owner should also inquire whether the financing party would be prepared to release the owner from any guarantees which she may have previously given in support of the company's financing arrangements. It will be crucial for the owner to obtain such releases in the event that her successor is willing to assume the financing which is currently in place. In addition to her personal guarantees, the owner may have to determine the existence of any guarantees which the company may have given to support the financial obligations of other parties, including those related to the owner, and to make an effort to either have such company guarantees terminated or limited to a specific dollar amount.

Some company liabilities are not readily limited or removed. A lawsuit against the company for a material amount may not be easy to settle and its continuing defence may be perceived by a successor as a huge drain on company resources with a very uncertain outcome. A material contract with a relatively long term may not be capable of amendment or early termination without the payment of considerable penalties.

UPGRADING OR REPLACING ASSETS

In addition to conducting various sales and promotions in order to reduce excess inventory and to strengthening collection efforts to shorten the length of time the company's receivables are outstanding, the owner may have to consider whether the condition of the company's physical assets might be a deterrent to a potential successor who is contemplating an acquisition. Initial on-site inspections by the successor should encourage, not dissuade, the successor in continuing with more detailed due diligence examinations of the company's assets and liabilities.

In order for the company's facilities to show well on inspection, the owner may decide to repair or replace malfunctioning or outdated machinery, equipment and vehicles, upgrade the company's computer software and hardware, and possibly renovate and refurnish its offices.

As a potential successor is unlikely to want to acquire any company asset which is held primarily for the personal benefit of the owner or her family and is not required in the operations of the company's business, the owner should attempt to identify any vehicles, recreational equipment, executive apartments, artwork, furniture and any other company assets held for only personal use and consider selling them or transferring them to a related corporation.

CORRECTING OR UPDATING RECORDS AND FILINGS

The holding of annual company meetings or signing of annual resolutions electing directors, appointing officers and approving financial statements may have generally been overlooked by the owner as a minor administrative inconvenience. Annual and other periodic government filings the company is required to make, and the renewal of any licences or permits necessary to carry on the company's business, may also have been ignored. But since a potential successor will want to be comfortable that the company has been properly administered before taking over, the owner should have the minute books and corporate records of the company reviewed to ensure that everything is up-to-date.

Given the possibility that the company was incorporated some time ago and may not have been properly organized at that time, the owner's review of the company's minute book ideally should go back to the date of incorporation, particularly with a view to confirming that all outstanding shares have been properly issued and that the share register correctly records all share issuances and transfers in the meantime. Such an exercise will invariably be undertaken by the lawyers for any successor carrying out due diligence investigations of the company. Hopefully any discrepancies which the owner may discover in her review can be rectified right away in order to avoid a later purchase transaction for the company being postponed or terminated because the successor came across such discrepancies before closing.

REVIEWING EMPLOYEE RELATIONSHIPS

Since a potential successor may be quite concerned that the company's employees may leave the company to work elsewhere as soon as the owner transfers her ownership, the owner should attempt to address this possible concern early on in the process.

One place to start is the use of employment contracts with all of the company's employees which specify the causes of termination and appropriate notice periods, require that all trade secrets and other company information be kept confidential, provide for an assignment to the company of the employee's intellectual property acquired while employed, and restrict the rights of the employee to solicit other company employees or to provide services to the company's customers after leaving. It may be necessary to pay current employees a bonus, provide some additional benefit or give them a promotion as consideration for their signing of such a contract. New employees should be required to sign such a contract as a condition of their employment.

Ensuring that key employees will stay around with the company after the owner leaves may also be accomplished by offering such employees various benefits such as group insurance and registered retirement savings plans, or by creating profit sharing, stock option, stock purchase, or phantom stock plans. Since the continuing involvement of such employees with the company can affect the value of the company, the owner should preferably have such plans in place before a potential successor considers acquiring the company.

REVIEWING SUPPLIER RELATIONSHIPS

Having supply contracts with suppliers, especially when alternative suppliers are scarce or non-existent, can be essential to putting the company in a saleable condition. However, supply contracts which make the company deal exclusively with a supplier for particular products or services can have a negative effect on the saleability of the company.

The owner should attempt to insert into such exclusive arrangements the right of the company to terminate them on relatively short notice, in the event that substitute products or services become available at a better price. Furthermore, the owner should attempt to remove any restriction against the company from assigning the supply contracts to a successor.

REVIEWING LANDLORD RELATIONSHIPS

A potential successor may be concerned that if the company operates out of leased premises, the applicable lease has too little time remaining under it or is capable of being easily terminated by the landlord. To ensure that the lease will not become a deterrent to a potential successor acquiring ownership of the company, the owner should review the provisions of the lease to ascertain what rights of renewal or extension exist and what events might permit early termination.

If the lease contains a "change of control" provision, requiring the landlord to consent to any sale of the majority of the company's shares or a substantial part of its assets, the owner may be facing the possibility that her successor may not be acceptable to the landlord, and thereby put the lease in jeopardy, unless she is able to get the landlord to amend or waive this provision.

REVIEWING CUSTOMER RELATIONSHIPS

Having written customer contracts, particularly those of a longer term or which can be terminated only after a lengthy notice period, can be essential to enhancing the value of the company. A potential successor will then be given some assurance that company revenues will persist after the sale is completed, as well as some understanding of what liabilities the successor may be assuming under possible warranties and other performance obligations.

As with supply contracts, the owner should attempt to remove any restrictions in any customer contracts which prevent their assignment by the company to a successor. Doing so can help to increase the company's value and remove any possibility that the acquisition of the business by any particular successor might threaten the continuation of the customer relationship.

PROTECTING INTELLECTUAL PROPERTY

If the company's value to a potential successor depends heavily upon the brand names which the company uses in the marketplace, the owner should attempt to obtain registered trademark protection for such names if she hasn't already done so. Applying for patent protection should be considered for any inventions which the company has made or funded which a successor may consider to be integral to the company's product line or operations.

The owner should ensure that all agreements with outside consultants contain their assignment of any intellectual property rights they may have acquired while providing services to the company, including all copyrights in any works they may author for the company, as well as their agreement to keep company information confidential.

REMEDIATING POLLUTED PROPERTY

A potential successor is likely to be deterred from acquiring ownership of the company if the company's plant is situated on polluted land. Only the successful remediation of the polluted condition may be sufficient to encourage the successor to seriously consider proceeding with an acquisition of the company.

The owner may attempt to merely quantify the amount of funds needed to remediate, expecting the successor to proceed with simply a reduction of the purchase price equal to the required cost of remediation. Such an approach may work if the company's strategic value to the successor greatly outweighs the environmental risks. However, it is quite unlikely that the owner will convince the successor to proceed with only a written assessment report from a qualified environmental expert which just sets out the environmental condition of the land and the work necessary to satisfactorily remediate.

AMENDING SHAREHOLDER AGREEMENTS

If there is a shareholder agreement in place, the owner should review it in order to determine the extent to which the sale of the company might be restricted. For example, it might provide "rights of first refusal", requiring a shareholder desiring to sell her shares to first offer them to the other shareholders, usually on a pro-rata basis to their existing holdings, before offering them to an outside party. Or it might provide "piggyback rights" which allow the other shareholders to have their shares included with the shares being sold by a shareholder to an outside party. Or it might provide "drag-along rights" which allow a selling shareholder to include the shares of the other shareholders when selling her shares to an outside party.

While piggyback rights can give minority shareholders the option to sell out, drag-along rights can require them to sell out. For the owner with a controlling interest in the company, rights of first refusal and piggyback rights in a shareholder agreement may be viewed as an impediment to selling, and the owner may have to re-negotiate the agreement with the other shareholders to have such provisions removed.

Although the current owner may wish to keep her options open in deciding who should be the most appropriate successor to the business, the shareholder agreement may contain various "call" provisions which might frustrate the owner's intentions in the event that they are activated before the owner has been able finalize her plans. For example, the agreement may provide that in the event that any shareholder (including the owner) becomes disabled, the other shareholders have a right to call for or acquire the shares of the disabled shareholder at a set price, which may or may not be fair market value at the time of the disability. For an owner who might prefer that her family members or perhaps long-standing employees should be able to acquire her shares, such call rights might prevent the family members or employees from ever acquiring her shares should she become disabled.

In addition to assessing the need to remove any call rights from the shareholder agreement, any "shotgun" rights in the agreement may have to be removed. A shotgun provision requires a shareholder to set a firm price at which she is willing to either sell her shares to the other shareholders or to buy their shares. The others then have the option of choosing whether to buy or sell at the specified price. As with call rights, shotgun rights once exercised can prevent the owner from transferring her shares to her chosen successor.

The owner may also have to consider whether there is a need for certain "family law" provisions in the shareholder agreement. Such provisions often require that each shareholder have a marriage contract, if married, which provides that a shareholder's spouse will not get the shareholder's company shares upon divorce or death.

In the absence of a shareholder agreement, an owner with a controlling interest might attempt to have such an agreement put into place which contains a drag-along clause, thereby enabling the owner to offer for sale 100 per cent of the company.

Valuation

In order to carry out many of the alternative actions suggested in this book, the current owner should first attempt to determine the company's fair market value. Whether the owner intends to transfer company shares to family members, or make shares available to employees or other shareholders, or negotiate the purchase price of shares with an outside party, the owner should retain a valuator to analyze the company and determine its fair market value using accepted valuation principles and methods. The valuator may also recommend various actions the owner might take to increase the company's value.

While there is no one, absolute definition of the term "fair market value" when used to describe what a particular business might be worth, it is often taken to mean the price that a buyer would reasonably be expected to pay, and a seller would reasonably be expected to accept, if the business were for sale on the open market for a reasonable period of time, and assuming that both buyer and seller had all the pertinent facts and that neither was under any compulsion to act.[1]

Determining the company's fair market value may be mandatory for the owner in certain circumstances. If a transfer to family members is intended, fair market value is often required to be used as the value for tax purposes regardless of any other values selected by the family for the transfer.[2] If a transfer to other shareholders is intended, an existing shareholder agreement may require that the transfer be made at fair market value. Even if a transfer to an outside party is intended, a valuator's determination of fair market value may appear to be necessary to allow the current owner to more objectively assess the adequacy of any offers to purchase which he may receive.

And objectivity is often what's needed in the circumstances. While the owner may well have a value in mind for the company which he firmly believes is an accurate reflection of what the company is worth, his assessment is likely based upon the company's past and present, and may be too wrapped up in sentiment, nostalgia and perhaps ego to provide an accurate reflection of the company's fair market value.

A valuator, however, focuses on the company's potential for the future, and attempts to determine the value of the company as if it's no longer in the owner's hands. A valuator assesses the company's transferable value and establishes what the company might be worth to another owner. To accomplish this, the valuator looks at how dependent the business is upon the current owner. A business which is heavily dependent upon the personality or specific skills of the owner is more difficult to sell.

But the valuator looks at a number of other things as well. The extent of customer concentration, the diversity of suppliers, the experience and skills of the management team apart from the owner, the effectiveness of the company's governance and reporting systems, and the severity of any specific industry or company risk factors are all analyzed by the valuator. The company's valuation can be negatively affected by its reliance on just a few customers or a few key employees, or by outstanding litigation or contentious labour relations.

Valuations will vary by the amount of independent review and analysis undertaken, and the amount of backup and verification required. A comprehensive valuation report will look at industry and economic factors and not just at the business itself. Some valuators have expertise in particular industries and types of businesses. A valuator may need to retain other specialists, such as equipment and real estate appraisers or compensation consultants, to assist in valuing certain assets or liabilities.

Yet valuation still comes down to working with numbers, and the valuator will attempt to arrive at some forecast of the company's future revenues and earnings, even though a considerable level of discretion may have to be exercised. The process is more art than science.

Since there is no open market to determine the value of the company's shares as exists for the shares of publicly traded companies, the valuator will normally use hypothetical or notional methods to arrive at a value for the shares while exercising a degree of professional judgment. The valuator's notional methods will be applied using certain assumptions and conditions that may not exist in an open market context. In the event that more than one valuator is retained, different valuators can arrive at widely differing valuations.

Often the financial statements of the company which are provided to the valuator will have to be adjusted by the valuator to more properly reflect the real value of the company to an independent, outside party. Discretionary expenses, non-recurring or extraordinary amounts, non-arm's length transactions and other dealings with related parties may all give rise to a need to adjust the company's earnings in order to arrive at an appropriate valuation.

Arriving at one value that can be used for all purposes is not an easy exercise, particularly in the case of a company which is owned and operated by just one or more family members. Such a company often poses specific valuation challenges, especially when the compensation paid to family members and the company's holding of personal use assets are considered.

NORMALIZING ADJUSTMENTS

The compensation paid to family members who are managing the company, often achieved by a mix of salary, bonuses and dividends, may be well in excess of what would be the market value of the services they provide. The total compensation paid to the owner and his family may be allocated in such a way among various family members that the deduction from the company's income is maximized and the total personal taxes paid are minimized.[3] To arrive at an accurate valuation for the company, it may be necessary to estimate the market salary that would have to be paid when hiring replacements for the owner and any other family members actively involved in the company.

Many expenses of a personal nature may have been charged through the company, including entertainment, travel and vehicle expenses. These expenses, or at least the non-business portion of them, may have to be added back into the income of the company in order to arrive at a proper valuation.

Other expenses may have been charged for services provided by related parties, such as rent or management fees, which may need to be adjusted to reflect more appropriate arm's length values. If the company has been financed by interest-free loans from family members, it may be necessary to assume more conventional financing from outside sources and add in expenses for interest at prevailing rates.

A similar approach may apply to many assets of the company which are of a personal nature, including artwork, furniture, equipment, vehicles and personal residences. If they are not needed for the operations of the company, they may have to be excluded from the company's valuation. Also to be excluded may be other assets which are held for investment rather than operational purposes, including real estate holdings, loans to family members and subsidiaries engaged in unrelated businesses.

These various adjustments for above-market compensation, personal expenses, non-essential assets, and related party services and loans, are sometimes referred to as "normalizing" adjustments. Although normalizing adjustments may be commonplace in the valuation of most businesses in order to eliminate expenses and assets which are not essential to ongoing operations or which entail payments to non-arm's length parties, the need for these adjustments tends to be greater in the context of family businesses in order to give the owners a realistic assessment of what an outside party might be prepared to pay.

VALUATION METHODS
There is no one method which a valuator will always use to determine a company's valuation. Assuming the business is viable and the company is intended to continue as a going concern and not be liquidated, the valuator may choose from a number of commonly used methods, one or more of which may be used in the particular circumstances.

The valuator may deem the "capitalized earnings" approach to be the most appropriate, and proceed to estimate the future after-tax income derived from the company's operations, which is then multiplied by a capitalization rate after being normalized as discussed above to arrive at the fair market value for the company. Or the valuator may use a "discounted cash flow" approach and discount the projected cash flows from operations for a number of years to arrive at the present value of those cash flows which will be received by the company in the future.

Or the valuator may calculate "adjusted book value" by adjusting the net book value of the assets and liabilities of the business to their respective fair market value. This method may be used when the earnings or cash flows of the business are not considered to reflect the fair market values of the underlying net assets.

While earnings based methods include non-cash amounts such as depreciation and amortization, cash flow based methods are concerned with the cash that will be spent or taken in by a company. Because valuators are trying to measure the economic benefit which shareholders will actually receive from a company, which usually comes by way of cash distributions, they may be more inclined to apply cash flow based methods unless future earnings and future cash flows for the company are expected to be roughly similar. Such similarity may occur in companies which are not capital intensive and have little depreciation expense.

Where cash flow based methods are applied to arrive at a company's value, the valuator may focus on the company's "discretionary" cash flows, which are determined net of capital expenditures, working capital requirements, and income taxes,[4] and on the rate of return or discount rate to be used. This rate reflects the time value of money as well as the opportunities and risks relating to the company's business and industry.

Whichever valuation method is used, the resulting valuation may then be supported by using a conventional "rule of thumb" multiple, or by comparing it with valuations for similar companies appearing in publicly available financial information. However, the use of these open market multiples can give rise to a misleading result, since the details of the various transactions which influence the multiples may not be readily apparent. The impact of the particular terms of the transactions on the prices paid, the respective negotiating strengths of the parties involved, and the extent of post-transaction "synergies" available to the buyers, are all relevant and should be known if used to support the company's "unique" valuation.

The valuation ultimately arrived at is more likely to be expressed within a range of values, and not as a specific number. But regardless of the method used in valuation, the valuator may not be able to reflect the synergies or influence on value which a particular buyer may have. This concern is discussed below in connection with the purchase price that may be paid.

If the valuation is being conducted to facilitate a transfer of ownership to the company's other shareholders, the valuator may be required to follow the methodology prescribed in a shareholder agreement if one exists. However, such agreements often lack the degree of guidance which a valuator needs, and sometimes contain inconsistent instructions which the valuator finds difficult to reconcile, particularly in connection with goodwill and the various possible discounts and premiums described below.

GOODWILL

In addition to making the normalizing adjustments, the valuator may wish to take into account certain other factors. The valuator may attempt to attribute some value to the "goodwill" of the business, which is an intangible asset representing the value of the business over and above its "net identifiable assets". The net identifiable assets include the tangible operating assets, which are required to carry on the business, along with its identifiable intangible assets, such as patents, trade names and copyrights, all net of liabilities.

Goodwill is essentially the aggregate of the company's non-identifiable or non-specific intangible assets. It may be a result of the particular product, service, location or other commercial feature of the business, or a result of the personal contacts, reputation, and efforts of key people in the company.

The valuator has to decide how much of the goodwill is commercial and how much is personal, since ordinarily only commercial goodwill is transferable when the company's ownership changes and has value as a result. The goodwill should be enduring, giving rise to earnings from future operations.

Although some goodwill may appear to be attributable to certain individuals while employed by the company, their goodwill may have no value if their roles can be performed by others if they should leave the company. However, in recognizing that some new owners, particularly family members or long-standing employees, are more likely than others to maintain or take advantage of an individual's goodwill, the price to be paid for goodwill may depend to some extent upon who is intended to be the new owner. Individual goodwill may be transferred, or at least protected, through the use of customer introductions, non-competition agreements, and consulting agreements.

VARIOUS DISCOUNTS AND PREMIUMS

In determining the company's fair market value, the valuator may want to consider the impact of any income taxes, professional fees and various additional costs which may be incurred by the company in implementing the changes suggested in this book and reduce the value accordingly. Yet other discounts may be warranted, especially when the company has more than one shareholder.

If the company is controlled by one individual, the valuator may deem a "key person discount" to be appropriate. This discount is the reduction in value resulting from the actual or potential loss of a key person in the business.

If the company has any shareholders holding 50 per cent or less of the company's voting shares, the valuator may attach a "minority discount" to their shares. The application of a minority discount can be complicated and involve a number of factors. It is intended to reflect a minority shareholder's inability to influence key company decisions and the value of his investment, including the payment of dividends and the approval of share transfers, often owing to the absence of a board seat.

The size of a particular minority holding can become important when viewed in relation to other holdings. A shareholder with a 20 per cent interest in a company with only one other shareholder is in a different position from a shareholder with 20 per cent of a company with 4 other shareholders each holding 20 per cent.

A minority discount can also be affected by the existence of a shareholder agreement affording buy-sell rights or a board seat to a minority shareholder, or by the existence of a number of related shareholders who are likely to act or vote the same way.

However, the size of a particular minority holding can be significant enough to result not in a discount but in a premium. Since a vote of two-thirds of all shareholders can be required for fundamental corporate changes,[5] a minority shareholder holding more than a third of the votes that may be cast at a shareholder meeting may enjoy a premium for "blocking power:"

A premium often reflected in valuations is a "control premium", which is afforded to the shareholder who is able to exercise control over the company. Control is normally achieved by holding shares with the right to cast a majority of votes at a shareholder meeting, and flows from the right to elect a majority on the company's board of directors. A control premium is the additional amount an investor would pay over the pro-rated value of a non-controlling interest to achieve a controlling interest.

In the event that the company has more than one class of shares, the fair market value determined by the valuator for the entire company using one or more of the valuation methods described above must then be allocated amongst the various share classes. This value allocation is often based upon the terms and conditions of each particular class. For example, if there is outstanding a class of preference shares which has a priority over the other classes to be paid out first upon the liquidation of the company, the allocation of the company's fair market value should take into account this priority in ranking.

LIMITATIONS OF VALUATION METHODS

Despite the importance of obtaining a valuation as described above, the current owner should nevertheless be aware that the valuation obtained may be quite different from the price that may be paid for the company in an open market transaction. Whatever fair market value may be determined by the valuator as the company's value, the price which the owner might receive from a prospective buyer may well be higher or lower.

In accordance with the above definition of fair market value, the notional valuation methods applied by the valuator generally attempt to arrive at the highest cash price available in an open and unrestricted market between informed and prudent parties who are acting at arm's length under no compulsion to act.

Yet these assumptions and conditions seldom exist in the open market context.

For example, having an open market from which no potential buyer is excluded and in which all potential buyers have the motivation and resources to act rarely occurs in an actual business sale. Having a market free from any statutory or contractual restrictions on a sale seldom applies to private companies which are usually subject to share transfer constraints in their articles of incorporation or shareholder agreements.

Assuming that the parties are well informed about the company and have all the facts that are relevant to determining its value is questionable, regardless of the amount of due diligence which has been undertaken. In an open market transaction, a buyer may not be fully informed about the company's financial position, business prospects or competitive pressures. Even assuming that the buyer is acting prudently can be flawed, since due diligence investigations are often prioritized and either shortened or sacrificed in practice because of time and cost considerations.

An assumption that the parties are under no compulsion to undertake a transaction often fails to reflect reality. In open market deals, sellers may be forced to sell because their business is failing, or because their health is failing, or both.

Two other assumptions inherent in the definition of fair market value deserve particular attention.

First is the assumption that the value will be the highest price, since without exposing the business for sale, the highest price can't be ascertained with any certainty due to the possible existence of special interest buyers who are willing to pay for expected post-acquisition benefits or synergies. Without open market negotiations, it is difficult to quantify with any accuracy how much a buyer would be prepared to pay for such synergies.

Second is the assumption that the value will be expressed in terms of cash. Transactions in the open market are frequently completed with just a portion of the purchase price being paid in cash, with the balance payable in shares of the buyer, under a promissory note, or under an "earn-out" formula requiring the company's earnings to exceed a prescribed threshold.

The questionable validly of each of these two assumptions in the open market context is discussed in greater detail below.

INFLUENCE OF BUYER SYNERGIES ON PRICE

While the definition of fair market value mentioned above means the highest price generally available in a marketplace consisting of all potential buyers, there may be a special buyer who will enjoy certain synergistic or strategic benefits in buying the company which are unavailable to other potential buyers. Such benefits may arise, for example, if the buyer is a direct competitor of the company, or is perhaps an existing company customer.

These synergies essentially represent an incremental value over the company's "intrinsic" value consisting of its net identifiable assets and goodwill as described above. This incremental value is unique to each potential buyer and may be based on additional revenues, cost savings or risk reduction that the buyer expects will result from combining the purchased business with its own existing operations.

The buyer will determine the amount of this incremental value representing its expected synergies and add some or all of it to the company's intrinsic value to arrive at a possible purchase price for the company.

However, the buyer will still have to adjust this incremental value by the costs to be incurred in realizing such synergies. These costs can include such things as severance payments, relocation expenses and re-structuring costs. For those synergies expected in the form of incremental revenues, the buyer should consider the additional costs necessary to generate those revenues, such as additional personnel, new equipment and higher levels of required working capital. These expenditures are ordinarily made "up front" soon after the transaction has been completed in the hope that the synergies will materialize as planned.

In deciding how much of the expected synergies it wants to pay for, the buyer can take into account any potential shortfalls in the company's cash flows which may occur after the deal closes and thereby reduce the purchase price being offered. By fully paying for the expected synergies, the buyer may later feel he paid too much if the post-acquisition benefits fail to materialize.

In other words, even though a buyer may be prepared to pay extra for these benefits, how much extra is very difficult for the valuator to deter-mine when applying standard valuation methods and is usually settled only during the purchase negotiations between the parties themselves.

INFLUENCE OF PAYMENT TERMS ON PRICE

In addition to the impact of buyer synergies on the determination of a purchase price for the company, the terms of payment represent another significant factor to be considered when explaining the likely difference between price and value.

While the above valuation methods applied by a valuator provide a possible "cash equivalent" price for the company, not all deals are com-pleted in cash on closing. Some exceptions have already been suggested. Payment may be made by way of shares of the buyer, or under the seller's "take-back financing" which permits the buyer to pay a number of pur-chase price installments over time pursuant to a promissory note. Pay-ment may also be made in accordance with an earn-out formula which requires the buyer to pay an additional amount only if the company exceeds certain financial targets after closing.

Furthermore, many buyers want to retain a portion of the purchase price as a "holdback" for a period of time after closing against which the buyer can offset any liabilities which were undisclosed at closing but which appear later on.

Each of these alternative forms of consideration which may be used to complete a transaction instead of paying the entire purchase price in cash on closing represent certain risks as well as rewards.

For the seller, the buyer's shares may drop in value after closing, or the buyer may default in paying some of the purchase price installments or the holdback to the seller when agreed upon, or the earnings of the company may plummet once the buyer takes over, thereby removing any chance of earn-out payments. The seller may require the purchase price to be increased to offset these risks.

The buyer, on the other hand, may regard these alternative forms of consideration as providing some extra protection to offset the overall risks of buying the company and as a way to avoid paying too much. After all, should the company's cash flows fail to generate a rate of return which exceeds the buyer's cost of capital when measured against the purchase price, the acquisition is likely to be regarded as a bad deal. Lower revenues or higher operating and financing costs than expected, or the inability to realize the synergies anticipated, can easily cause this to happen.

OTHER INFLUENCES ON PRICE

To understand the gap between the company's valuation and the price to be paid to acquire the company, the owner has to understand more than just the buyer's potential synergies and the various forms of consideration.

The owner will also have to keep in mind that a negotiated purchase price is generally influenced by a number of additional factors which are not reflected in the notional methods used by the valuator. These include the competitive bidding environment, the relative importance of the transaction to the parties and the availability of alternatives to it, the sense of urgency felt by the parties to complete the transaction, and their respective negotiating power and ability.

And, significantly, the other terms of the deal.

For example, various representations, warranties and indemnities from a seller, or non-competition agreements and employment contracts with the seller and the company's senior officers, can allocate some of the risk, as well as the rewards, of the transaction between the buyer and seller, and can greatly influence the amount of the purchase price to be paid.

The price may also be affected by whether the transaction is structured as the sale of assets or the sale of shares, a distinction described in more detail in the *Transfers to Outside Parties* chapter. Buyers usually prefer to buy the assets of a company in order to avoid hidden liabilities and for certain tax advantages, whereas sellers usually prefer to sell shares for their own tax benefit. However, the buyer may benefit from a purchase of shares if the seller is prepared to reduce the purchase price while allowing holdbacks or other protection mechanisms that reduce the risk of the buyer assuming hidden liabilities.

The particular type of business operated by the company can create specific valuation challenges and increase the likelihood that the eventual purchase price negotiated in the open market context will vary considerably from the valuation given.

For example, while many of the foregoing factors which influence price are generally applicable to all kinds of businesses, franchises, along with dealerships and distributorships, present certain difficult valuation problems. Because trademarks are usually involved, the scope of the trademark license granted to a franchisee and whether it is exclusive or non-exclusive must be considered. Furthermore, the risk of non-renewal of the franchise agreement, the restrictions on franchise transfer, and the franchisor's rights of approval of proposed transferees must be taken into account in determining value.

What can be more problematic in the valuation of a franchise is the impact of the franchisor's right of first refusal which can be a serious impediment to marketability. When a franchisor holds such a right, a potential buyer of the franchise from the franchisee will be concerned that the franchisor is always a potential bidder, and the franchisor is likely to know more about the available franchise than any other outside party. As a result, an outside buyer might have to spend a lot of time and money in order to come close to matching the franchisor's knowledge of the available franchise. Without that knowledge, the outside buyer may offer either too little and risk losing out to the franchisor, or too much and risk making a bad deal in acquiring the franchise.

In light of all of the many factors outlined above which can affect the price ultimately payable by a buyer for the company in the open market, the valuation initially obtained may serve only as a rough guide for the owner in predicting how much he will eventually receive for his shares in the company after he embarks on the process described in this book.

Reorganization

In addition to obtaining a valuation of the company, the current owner may consider whether the company and its business should be "reorganized". A reorganization may involve creating additional classes of shares, exchanging existing shares for new shares, incorporating a new holding company, exchanging assets and shares between both companies, and even paying dividends.

The main goal of a reorganization is generally to minimize any taxes that might arise when carrying out many of the steps for succession which are discussed in this book. A reorganization may not only allow the owner to use her lifetime capital gains exemption described below, but it may also ensure that any consideration paid to her is received as a capital gain and not as more highly taxed income.

A reorganization, however, may provide other benefits to the owner at the same time. It may protect some of the company's assets against possible attacks from company creditors if such assets are transferred elsewhere, perhaps to another corporation which in turn leases the assets back to the company. The company's real estate, for example, may be protected this way.

Reorganizing the company may also make it more attractive to a potential successor by leaving it with only those assets which the successor really wants to acquire, and possibly with only those liabilities which the successor is prepared to assume. The company may be reorganized simply to separate business assets from any assets which are not necessarily integral to operating the company's business.

From the owner's perspective, a reorganization can be used to leave the company with only those assets which she wants to pass on to her successor, while transferring to a related company those assets which she wants to keep for herself.

LIFETIME CAPITAL GAINS EXEMPTION

The first objective the owner might have is to take advantage of the lifetime capital gains exemption[1] which can reduce the amount of taxes she may have to pay in the event that she disposes of her shares, or which her estate may have to pay because of the deemed disposition of the shares occurring upon her death.[2]

The exemption is available only to individuals resident in Canada, and shelters from tax a maximum of $750,000[3] in capital gains arising from the disposition of the shares of a qualified small business corporation, or QSBC. It is not available to the company upon the sale of any of the company's assets, nor is it available upon the redemption by the company of the company's shares.

In order for the shares of a company to be QSBC shares, three tests[4] generally need to be met: the company had to be a "small business corporation" on the disposition of the shares which is defined to be a Canadian-controlled private corporation carrying on an active business primarily in Canada;[5] the shares cannot have been owned by anyone other than the person disposing of them or by a related person during the two year period preceding the disposition; and during those two years, at least 50 per cent of the fair market value of the assets of the company had to be used principally in an active business carried on primarily in Canada by the company or a related company. A company which is winding down, selling off its assets and investing the sale proceeds, is not carrying on an active business.

PURIFICATION OF THE COMPANY

There are a number of qualifications to each of these three tests which need to be considered but which are beyond the general scope of this chapter. However, in order for the company to be a small business corporation on the disposition of the shares, at least 90 per cent of the fair market value of the company's assets must be used principally in an active business carried on primarily in Canada by the company or a related company which may not consist of a specified investment business or personal services business.[6] Non-active assets often consist of excess cash, securities and other investments which generate non-business income.

If the company meets the above two year, 50 per cent test but its active assets will fail to comprise at least 90 per cent of the fair market value of its total assets at the time of the proposed disposition, the owner may consider "purifying" the company. Purification essentially involves the removal of non-active assets so that the company may again qualify as a small business corporation. How the owner will actually purify the company will depend upon whether or not the non-active assets have accrued unrealized capital gains.

Non-active assets without accrued gains may simply be removed tax-free from the company to allow it to comply with the 90 per cent test. For example, if surplus cash might threaten the company's ability to comply, especially if such cash is used to earn investment income, the company might decide to use some of the surplus to buy equipment and inventory, or prepay various business expenses such as rent and taxes. It may also decide to increase salaries and bonuses to employees, pay dividends to its shareholders, or retire outstanding debt and other liabilities.

Where the non-active assets have accrued gains, the owner may have to consider a reorganization to accomplish their removal on a tax efficient basis.[7] If the company's non-active assets have little accrued gains, the owner might transfer her company shares to a new holding corporation, and the company would then redeem or repurchase such shares by transferring the non-active assets to the holding corporation.

If the company's non-active assets have significant accrued gains, a divisive reorganization or "butterfly" might be used to complete the asset transfers. A butterfly often comprises the following four general steps.

First, the owner incorporates a holding corporation and transfers some of her company shares to the holding corporation in exchange for shares of the holding corporation. The owner elects to have that transaction completed as a tax-deferred rollover. The total value of the company's shares transferred to the holding corporation will equal the value of the non-active assets being removed from the company.

Second, the company then transfers the non-active assets to the holding corporation, receiving in return preferred shares issued by the holding corporation which are redeemable and retractable for an amount equal to the value of the non-active assets. The parties elect to have the transfer treated as a tax-deferred rollover.

Third, the company then redeems its shares held by the holding corporation for a promissory note, and the holding corporation redeems its preferred shares held by the company for a promissory note of the same value.[8] Fourth, both promissory notes are then set off against each other and cancelled.

Upon the completion of these four steps, the company holds only active assets, and the holding corporation holds only non-active assets. The owner ends up owning both the company and the holding corporation, and is then able to use her available lifetime capital gains exemption when she transfers her company shares.

It is important that these purification steps are carried out before the owner's successor has been identified. If these steps occur in contemplation of the sale of the company's shares to an unrelated buyer, the share redemptions in the third step that would otherwise be deemed to be tax-free inter-corporate dividends may instead be treated as taxable capital gains.[9]

A similar purifying reorganization can also take place so that the 50 per cent test can be met, if necessary, keeping in mind that such a reorganization would have to take place at least two years before the disposition of the shares.

CRYSTALLIZATION OF EXEMPTION

Once the company has been purified in order to make its shares eligible as QSBC shares, the owner may decide to "crystallize" or "lock-in" her available lifetime capital gains exemption by disposing of her shares in order to generate a capital gain which is then sheltered by her exemption. Crystallization essentially allows the owner to use her exemption now instead of running the risk that she may later lose it, either because of possible legislative changes or because the company fails to meet the asset tests described above in the future and ceases to be a QSBC.

The exemption may be crystallized by the owner simply transferring her shares to a third party, which may include a family member, trust or a holding corporation, although such a transfer should not take place if the fair market value of the shares is more than the owner's available capital gains exemption room.

If the fair market value is more, then the owner wanting to crystallize her exemption might exchange her company shares for new shares of the company and elect an exchange amount equal to her available exemption room.[10] Alternatively, she might transfer her shares to a holding corporation and elect the proceeds of the disposition to be equal to her available exemption room.[11] Using a holding corporation, however, may trap any proceeds from an eventual sale of the company in the holding corporation because paying out the proceeds will result in a taxable dividend to the owner.

Since the exemption is available to individuals resident in Canada, it can be quite useful when the owner and all of her family members are shareholders of the company. The number of individual exemptions will then be multiplied amongst the family and the overall tax savings can be increased accordingly.

Consequently, the owner may attempt a form of reorganization to expand the company's ownership. She may transfer her shares directly to individual family members[12] or to a family trust, or alternatively, she may create an "estate freeze", which is described in more detail in the next chapter. Either way, her family members will then be able to apply their own capital gains exemptions to reduce the tax payable on any increase in the value of the company between the time of the reorganization and the time of an eventual sale.

Any reorganization intended to increase the capital gains exemptions available should take place long before any sale of the company to an outside party in order to provide enough time over which the value of the company can appreciate substantially to allow the maximum exemptions to be taken.

DIVIDING ASSETS

Although the steps described above in removing non-active assets may be undertaken to purify the company so that it qualifies as a small business corporation, they may also be undertaken to meet the anticipated demands of a potential purchaser of the company. They may make the company more saleable, regardless of whether the owner is able to take advantage of the lifetime capital gains exemption on the sale of her shares.

Such steps may also help the owner to remove from the company certain assets which the owner wants to keep after the company is sold to an outsider. This is often the case when the company is using a valuable parcel of real estate in a prime location, and the owner wants to acquire it from the company for the purpose of leasing it back to the company after the sale. Similarly, the owner may want to acquire certain intellectual property used in the business, perhaps the patent upon one of her inventions, which she would like to then license to the company.

It therefore becomes necessary that the company own only the assets which are to be included in the business being sold. These business assets, in other words, need to be separated from the company's non-business assets. But if the non-business assets have appreciated since their acquisition by the company, there will be tax payable by the company to the extent of such appreciation if they are transferred directly to the owner or a corporation related to the owner.

However, by using the butterfly technique described above, a reorganization of the assets can be carried out tax-effectively to have the business assets reside in one corporation and the non-business assets reside in another, with both corporations each controlled by the owner. While a butterfly reorganization can achieve this result, it should not, as cautioned above, be undertaken as part of a series of transactions which include the sale of the business to an arm's length buyer. If no such sale is contemplated, reorganizing the assets this way will enable the owner to divide up the various assets without the adverse tax consequences of a direct transfer to the owner.[13]

REDUCING THE CAPITAL GAIN

If the lifetime capital gains exemption is not available to the owner, the owner may still achieve a reduction of the capital gain on the disposition of her company shares by first removing "safe income" from the company in order to reduce the value of her shares. A safe income "strip" often involves three steps.

The first step requires the owner to transfer her company shares to a new holding corporation on a rollover basis in return for shares of the holding corporation.[14] As a second step, the company then pays a dividend to the holding corporation out of the company's retained earnings or safe income on which tax has already been paid. This dividend reduces the value of the company's shares. In the third step, the holding corporation then sells the shares to the successor for a reduced price reflecting the reduction in the company's value caused by the safe income dividend.[15]

As an alternative means of reducing the value of the owner's shares, funds might be removed tax-free from the company though the payment of capital dividends directly to the owner provided such dividends are paid out of the company's capital dividend account, a notional account comprising among other things the non-taxable portion of any capital gains earned by the company and the amount of any insurance proceeds received exceeding the adjusted cost base of the policy.[16]

Transfers to Family — Part I

In considering possible successors to the company's business, the current owner's first thoughts are usually to the members of his own family and their respective willingness and ability to be an owner, manager, or both. He must carefully consider whether all members of the family should be treated equally, especially if some members of the family are already quite involved in the company's operations.

In deciding whether a particular child is the logical successor, numerous questions will need to be asked, and the answers may not come easily. Does the child have the experience and skills necessary to run the business? What will happen to the relationship between the current owner and child once the child becomes the owner, or to the relationships with other children who are not selected? If more than one child is selected, how well will the selected children work together, especially if the current owner ceases to be involved?

The owner may be able to wait a while before having to decide which, if any, of his children are suitable successors. He may have suggested that they acquire some needed skills or experience by working somewhere else. Or he may have tested their abilities by first giving them smaller roles to play within the company. His assessment of their abilities to be both a manager and an owner will ideally be based upon how well they have performed a variety of tasks.

But deciding upon any successor cannot be made without regard to the owner's personal financial circumstances.

If the owner has enough financial resources unrelated to the company, he may simply decide to leave his company shares to some or all of his children in his will and continue to hold on to his shares in the meantime upon his retirement while the company is operated by professional managers from outside the family. Waiting to transfer his shares to his children as an inheritance upon his death will make his estate liable for any capital gains taxes then arising.[1] Using a will to transfer his shares upon his death is discussed in the next chapter.

GIFT OF SHARES

Instead of deciding that the transfer of his shares should be delayed until after his death, the owner may be in the financial position to simply give all of his company shares to his children while he is still living and then pay the capital gains taxes owing.[2]

Such taxes may arise because he is deemed upon the gift to have disposed of his shares at their fair market value and to have received such value in return.

Depending upon the company's valuation, and the amount of his $750,000 lifetime capital gains exemption still available to him, it is possible that no such taxes will become payable, in which case an outright gift of his shares may then make sense.

However, if the shares are worth considerably more than the owner's available exemption, the excess gain will be taxable. One-half of the excess gain will be included in the owner's income and taxed at his applicable marginal rate. In such circumstances, giving the shares away to his children should be avoided.

While the owner may believe that the fair market value of his shares is less than the amount available to him under his lifetime capital gains exemption, there is nonetheless the possibility that the Canada Revenue Agency might determine a higher fair market value for his shares and assess capital gains tax accordingly on the gift. Since gifts of private company shares to family members are likely to be more closely examined than transfers to arm's length parties in the Agency's assessment of tax payable, the owner may face unexpected taxes after the gifts have taken place.

SALE OF SHARES

Giving away his shares will not be an option for the owner who requires additional capital in order to retire successfully. While he may not necessarily need the capital provided by the sale of the company, he may need the income such capital might produce. It may therefore be possible for his children to acquire his shares without paying him what outside buyers might pay so long as they agree to pay him what he would have made as investment income if he had sold the company to an outside buyer and invested the sale proceeds.

However, as with a gift of his shares, any sale of his shares to his family will be deemed to be made at fair market value, regardless of the amount the owner may receive. He will therefore be required to pay capital gains tax on the difference between the cost of his shares and the fair market value he is deemed to have received, subject to a reduction for the amount of his lifetime capital gains exemption still available to him. Unfortunately the children buying his shares for less than fair market value are only allowed to treat as their tax cost for the shares the amount they actually paid.[3]

Selling his shares to some of his children for cash, assuming they already have it or can borrow it, has the advantage of providing the owner with the funds he might need for retirement or might need to give to his other children who will remain unconnected with the business. With a cash sale, any capital gain arising will be included by the owner in his income for the year of the sale, less the amount of his available lifetime capital gains exemption.

Providing instead for payment of the purchase price to be deferred may not give the owner immediate access to funds which he needs, but may be the only way his children can afford to buy him out. If payment of the sale price includes a promissory note payable to the owner which permits installments to be made over time, the owner may be able to claim a reserve for the unpaid sale proceeds which requires that only a portion of the gain be taxed in the year of sale. Claiming a reserve ordinarily permits the applicable capital gain to be spread out over a period of five years, although in the case of a sale to a child, the owner may be able to claim a reserve covering 10 years.[4]

ESTATE FREEZE

If the owner has decided to transfer ownership of his shares to his family, he may attempt to make the transfer by way of an "estate freeze" and thereby reduce the taxes that he might otherwise pay if he made an outright gift or transfer,[5] or which his estate might pay upon the deemed disposition of the shares upon his death.[6]

An estate freeze is particularly useful when the owner doesn't need cash proceeds from a sale of his shares. It allows his children to acquire equity in the company for a nominal investment. It also permits the splitting with his adult children of any future earnings of the company and any gains realized on a subsequent sale of the company's shares. Any future increase in the value of the company's shares accrues to the benefit of the owner's family. When used as a tool in estate planning, a freeze may save enough in taxes owing upon the death of the owner to mean the difference between having to sell the company's assets to satisfy the tax liability and being able to keep the company operating as usual.

The freeze essentially limits the tax liability that arises on death by fixing the owner's shares at their value when the freeze is implemented. It defers a portion of the tax that would otherwise have been payable on the owner's death since the tax on future growth in the value of the shares isn't payable until his children dispose of their shares.

When an estate freeze is put into place, the current owner usually exchanges his common shares with the company for redeemable preferred shares. His children, or a family trust for their benefit as described below, then subscribe for common shares for nominal value. The owner's interest in the company is fixed at the redemption value of his preferred shares, and the children then get the benefit of any future increase in the value of the common shares. The redemption value of the preferred shares is usually fixed at the fair market value of the common shares being exchanged in order to avoid a benefit being conferred on the children by the owner.[7]

In addition to providing both the company and the owner with the right to redeem the preferred shares, such shares often provide preferential dividend rights, requiring that any dividends on the preferred shares be paid before any dividends on the common shares. The dividends on the preferred shares, often set at a particular percentage of the redemption amount, may be either discretionary, as deemed desirable by the company's directors, or mandatory. The preference shares usually have priority over the common shares in any return of capital upon the company's liquidation, and may have voting rights to allow the owner to maintain voting control as discussed below.

Ordinarily the capital gain or loss incurred upon the exchange of his common shares for preferred shares can be deferred, since the cost of the preferred shares is deemed to be the same as the adjusted cost base of his common shares. The owner's gain on the common shares will effectively be taxed when the preferred shares are eventually disposed. However, the freeze can be implemented in a slightly different way which allows the owner to elect that the share exchange takes place for more than the adjusted cost base of his common shares so that he can create a capital gain and crystallize his lifetime capital gains exemption, as discussed earlier in the *Reorganization* chapter.[8]

If the owner will not have an immediate need for the proceeds resulting from his redemption of the preferred shares to fund his retirement, he may be able to defer the tax that would otherwise be owing upon the share redemption by transferring his preferred shares to a new holding corporation which he might create. The share transfer could be made with no immediate tax consequences so long as he receives shares from the holding corporation,[9] and the proceeds resulting from any subsequent redemption of the preferred shares by the company would result in the holding corporation receiving a tax-free deemed dividend from the company. These proceeds could then be invested by the holding corporation, which would pay the applicable corporate tax on any investment income. Should the owner need additional funds later on, the holding corporation could pay dividends at that time to him, and he would then be liable to pay tax on the dividends he receives.

Another use of a holding corporation in carrying out an estate freeze might also be considered by the owner. Instead of exchanging his common shares for preferred shares in the company, the owner might set up a new holding corporation and transfer his company shares to the holding corporation in return for preferred shares of the holding corporation. His children are issued in turn common shares of the holding corporation.[10] However, such an approach may not be as tax-effective if the holding corporation cannot meet the tests of a QSBC when the children are given the opportunity to sell their shares and are then unable to use their lifetime capital gains exemption.

It should be kept in mind that the $750,000 lifetime capital gains exemption can be multiplied among a family holding shares of a QSBC should each family member be able to use his respective exemption in the disposition of QSBC shares. Adding more individual family members as shareholders therefore increases the number of available exemptions. This is just another reason for implementing an estate freeze even though the owner may wish to eventually sell the company to an outside party, particularly when he feels the company may substantially increase in value. The freeze then becomes merely an interim step to multiply the number of capital gains exemptions available upon an outside sale rather than the means used by the owner for a final ownership transfer to his children.

RETAINING CONTROL

The preferred shares received by the owner on a freeze are often voting shares which give the owner the ability to continue to control the company, at least until a certain percentage of his preferred shares are redeemed by the company.

Alternatively, the owner may be issued a separate class of voting special shares in addition to being issued the preferred shares. This separate voting class of shares can allow the owner to maintain control of the company even after his preferred shares have been redeemed. The owner's control may be reinforced by a shareholder agreement which affords him the right to appoint a majority of the company's directors or to veto certain company decisions, such as the declaration of dividends or issuance of shares.

The shareholder agreement can also be used to impose various restrictions upon the children who have acquired company shares under the freeze. While such restrictions may appear to be undesirable when planning for a sale to a third party as discussed above in the *Putting the Company in Saleable Condition* chapter, they may be necessary to ensure that the company is in "good hands" when continuing under family ownership. The agreement might therefore provide for rights of first refusal and various buy-sell rights, including call rights which might give those children who are actively involved in the company a right to buy the shares of those children who aren't.

A more comprehensive description of these rights and restrictions can be found in the chapter *Shareholder Agreements*.

ENSURING LIQUIDITY

When receiving the preferred shares under a freeze, the owner is often concerned that the redemption value will not be enough to retire on. In order to provide the owner with funds if and when necessary, the owner and the company often enter into an agreement requiring the company to repurchase or redeem the owner's preferred shares over time in accordance with a series of prescribed dates or milestones. The amounts received by the owner under this redemption schedule will usually be taxed as deemed dividends.[11]

The owner might also receive funds by way of actual dividends, since the preferred shares issued to the owner often provide for a discretionary dividend which permits the directors to pay dividends to the owner sufficient for his needs before paying dividends to the children or the family trust on the common shares.

Either way, whether through share redemptions or dividends, the owner may not be able to receive adequate funds quickly enough for retirement purposes. The business may simply not be capable of generating sufficient funds for the redemption of his shares or payment of dividends. For this reason, an estate freeze may not be appropriate for the owner who has an immediate need to realize upon the value he has built up in the company. In some instances, the owner may have left it too late to establish an estate freeze which will be able to satisfy his financial objectives.

However, in setting up an estate freeze, the owner will at least learn how much his interest in the company is worth and how much tax will likely be payable on his death when his interest is deemed to be disposed. He can then address how the tax might be paid by his estate, hopefully without requiring a sale of the company or a significant portion of its assets.

Implementing an estate freeze often involves the purchase of life insurance which can help in satisfying the tax liabilities arising on the owner's death. The insurance proceeds can be used to pay the taxes owing on the accrued gains on the owner's preferred shares which are deemed to be disposed upon his death. Insurance proceeds can also be used to fund the company's redemption of the owner's preferred shares and thereby avoid the possibility of having to sell some of the company's assets to generate sufficient monies for the redemption. The surviving spouse of the owner may also receive insurance proceeds as a replacement for the distributions from the company previously received by the owner.

A more comprehensive description of the role played by insurance in funding the purchase of the owner's shares upon his death appears in the following chapter.

FAMILY TRUSTS

Despite the tax-savings which may result from the implementation of an estate freeze, the freeze may actually prove to be an obstacle to carrying out the business succession which the owner might prefer later on. Since many freezes treat all of the owner's children equally, and provide each of them with a similar number of common shares of the company, the child who may eventually turn out to be the most logical and capable successor may be forced to negotiate with the other siblings to buy their shares.

The owner, if still living, might then try to encourage the others to sell out, or at least come to some "first amongst equals" solution for the overall benefit of the company, using the argument that a single successor can minimize the conflicts that tend to arise when there are multiple leaders. The others may simply refuse to do so, especially when selling their shares to the chosen successor might trigger a capital gains tax liability which was intended to be deferred when the freeze was set up.

One way to avoid this situation from arising is through the current owner's use of a family trust with discretionary distribution powers to hold the common shares instead of providing for the children to hold the shares directly. While the owner would still exchange his common shares for preferred or "freeze" shares of the company, the common or "growth" shares would be issued to the family trust. The trustees of the trust would then be given the power to distribute the trust property, such as the shares, when and to whom they feel appropriate. They are thereby allowed to benefit a beneficiary disproportionately, or perhaps exclude a beneficiary altogether.

They are also allowed to distribute income earned by the trust to any one or more of the beneficiaries in their discretion.

The family trust in these circumstances is an "inter vivos" trust, created while the owner is still alive to hold company shares and other property for the benefit of his family. It is different from a "testamentary" trust, which may be created under the owner's will as a means of ultimately transferring his shares and other property to his family members after his death. Testamentary trusts are discussed in the next chapter.

Unlike a corporation, a trust is not a separate legal entity but is instead a legal relationship or obligation involving a trustee who holds and deals with property for the benefit of the beneficiaries. The person who creates the trust is usually referred to as the "settlor". The trustee's main obligation is to carry out the instructions of the settlor as contained in the terms of the trust. These terms are described in greater detail in the *Family Trust Agreements* chapter.

Certain features of trusts make them quite useful in the succession planning context. Their separation of legal and beneficial ownership of the trust property, their ability to provide for a number of successive beneficial interests spanning a considerable period of time, and the discretion they can offer the trustees when dealing with the trust property, including how and when the beneficiaries may actually receive a benefit, can help the owner accomplish his overall business succession objectives. Trusts can be used to provide the owner's children with the enjoyment of property without the powers of management or control.

Even though a trust may not be a separate legal entity, it is nonetheless treated as an individual for tax purposes.[12] It is therefore subject to tax on the taxable income it earns from property or a business, although it can flow such income to its beneficiaries so that the beneficiaries, not the trust, pay the tax owing on any "flowed through" amounts.[13] The trust is allowed a deduction for the amounts paid to the beneficiaries when calculating its income for tax purposes.[14]

Although commonly used in estate freezes, when a family trust acquires new common shares of the company after the owner has exchanged his own common shares for preferred shares, a family trust can also be used to acquire all of the owner's common shares directly from him. As described above in connection with the gift or sale of his shares to his children, a family trust acquiring his shares will be deemed to have acquired the shares at their fair market value, and the owner will be deemed to have disposed of the shares at their fair market value.[15]

If the value of his shares is less than the amount still available to him under his lifetime capital gains exemption, he may consider an outright transfer of his shares to a family trust rather than creating an estate freeze. However, he should not be the sole trustee of the family trust in order to avoid the possible attribution back to him of any capital gains or income earned by the trust in connection with the shares.[16] Often the trustees of a family trust include the owner, his chosen successor and a third party familiar with the family's affairs.

Although a trust established as a family trust involving the owner's children may be more commonly used by an owner for business succession, he may also consider using a trust established for the benefit of his spouse. The owner may elect to transfer his shares to a qualifying spousal trust at his adjusted cost base on a tax-deferred rollover basis,[17] or elect not to claim the rollover so that the transfer will take place at fair market value.[18] In order for a spousal trust to qualify for rollover treatment, the spouse must be entitled to receive all of the income of the trust that arises before her death, and during the spouse's lifetime, no other person may receive any of the income or capital of the trust.

Even though an inter vivos trust may be established by the owner to hold his shares and possibly his other property for the benefit of his family members, the trust cannot hold the property for an indefinite period as a way of deferring the taxation of capital gains. A trust is deemed to have disposed and then reacquired its capital property every 21 years for proceeds equal to its fair market value.[19] Consequently trust property which has appreciated in value is often distributed to the beneficiaries on a tax-deferred basis[20] before the 21-year period has expired, assuming the trust deed or other instrument creating the trust allows for such a distribution to take place.

Whether the family trust acquires the owner's common shares directly from him or acquires new common shares of the company upon an estate freeze, the trust can still be used to ensure that the ownership of the company ends up in the hands of the beneficiary who deserves to control and ultimately own the company. With just one beneficiary as the intended successor, the shares can be distributed to that beneficiary on a tax-free basis and no capital gains will be realized until the beneficiary eventually disposes of the shares. The beneficiary acquires the shares at the adjusted cost base of the trust.[21] Even thought the trust is deemed to dispose of its assets after 21 years, the trustees are given considerable time before being required to select which beneficiaries ought to acquire the shares.

If the owner wishes for each of his children to be involved in the company, a family trust can still be used to multiply the number of lifetime capital gains exemptions used among the family. Each child receiving the company's shares from the trust can shelter the proceeds eventually received upon the sale of such shares from capital gains tax up to the amount available under the child's own lifetime exemption.

A family trust with discretionary distribution powers can also be used for income-splitting purposes. The trustees might distribute dividends to the children on a discretionary basis so that income can be made available to the children without giving them control of the company.

Furthermore, a family trust may be used to provide some measure of creditor proofing. A trust holding the common shares can protect the shares from being attacked by the children's creditors.

A family trust can also be used to avoid the consequences of children predeceasing the owner. If the owner's common shares, or the new common shares created upon a freeze, are transferred directly to a particular child, and that child then dies, the shares will be dealt with under the child's will and could end up being transferred to someone the owner might regard as an unsuitable successor. Having the shares held instead by a family trust enables the trustees to decide who should receive the shares, as the shares are governed by the trust agreement which can reflect the owner's wishes in the event of a child's death, and not the deceased child's will.

If the parents are included as additional beneficiaries of the family trust, an estate freeze which uses a family trust can effectively be "reversed" if the children turn out to be unsuitable successors or if an irreconcilable intra-family dispute appears to threaten the viability of the company. The trustees might then exercise their discretion to distribute the company's common or "growth" shares to the parents who would then consider other alternatives in dealing with them. Reversing a freeze in favour of the owner may also be appropriate in the event that the value of the company has appreciated considerably after the freeze was created and the redemption value of the owner's preferred or "freeze" shares is inadequate to meet his needs in retirement.

If the owner and his spouse are the only trustees of the family trust, they will clearly have a conflict of interest in exercising their discretion to distribute trust assets to themselves as beneficiaries. Even though the deed establishing the trust may permit such distributions to be made despite the conflict, the children may nonetheless bring legal proceedings to overturn them. It is therefore preferable for the trust to have a third trustee, thereby allowing the parents to abstain from voting on any distributions in their favour.

DIFFERENT VS. EQUAL TREATMENT OF CHILDREN

In setting up an estate freeze or family trust, the owner may have to decide which of his children should benefit from the growth of the company's business. He may wish to favour those children who are active in the company over those who are not. This favouritism can be accomplished by different means.

If an estate freeze is established by issuing new company shares directly to the owner's children, different classes of shares may be issued to different children. For example, those children less involved or less capable in managing the company might receive shares with rights to dividends but not rights to vote except in the event that the company is to be sold to an outside party.

However, deciding how much of the company's profits should be paid as dividends on their shares can be a challenge, especially if the owner wishes that all children be compensated as equally as possible. While the non-active children may be looking to the company for generous dividend income, the active children may prefer to reinvest the profits in the company to finance further growth. Giving the non-active children a preference over the active children to a specified annual dividend can create considerable dissension amongst the family, since the active children may feel they are working very hard and making personal sacrifices in order to pay their non-active siblings first.

If new company shares are to be issued to a family trust when a freeze is established, the owner will have to determine which of his children should be the beneficiaries of the trust in order to eventually receive the "growth" shares created under the freeze. Those who are not involved in the company could be excluded as beneficiaries. Often a family trust supporting a freeze will name as beneficiaries not only the chosen successor but also the successor's children and spouse, although a spouse who is separated from the successor is usually excluded as a beneficiary.

Although all of the owner's children may initially be made beneficiaries of the family trust created to support an estate freeze, the trust may continue to include as a beneficiary only the chosen successor after a particular period of time. While having the non-involved children as beneficiaries allows them to share in the proceeds of a company sale occurring in the short term after the freeze is set up, dropping them as beneficiaries later on provides the successor, who is likely to still be involved in the business, with the benefits of increasing the company's sale value.[22]

Equalizing how his children are financially treated may be accomplished by the owner through other means. Assets of the company which are not integral to the company's business operations such as real estate can be transferred to another corporation owned by those children not chosen as the company's successor. Even if each child is willing and qualified to be a successor, equalization may still be possible if the company's assets and operations can be divided up amongst separate corporations, each owned by a different child, or alternatively divided up amongst separate divisions of the company, each managed by a different child.

If the current owner provides for just one child to become the successor of the business, and if the size and diversity of his other holdings are sufficient, he may also be able to equalize the entitlements of all of his children when he dies. Since the preferred shares which he receives when the freeze is created might be transferred to the successor under his will, the will might then contain what is called a "hotchpot" clause, which specifically excludes the successor to the company from additional benefits under the owner's estate.

ARM'S LENGTH TREATMENT

While an estate freeze may be used as part of a current owner's plan to transfer ownership of the company to the members of his family, he may decide instead to deal with his chosen successors as if they were unrelated to him and follow the procedures outlined later in the *Transfers to Outside Parties* chapter.

While such procedures may not provide the same tax advantages and generally entail the use of a negotiated purchase and sale agreement and due diligence investigations, such an "arm's length" approach may be appropriate in certain family situations. The owner may feel that a freeze might be difficult to implement because of certain rivalries and distrust among his children, and that his best form of exit might be to simply sell to the child who is the highest bidder.

Furthermore, implementing an estate freeze may not provide him with enough to retire on, or at least not enough when he wants to retire. His wishes for an early exit may make him too late for a freeze. Even though the redemption value of the preferred shares he would receive on a freeze is usually equal to the fair market value of his common shares in the company, the company may not be in a position to redeem the shares for quite a while. He may wish to obtain something more right away. Treating his children as outside parties may yield a purchase price, payable to him immediately, well in excess of the redemption amount he would eventually receive under a freeze.

FAMILY LAW CONSIDERATIONS

Any decisions which the owner may make regarding the transfer of his company shares to his family members may have to take into account the impact of applicable provincial family law.[23]

In short, if his chosen successor is married, the owner should be aware that his successor's spouse may have certain rights relating to the value of those shares after the transfer in the event that the successor and his spouse separate. Any appreciation in the value of the shares once transferred to the successor may end up being subject to equal division between the spouses.

However, while shares sold to his successor may be subject to such division, shares which he gives to his successor may not. The value of certain types of property is not subject to division between spouses, such as property acquired by gift or inheritance after the date of marriage and income earned from such property.[24]

Upon separation, an equalization payment is ordinarily required to be made by the spouse with the greater value of assets to the spouse with the lesser value. Such a payment attempts to ensure that the value of assets accumulated by the spouses during their marriage is evenly divided between them regardless of which spouse owns the assets when the marriage breaks down. The equalization process allows the spouses to effectively share the increase in the value of their assets during their marriage.

However, the process also creates the possibility of a married successor being required to sell the company shares acquired from the owner in order to satisfy an equalization obligation, thereby frustrating the owner's original intentions for ownership succession.

Transferring the owner's company shares to an existing family trust which includes the successor as a beneficiary will not take the value of the shares outside of the equalization calculation if the successor was already a beneficiary at the time he was married. The successor's beneficial interest in the trust, even a discretionary trust, is still property to be included in the calculation, although determining its value may be a challenge.

Protecting the company shares from an equalization obligation is often accomplished by means of a marriage contract which excludes a spouse's shares from the equalization calculation. While many married couples have marriage contracts, many don't. Those who do cannot always depend upon such contracts being fully enforceable by the courts, since enforceability often depends upon complete financial disclosure being made at the time the contracts were entered into. Furthermore, because the personal circumstances of the spouses may become quite different, variation of a marriage contract after separation is often justified.

For the chosen successor, a marriage contract may not be an option, particularly if the successor is already married or is disinclined to exchange personal financial information. However, the company shares can still be protected in the absence of a marriage contract if they are given directly to the successor after the successor becomes married. Alternatively, they might be transferred to a family trust created after the successor is married, since a beneficial interest in the trust acquired by the successor as a gift after the date of marriage will be excluded from an equalization calculation.

This need for the share transfer to be a gift to the successor after marriage rather than a purchase by the successor after marriage in order to achieve an exclusion from an equalization calculation has implications for the standard estate freeze. Ordinarily the owner's children, as described above, subscribe for newly issued common or "growth" shares of the company for only nominal consideration, often just $1 a share. But their subscription is effectively a purchase, not a gift, taking their common shares outside of the definition of property excluded from the equalization calculation.

Consequently, to avoid potential family law concerns, an estate freeze might be established differently, with the owner exchanging his common shares in the company for new preferred shares as well as new common shares, so that the new common shares might then be given to his children. This gift might also provide that any income thereafter earned from the shares would also be exempt from the property used to determine a married child's equalization payments.

Transfers to Family — Part II

Instead of the current owner transferring ownership of the company to her family members by way of an estate freeze following the approach described in the previous chapter, or alternatively giving them her shares in the company and paying the capital gains taxes that may then be owing, or even selling them her shares in return for certain payments over time, she may decide to wait and provide for the share transfer to take effect upon her death.

Providing for the transfer of company ownership on her death to her chosen successor is usually accomplished by the owner in her will.

However, it is possible for the owner to accomplish the ownership transfer upon her death without having made a will. If she dies "intestate" or without a will, her shares in the company and the rest of her property will be dealt with in accordance with applicable provincial law governing intestate succession. If her chosen successor is her only living relative, ownership of the company may end up with her successor, thereby achieving the same result which a will would have achieved.[1]

A similar result might also be achieved using various "will substitutes", such as "alter ego" and "joint partner" trusts which designate her successor as a contingent beneficiary, or "joint ownership" under which she holds the shares jointly with her successor. These will substitutes, which are discussed below in connection with avoiding probate fees, have certain disadvantages over using a will to transfer share ownership.

Although it is generally assumed throughout this book that the current owner wishes to transfer her shares while she is still alive, often for the reason that she needs the capital and income arising upon the transfer of ownership to fund her retirement from the business, this chapter will assume that the owner wishes to transfer ownership of her shares upon her death.

While the owner's will may also be used to accomplish the equalization of her assets among family beneficiaries as mentioned in the previous chapter, or provide for the disposition of all of her assets including her preferred "freeze" shares in the company should she unexpectedly die before her plans for business succession are fully carried out while she is still alive, she may nonetheless select her will as the only means by which she transfers ownership of her shares.

Even if she has no assets other than her company shares, or even if her only other assets are jointly-held which automatically pass to her joint owners upon her death, she may still decide to use a will to transfer her shares.

But in deciding to transfer her shares by means of a will, she necessarily faces the general rules and practices applicable to will planning, drafting and execution. Her estate trustees, commonly referred to as executors, will face the rules and practices applicable to estate administration once she dies.

This chapter will describe the process which the owner will experience, often with the guidance of her lawyer, in the preparation of her will in order to transfer her company shares and other assets to her family following her death. This will planning process is different from the process she experiences in setting up a family trust, described in the previous chapter, to hold company shares and to operate independently from her will.

WILL PREPARATION PROCESS

If a lawyer is engaged to help in the preparation of the owner's will, the process recommended by the lawyer for the owner to follow, perhaps with some insistence, is often more complicated than if the owner attempted to draft her will on her own without a lawyer's input.[2]

A lawyer generally has a number of obligations to satisfy when preparing a will for the owner.

In addition to determining whether the owner has the necessary mental capacity to give the lawyer sufficient instructions regarding the will, the lawyer must ensure that the instructions are not the result of duress or undue influence exerted upon the owner by others. The lawyer will also attempt to confirm that the owner has the requisite ability or authority to dispose of her property, often by requesting at the outset a complete and accurate inventory of the property. The lawyer may also provide the owner with relevant advice on any adverse tax implications and other limitations which may affect the property distributions proposed. And the lawyer will try to ensure that certain statutory formalities regarding the execution of the will are met and that the owner fully understands and approves the contents of the will.

These obligations of the lawyer give rise to a number of specific procedures which the owner may not fully appreciate but which are recommended by the lawyer to establish that that the owner's wishes can be carried out and that the will can withstand a possible attack by those claiming an interest in the owner's estate.

PRELIMINARY INVESTIGATIONS

In satisfying the obligation to ensure that the owner has the mental capacity to understand the extent of her assets and the dispositions to be made, the lawyer may seek outside expertise, perhaps a medical doctor or psychologist, to confirm the owner's capacity to make a will.

To confirm that the owner is giving her instructions for the will in the absence of any undue influence exercised by others, the lawyer may require that the owner meet with the lawyer to discuss the will without anyone else being present, with the exception of an independent language interpreter if necessary. The lawyer will have the same concern later on, insisting that none of the beneficiaries under the will is present when the will is executed.

In determining whether the owner has the authority to make the various dispositions of assets designated in the will, the lawyer will usually request a detailed description of the owner's assets, including their value, location and ownership. Although the owner is often reluctant to provide such details, perhaps out of desire for complete privacy of her financial affairs, there are a number of reasons for the lawyer's request.

The lawyer may be attempting to determine which assets are under joint ownership, which will take them outside of the estate covered by the will, or how such assets will be valued for the purposes of income tax or probate fees. The lawyer may request to see the title documents for the owner's real property to ascertain if it is held jointly by one or more persons.

The lawyer may also be trying to establish if any of the assets might be governed by the laws of another legal jurisdiction which might limit or prevent the owner's disposition of such assets in her will.

Perhaps the lawyer may be investigating whether another agreement, such as a separation agreement, marriage contract, partnership agreement or shareholder agreement, will bind the owner's estate to deal with a specific asset differently from the way intended by the owner under the will. Other agreements previously signed by the owner may subject her company shares to a trust or pledge, or impose certain buy-sell requirements or restrictions on transfer. For an owner who has previously signed a separation agreement, and may not be able to precisely recall the support and property obligations that may be imposed upon her death, the lawyer will usually request to see the separation agreement.

The lawyer will also ask the owner a number of more personal questions which the owner may not be particularly comfortable in answering. For example, the owner may be asked if she is living in a common law relationship, or is intending to be married or re-married, or if her children are married or are living in a common law relationship. She may also be asked if she has any children who are disabled, or any "dependants" who are not part of her immediate family. The lawyer's goal in asking such questions is often to determine the potential liabilities to disappointed relatives who are not provided for.

LIMITATIONS ON PROPERTY DISPOSITIONS

The owner does not have complete discretion through her will to dispose of her property entirely as she sees fit. Her "testamentary" freedom is limited to a certain extent by provincial family law, which governs the property rights of legal spouses, and provincial dependants' relief legislation, which covers dependants' support on death.

While the following comments are based upon the Ontario *Family Law Act*[3] and *Succession Law Reform Act*[4] which deal with spousal property rights and dependants' support rights, respectively, comparable laws in the other provinces, though far from identical, give rise to somewhat similar issues, concerns and restrictions affecting the owner's right to dispose of her property, including her shares in the company, through her will.

In short, whatever the owner may intend to accomplish in her will, her intentions may be frustrated by a matrimonial property claim or dependant's support claim.

Dependants' relief legislation is designed to ensure that certain persons who were financially dependant upon a deceased during her lifetime are not placed in dire circumstances upon her death because she failed to make adequate provision for them. Potential claimants for relief must have had a certain relationship with the deceased, such as a legal or common law spouse, parent, grandparent, child, grandchild or sibling. They must also have been receiving, or been entitled to receive, support from the deceased immediately prior to her death and the deceased must have inadequately provided for them upon her death.[5]

In exercising its discretion when assessing a dependant's claim for relief, a court may consider moral as well as financial issues, and may attempt to achieve a more equitable sharing of family wealth. In determining the amount of support, the court will look at a number of factors, including the dependant's age and health, current assets and means, capacity to be self-supporting, and accustomed standard of living.[6]

In addition to being possibly overturned by a dependant's relief claim, an owner's disposition of particular property in her will can also be overturned by a matrimonial property claim, since a marital relationship ends upon the death of one of the spouses. In the absence of a marriage contract, a surviving spouse can choose between accepting an entitlement under the deceased's will or claiming an "equalization payment" representing a sharing of the spouse's property. If a will leaves less than 100 per cent of the deceased's estate to the surviving spouse, there is, at least theoretically, a risk that the spouse will choose to make an equalization claim.[7]

Since a married owner's disposition of property, including her shares in the company, by way of her will is vulnerable to a possible equalization claim, there is an advantage to the owner in having a marriage contract with her spouse under which her spouse gives up any right to make an equalization claim. Given that an enforceable marriage contract usually requires full financial disclosure and independent legal advice to be to given to both parties, the likelihood of obtaining such a contract may be small, especially for the owner with a long-standing marriage.

The concern over possible equalization claims does not apply only in respect of the owner's spouse but also to a present, or future, son-in-law or daughter-in-law, if the owner wishes to pass on her property as an inheritance, including her company shares, to her children.[8]

IMPACT OF PROBATE FEES

In deciding to use a will as the means for distributing her shares in the company to the members of her family, the owner will likely be advised of the impact of certain probate fees that may be payable by her estate following her death.

Probate fees, which are sometimes referred to as estate administration taxes, are charged in connection with the issuance of a certificate for the appointment of an executor or trustee for the estate, often described as "getting probate".[9] Probate fees are generally calculated on the value of the assets which are transferred by means of a will "proven" by a court as the last valid will of the deceased.

In order to reduce an estate's exposure to probate fees, a practice of using multiple wills has evolved. Those assets which require, either legally or practically, a probated will to transfer ownership of them from the deceased to another person are contained in one will which is to undergo probate. A second will is prepared which contains those assets which do not require the will to be probated in order to transfer ownership.

Unlike investment securities, real property, and other assets contained in a will which often require the will to be probated in order to complete a transfer of their ownership, the shares of a private corporation usually do not. The owner, therefore, may be advised to create a second will, which will be unprobated, to cover only her shares in the company, especially if the shares have considerable value and would otherwise attract a relatively large amount of probate fees.

As an alternative to using a second will to avoid probate fees on the transfer of her shares, the owner may be tempted to place her shares in joint ownership with the child she wishes to acquire the shares on her death. By having ownership of the shares in their joint names with a right of survivorship, the surviving child would acquire outright ownership of the shares upon the owner's death without any need to probate the owner's will, since the shares would not be dealt with under the will.

However, there are certain disadvantages to the owner in using joint ownership as an alternative to a second will. The child's interest may become subject to claims from the child's creditors, thereby subjecting the shares to a possible forced sale. Furthermore, the owner's transfer to joint ownership may result in a taxable disposition, triggering possible capital gains taxes payable by the owner.[10] Moreover, if the owner has other children who are not made co-owners, there is the possibility that the co-ownership may be overturned if the other children successfully prove that the co-owning child was intended not to hold the shares outright as a gift but merely in trust for the owner's estate and for the benefit of all of the surviving children.[11]

Another alternative to using a second will to avoid probate fees is the transfer by the owner of her shares along with her other property to an "alter ego" trust or "joint partner" trust on a tax-free rollover basis.[12] While both such trusts must be created by an individual at least 65 years of age, an alter ego trust is a trust under which that individual is the only person able to receive the income or capital of the trust before her death, whereas under a joint partner trust, the individual and her spouse must be the only persons entitled to receive the income or capital of the trust up until the death of the surviving spouse.[13]

Both of these trusts then provide for "contingent" beneficiaries such as the individual's children to receive the income and capital of the trust after the death of the individual, in the case of the alter ego trust, and after the death of the surviving spouse, in the case of the joint partner trust. However, while these trusts may avoid probate fees, they are taxed as "inter vivos" trusts which can incur a higher rate of tax than if the same assets were included in a "testamentary" trust in the owner's will, as described below.[14]

IMPACT OF INCOME TAXES

In addition to addressing the impact of possible probate fees on the disposition of her shares in her will, the owner will also have to consider the impact of income taxes which will arise on her death. Although mentioned in the previous chapter as a reason for pursuing an estate freeze as an alternative to disposing of her shares by way of a will, such taxes are briefly repeated here in the context of will planning.

Since the owner is deemed to have disposed of all of her capital property, including her shares, immediately before her death at its then fair market value, any capital gain arising is to be included in the tax return for the owner's year of death. However, any transfer of the property to the owner's surviving spouse or common-law partner, or to a trust for their exclusive lifetime benefit, will take place at the tax cost of the deceased owner unless the estate trustee elects otherwise.[15] If the owner still had available on her death some of her lifetime capital gains exemption, the trustee will often elect a value for the share transfer which uses up the remaining exemption.

The income taxes which arise on death are determined, in practical terms, on two separate taxpayers, one being the deceased owner for the period up to her death, and the other being the owner's estate for the period after her death. The estate is taxed as a trust, and will pay tax on any income earned by the estate after the owner's death and before the distribution of the estate to the beneficiaries.[16]

In the case of the owner's shares in the company, or for that matter any other assets, which are specifically directed to a named beneficiary, the capital gains tax liability arising on the owner's death does not follow into the hands of the designated beneficiary, but instead becomes a liability of the estate. Other estate assets may therefore have to be used to pay the taxes owing. Since this can easily result in a distribution of estate value among two or more beneficiaries which can be quite different from what the owner intended to be accomplished by her will, the owner may decide that the will should impose upon the recipient of a specific asset the tax liability for that asset.

Perhaps more significantly, if the capital gains tax liability incurred by the estate on the deemed disposition of the shares is greater than the value of the other estate assets, it is possible that the shares may have to be sold to a third party for cash consideration instead of being transferred to the intended beneficiary in order to pay the taxes owing. To address this possible shortfall which can overturn the owner's attempt to transfer her shares in the company to her intended beneficiary, the owner, or the beneficiary, should arrange for insurance on the owner's life to be payable on her death which is sufficient to satisfy the tax liability, as discussed in more detail below.

Because the failure of an estate to pay the income taxes arising on the death of a taxpayer imposes a personal liability on the executors,[17] executors ordinarily make only interim distributions out of the estate and retain a reserve which is more than sufficient to meet the anticipated taxes when finally assessed. Alternatively, the executors may decide to distribute the entire estate to the beneficiaries before the final taxes have been paid provided that the beneficiaries agree to indemnify the executors for the taxes ultimately payable.

APPOINTMENT OF EXECUTORS

Although this chapter is primarily intended to deal with the owner's disposition of her company shares by way of a will, the need for the appointment of a suitable estate trustee or executor which applies in connection with other asset classes when planning a will should still be kept in mind by the owner when considering the inclusion of her shares. Depending upon how the shares are dealt with in the will, the executor's role may be quite demanding.

In addition to collecting and protecting the estate's assets, paying its creditors, carrying out specific bequests and then distributing the residue of the estate, the executor may have to establish and administer one or more trusts for a number of beneficiaries. The executor may have the power to accumulate and distribute income earned by the estate, encroach on its capital, borrow on its behalf and generally keep its assets fully invested. By including the owner's company shares as part of her estate, whether for outright disposition to a family member or for inclusion in a trust to be established for family members, the selection of an appropriate executor can raise certain issues.

For example, if the shares are to be placed in a trust which is to oversee the business operations of the company until the owner's children as beneficiaries are old enough to take over, the executor should have sufficient business skills and experience to perform that role. Or if the shares are to be placed in a trust which may run for many years, as may occur when a trust is established for a disabled child with a normal life expectancy, a trust company instead of an individual may be a more appropriate executor.

Furthermore, if the shares are not to be transferred to a designated beneficiary but are to be dealt with under the buy-sell provisions of an existing shareholder agreement involving the company, the executor who is selected may have a conflict of interest. This conflict may arise when a trusted business partner of the owner, who may even own shares in the company, is selected as the owner's executor, and the buy–sell provisions allow for the partner's purchase of the owner's shares. The executor would then be placed in the conflicting roles of both buyer and seller of the owner's shares.

A similar conflict might arise in the event that the owner's surviving spouse is selected as the executor. Should the spouse choose to make an equalization claim against the owner's estate, as discussed above, she will then be required to forfeit her right to serve as executor. To avoid these circumstances occurring, the owner should either refrain from naming his spouse as executor, or naming one or more additional persons to act as executors along with, or as an alternative to, the surviving spouse.

Selecting a non-family member to act as an executor may have monetary implications for the owner's estate. While all executors may be entitled to be compensated for their time and trouble in administering an estate, a deceased's family members seldom charge executor fees, usually because they are entitled to receive some share of the estate. Fees which "outsiders" might earn for serving as executors may amount to 2.5 per cent of estate receipts and 2.5 per cent of estate disbursements, along with an annual fee of 2/5 of 1 per cent of the estate assets under administration.

It is preferable that the executors be Canadian residents, since non-resident executors are generally required to post a bond in order to obtain probate of the will, and the residence of the estate for tax purposes is often determined by the residence of the executors.[18] This is particularly important for the estate's holding of the owner's company shares in order to ensure that the company remains a Canadian-controlled private corporation and the shares maintain their status as a qualified small business corporation or QSBC shares, as described in the *Reorganization* chapter.

DESIGNATION OF BENEFICIARIES

In deciding to use her will to dispose of her company shares to her "family", and if the owner wishes to designate a class of beneficiaries in terms of their relationship with the owner, the owner should be aware that step-children are not ordinarily regarded as "children", and step-siblings are not ordinarily regarded as "brothers" or "sisters". Depending upon the intentions of the owner, the will may be used to specifically confirm whether such persons are to be included, as well as confirm that persons born outside marriage are to be excluded.

Consequently, it may be preferable to use the names of specific individuals, along with their city of residence, to designate beneficiaries instead of designating beneficiaries simply by class. If the owner wishes to designate by class, it may be preferable for the will to "close" the class at the date of the owner's death rather than at some later date which can create practical problems in administering the estate.

Should the owner designate one or more of her children as the beneficiaries to receive her company shares, but it turns out she has previously disposed or otherwise encumbered her interest in her shares to a third party, perhaps by way of a shareholder agreement, the prior disposition will cause the bequest to her children to fail or "adeem". However, unless the will provides to the contrary, the children may then be entitled to the owner's interest in any property substituted for the shares. Such substitute property might consist of any cash proceeds resulting from the sale of the shares, and any promissory notes given as part of the purchase price.[19]

If the owner intends for her shares in the company to go to a particular child, she needs to consider the possibility that the child may predecease her, and perhaps provide for a "gift over" to some other beneficiary as an alternative. As a general rule, a testamentary disposition will lapse if the designated beneficiary dies before the "testator" who made the will. Unless the will provides to the contrary, a bequest to a beneficiary who predeceases the testator will fall into the residue of the estate.[20]

A bequest to a class of beneficiaries, such as the testator's children, however, is not subject to this lapse rule, and if one or more members of the class should predecease the testator, the bequest shall pass to those other members still alive when the testator dies. Another exception to this lapse rule applies to any bequest to a child, grandchild or sibling of the testator who predeceases the testator but who leaves a spouse or children. Unless the testator's will otherwise provides, the bequest then passes to the surviving spouse and children of the intended beneficiary as if the beneficiary had died "intestate" without a will.[21]

TESTAMENTARY TRUSTS

The owner may not intend for her will to provide for the outright distribution of her shares and the rest of her property upon her death but instead require that her property be held "in trust" after her death for a certain period of time or until the occurrence of a particular event, such as a child reaching a prescribed age.

This form of trust created in a will which is designed to take effect upon the owner's death is called a "testamentary trust", as opposed to an "inter vivos" trust which takes effect while the owner is still alive, as described in the previous chapter.

Should the owner decide to establish one or more testamentary trusts in her will, she may have to consider some additional issues.

For example, the estate trustees or executors will have to keep the estate's assets invested during the existence of the trust, and the owner may wish to set out certain investment guidelines or rules to be followed, although the owner is under no requirement to do so.[22] The guidelines may designate the various asset categories which the estate may hold and fix the maximum percentage which may be invested in each category.

The owner may also have to consider if she wants a beneficiary to receive the income derived from the property being held in trust, such as dividends which might be declared on the company's shares. If the trust property is likely to generate substantial income over time, the owner may prefer to direct the trustees to pay out to the beneficiary only such amount as they deem appropriate and to reinvest the rest of the undistributed income.[23]

Testamentary trusts can provide a safer alternative to specific bequests in her will of money or property, particularly if the owner is concerned that such assets might be irresponsibly squandered away should her children receive such assets directly. By holding back some or all of a child's inheritance in trust, it may be spread out over time in a number of separate distributions, perhaps coinciding with prescribed birthdays. For example, a child's inheritance might be distributed in three installments falling on the child's 18th, 25th and 30th birthday.

There may be certain restrictions on how long the trust property may remain in trust before being transferred by the trustees to the intended beneficiary.[24] There may also arise circumstances when the beneficiaries can accelerate the distribution to them of the property being held in trust on their behalf, regardless of the testator's wishes for a longer trust period.[25]

A testamentary trust provided in the owner's will can serve as a conduit for tax purposes as it "flows" income out to the beneficiaries. The amounts distributed constitute income to the beneficiaries, and in order that the trust is not taxed on the same income, the trust is allowed to deduct from its own income all amounts flowed through to the beneficiaries.

Unlike inter vivos trusts which are taxed at the top marginal rate on any trust income not paid out to the beneficiaries, testamentary trusts pay tax at graduated rates. This difference in tax treatment can encourage an owner to establish a number of income-splitting trusts in her will, each in favour of a particular family member instead of creating inter vivos trusts for them.

Although a transfer of the owner's shares and the rest of her property to a testamentary trust generally results in a taxable disposition,[26] a deferral of tax may be available and the property may be transferred at the tax cost of the deceased owner when her property is transferred to a qualifying spousal testamentary trust, as mentioned above, unless the executor elects otherwise. As a result, the owner's will may transfer her assets which have appreciated in value, such as her company shares, to a spousal trust to avoid paying tax on the gain, unless her lifetime capital gains exemption is still available. The remainder of her assets which have not appreciated in value, such as term deposits, may then be transferred by the will to a family trust.

ESTATE FREEZE ON DEATH

Although an estate freeze is ordinarily implemented by the owner while she is still alive as described in the last chapter, she may decide to defer the freeze until her death, instructing the trustees of her estate in her will to cause the company to issue the necessary common and preferred shares to her designated beneficiaries.

While she may designate all of her children to receive an equal amount of the preferred fixed value or "freeze" shares, she may then designate only her chosen successor, perhaps the one child who is actively involved in the business, as the beneficiary entitled to receive the common or "growth" shares. In such circumstances, all of her children would share in the company's value at the time of her death but only her child running the business would be given the right to benefit from the company's future growth.

If the owner has considerable other assets, the will may not provide for an equal sharing of the preferred shares amongst all of the children, leaving most of those shares to the owner's successor. The other children who were not involved in the business would be given instead a larger share of the owner's other assets.

FORMALITIES IN WILL SIGNING

A will is generally required to be signed at the end by the testator and at least two witnesses, although another person may sign it on behalf of the testator in the testator's presence.[27] Since the testator must sign or acknowledge her signature before at least two witnesses who are present at the same time, all of the signing parties are usually in the same room at the same time when each signs.

The witnesses should not be beneficiaries under the will or a spouse of a beneficiary. If they are, any disposition in the will to the beneficiary will be void unless a court rules that the beneficiary or spouse did not exercise any undue influence upon the testator.[28]

An exception to these formalities is provided for a "holograph" will which is entirely in the testator's own handwriting and signed by the testator at the end without any witnesses. This kind of will is generally made in emergency situations when a lawyer cannot be involved or independent witnesses are not available.[29]

Once the will is signed, one or more copies may be prepared and "notarized" for retention by the lawyer and others as back-up in the event that the original will cannot be located when the testator dies. If the original has been kept by the testator and cannot be found, there is a presumption that the will was destroyed unless a court determines otherwise.

USE OF INSURANCE

While this chapter has focused on how the owner might use a will to transfer her company shares and other assets to her family following her death, the owner might use insurance to ensure that the transfer in the will can be carried out as intended. In the absence of suitable insurance coverage, the impact of taxes arising upon her death may frustrate what she wants the will to achieve.

As mentioned above, if the capital gains tax liability incurred on the deemed disposition of her shares is greater than the value of her other assets when she dies, the owner's shares may have to be sold to a third party for cash in order to pay the taxes owing instead of transferred to her intended beneficiary. To address this possible shortfall, insurance might be obtained on the owner's life which is sufficient to satisfy the tax liability.

Upon the owner's death, the insurance proceeds received could be used to pay the capital gains taxes owing and any other liabilities of the estate then due, as well as provide additional funds which could be distributed by the owner's estate in accordance with the will to various family members, including those not involved in the business.

In addition to providing funds to be used for the payment of capital gains taxes, insurance can provide funds to be used for the purchase or redemption of the owner's shares upon her death. Even if the owner's will does not provide for a transfer of her shares to her successor as a designated beneficiary under the will, insurance can be used to provide the successor with enough funds to purchase the shares upon the owner's death.

In considering what insurance coverage should be obtained, the owner and her insurance advisor will likely address what type of insurance policy is most appropriate in the circumstances, who should be the policyholder, and who should be designated as the beneficiary under the policy. While the policyholder might be the owner, her successor, or another family member, the policyholder might instead be the company itself or even another corporation which holds company shares. The beneficiary under the policy might be the policyholder or someone else, including the owner's estate. Assuming that it is the owner's life which is insured under the policy, upon her death, a tax-free death benefit will flow to the designated beneficiary.

The owner's desire for her shares to be purchased or redeemed upon her death, preferably by way of an immediate payment which can be used by her estate to pay any capital gains taxes owing and make equalization payments to those family members who are not involved in the business, can often be met by way of a company held insurance policy on the life of the owner. Upon the owner's death, the company receives a cash death benefit under the policy at least equal to the fair market value of the owner's shares, assuming that amount is within the policy limits, and then uses the cash received to purchase the owner's shares from her estate.[30]

Transfers to Employees

Once the current owner realizes that his family members will not be the appropriate successors to the company's business, he may consider a succession plan involving the company's employees. Transferring ownership to the employees instead of outside parties can provide a number of advantages.

A possibly higher sale price may be the biggest advantage. It's not unusual for a current owner as well as an independent valuator to value the company at more than what an outside party may be prepared to pay. However, employees thoroughly familiar with the company's business may feel the higher value is reasonable in their circumstances. They may not be compelled to achieve the same rate of return on their investment as an outside corporate buyer might be required to achieve. Consequently, employees are sometimes considered the only buyers who might pay what outsiders won't.

But there are a number of other reasons why the owner should consider employees as possible successors in addition to their preparedness to pay a higher price. Since employees are more likely than an outsider to want to keep their jobs, salaries and benefits intact, an owner wanting to minimize lay-offs may feel more comfortable with employees as his successor. If the purchase price is being paid in installments over time, the owner may feel it is more likely to be paid if the business continues to be operated as before with the employees in charge.

A transfer to employees may involve few disruptions to day-to-day operations and may reduce the risk of upsetting suppliers and customers. Having been involved with the business, the employees may be less inclined to sell the business or major parts of it in a "quick flip", or combine it with other businesses in a search of "strategic synergies".

Furthermore, the owner may feel that there is less risk in providing confidential information about the business to employees as potential buyers than to third party competitors who might be tempted to unfairly use the information for their own purposes should a sale not take place.

However, whether or not the employees eventually buy the owner out, considering the employees as possible owners may just be good business. Providing employees with some ownership well before the owner wishes to relinquish control can serve as a strong incentive to those employees to remain productive and committed to the success of the company.

In deciding which employees may be the logical successors to the business, the current owner will need to ask some of the same questions he may have asked when considering his family members as possible successors. Which employees have the necessary experience and skills to be the successor, and will they have the respect of the other employees upon becoming the owner? Which employees are prepared to assume the risks of ownership in addition to the responsibilities of management? If a number of employees wish to become successor owners as a group, can they organize themselves effectively? Will the current owner have to be involved with the business after the ownership has been transferred?

FINANCING THE EMPLOYEE BUY-OUT

Depending on the strength of the company's business and the personal creditworthiness of the employees wishing to buy the owner out, conventional financing from institutional lenders or other financiers may not be readily available. The employees may not have sufficient financial resources of their own to acquire ownership, or sufficient credibility with outside financiers to obtain the required financing.

The owner may therefore have to provide the employees with "take-back" financing as an alternative. Such financing is often provided by the owner accepting payment of the purchase price in a number of installments over several years. Security for the unpaid installments may be given to the owner by means of a pledge of the purchased shares or a charge over the company's assets.

Some employees may feel that it is the owner's obligation to assist them in financing their purchase since if it weren't for their own personal efforts throughout the preceding years, the company wouldn't have become as valuable as it has. Since some may believe that they brought in many of the customers, or were responsible for setting up many of the operations, they may feel that the owner still owes them something and therefore expect the owner to help them buy the company.

Whatever sentiments some employees may have regarding the owner's role in preparing for an employee buy-out, any decision by the employees to buy will usually be influenced by a number of financing questions. It is because of these financing questions that employee buy-outs can require more time to negotiate than a sale to an outside party.

How will the employees be able to pay the purchase price? Will the purchase price be firmly established at the outset? Will the purchase price be subject to various conditions and adjustments after the employees take over, including an adjustment based upon the future earnings of the business? Can they pay off the purchase price over time? How will their purchase be financed? The greater the number of employees who wish to be part of the buy-out group, the more complicated the financing and ongoing control issues will become.

Depending upon the answers to these questions, the transfer of the owner's shares may be carried out in a number of different ways. All of his shares may be transferred to the employees at the same time, even though he may receive payment for the shares from the employees in later installments instead of being paid one lump sum for the entire purchase price.

Alternatively, his shares may be transferred in a series of installments or "tranches" over time, with payment for each tranche being made by the employees when the tranche is transferred. This approach will allow the owner to remain a shareholder and continue to share in the company's profits, although his percentage interest in the company will be declining as his shares are eventually transferred to the employees.

Instead of the owner's shares being transferred to the employees, and if the employees already own some shares of the company, his shares may be purchased by the company, either all at the same time or in tranches. Payment of the purchase price may be made by the company in one lump sum or over time in installments. In agreeing to a deferral of the payment of the purchase price by the company, the owner will be relying upon the continuing profitability of the company to support the payments. However, by transferring his shares to the company instead of transferring them to the employees, the owner may not receive favourable capital gains tax treatment, as mentioned below.

If the employees are able to obtain some of the required purchase financing from an institutional lender or other financier, the terms of any take-back financing from the owner which is needed to make up the difference between the amount of the institutional financing and the purchase price may not be to the owner's liking. As discussed below in connection with the deal process, the owner may well have to postpone his rights to receive payment, and to subordinate any security he may be granted, in favour of the financing institution.

EMPLOYEE BUY-IN

Instead of using an employee buy-out to acquire the current owner's shares directly from the owner, the employees may acquire company shares over time through an employee share purchase plan or employee stock option plan. Acquiring shares in this manner as an employee "buy-in" will dilute the current owner's interest in the company but will not provide the owner with any proceeds for his own shares until they are eventually either acquired by the employees or, more likely, redeemed by the company.

The employees' acquisition of shares directly from the company can be assisted through a "freeze" of the company as discussed earlier in the *Transfers to Family – Part I* chapter. By providing for the current owner to receive redeemable preferred shares, the employees are then able to acquire the common shares of the company for considerably less than they would have to pay for all of the shares, thus easing their need for financing. However, the owner may then require that his preferred shares be redeemed by the company over a fairly short time period after the employees take over. In such circumstances, the owner will run the risk that the company may not be financially able to redeem his preferred shares when the time comes.

However, if the employees acquire their shares in the company directly from the company instead of from the owner, they may face specific tax consequences. The difference between the amount paid or to be paid for the shares and the fair market value of those shares will be treated as a taxable employment benefit.[1] However, if the shares have only a nominal market value, such as occurs upon a freeze when most of the company's value is ascribed to the preferred shares acquired by the owner, the taxable benefit to the employees should be insignificant.

If the employees become shareholders in this manner, the owner will likely insist that they become parties to a unanimous shareholder agreement covering their rights and obligations as shareholders. Although described in much more detail in the *Shareholder Agreements* chapter later in this book, the agreement to be signed by the employees upon acquiring shares from the company should address what happens to their shares in the event that they cease to be company employees, or they die or become disabled.

For example, they may be required to sell their shares back to the company, or alternatively, sell to the owner at a specified price. Furthermore, they may be given the right to buy the owner's shares at a set price upon the owner's death.

EMPLOYEE TRUST

If more than just a few employees are intended to become shareholders of the company, the shares to be owned by the employees could be held by a trust, with the employees being the beneficiaries of the trust. If the trust agreement so provides, the shares held by the employee trust could then be voted as a "block" in accordance with the wishes of a majority of the employees expressed at a meeting of beneficiaries. The trust agreement could also provide that any poll taken of the employees could be taken on a "one person, one vote" basis instead of being based upon the employees' proportionate holdings.

In addition to providing collective voting power, an employee trust which allocates the shares to employees over time can have tax advantages. Since an employee beneficiary is deemed to have acquired the shares when they are acquired by the trust, presumably at a nominal value, instead of later on when they are allocated to the employee by the trust and have a higher value, only the lower value will be attributed to the employee as a taxable benefit.[2]

CAPITAL GAINS

If the current owner transfers his shares in the company to an employee group or employee ownership trust, he will realize a capital gain if his sale proceeds exceed his adjusted cost base of the shares. The amount of tax he will have to pay on the gain will depend upon the amount remaining available to him under his lifetime capital gains exemption.[3]

However, if his shares are purchased by the company, the sale proceeds he receives from the company may be deemed to be a taxable dividend instead of a capital gain, thereby depriving him of the use of his lifetime capital gains exemption to shelter the sale proceeds from tax.[4]

If the owner transfers his shares to the employees or to an employee ownership trust in installments, the owner will be entitled to claim a reserve for the unpaid sale proceeds and corresponding capital gains which may be spread out over a period of up to five years from the sale.[5]

Receiving the purchase price in installments and claiming a reserve would ordinarily be considered by an owner who ceased to have any availability under his lifetime capital gains exemption. This reserve can also be taken by the owner in the event he sells his shares to another shareholder or to an outside party in installments.

For example, if the employees are entitled to pay for their shares over five years in equal installments, the owner would then include in his income only one-fifth of the total capital gain in each year. However, in order for the reserve to be available, term promissory notes, not demand promissory notes, should be used to evidence the unpaid installments.

If the owner was issued preferred shares in the company upon a freeze which are held by his personal holding corporation, it may be possible for the holding corporation to receive tax-free inter-corporate dividends upon the redemption of the preferred shares, provided that "safe income" is paid out, as discussed in the *Reorganization* chapter.

DEAL PROCESS

The transfer of the owner's shares to certain key employees or even to an employee group may involve considerably less documentation and due diligence than would ordinarily be expected on a sale to an outside party.

While the establishment of a trust for the benefit of an employee group and the requirements for external financing can be complicated, the documentation required to transfer the owner's shares to the employees individually or to an employee trust can be relatively short. Such documentation may entail only a minimum number of warranties from the owner and provide for nothing more than the delivery of the owner's endorsed share certificates in exchange for the employees' certified cheque in order to complete the transfer.

The need for the employees as buyers to engage in comprehensive due diligence is generally reduced if they are already thoroughly familiar with the assets and liabilities of the business. Although they will attempt to confirm the ability of the owner to transfer good title to his shares free from the claims of any other party, they should be able to avoid reviewing numerous company documents which they may well have reviewed in the past.

However, such minimal due diligence is unlikely to satisfy the bank or other institutional lender which may be financing the employee purchase. The lender will probably want to investigate the company to the same extent as an outside purchaser, and request considerable information about the company before deciding whether or not to advance funds. Since such requests will be passed along to the owner from the employee buyers for assistance in responding, the owner may well resent such requests being made because of the time required to properly respond. However, the owner's cooperation is needed nonetheless to ensure that the purchase will be financed and that the owner will receive the purchase price at closing.

Depending upon the extent of the employees' knowledge of the company and the amount of personal trust they have in the current owner, the employees may feel more comfortable following the procedures generally used in ownership transfers to third parties, which includes numerous due diligence investigations and a comprehensive purchase and sale agreement. The *Letters of Intent*, *Due Diligence* and *Purchase and Sale Agreements* chapters which appear later in this book describe the kinds of additional protection which the employees may feel is necessary in their circumstances.

If the employees who wish to buy out the owner are able to obtain purchase financing from a bank or other institutional lender, they may well incorporate a new corporation or "newco" for borrowing purposes to serve as their "acquisition vehicle", whether or not additional take-back financing from the owner will also be needed to fully fund the purchase.

If funds are to be provided by the lender to an employee newco, the loan transaction will likely adopt the leveraged buy-out model. This model ordinarily requires the acquisition debt to reside with the entity generating the earnings from the acquired business so that the interest paid on the debt can be deducted from the earnings for tax purposes. Consequently, newco will borrow the purchase funds from the lender to acquire the owner's shares of the company, and then amalgamate with the company. The required amalgamation will then combine the acquisition debt taken on by newco with the assets and business of the company in one continuing, amalgamated corporation. The lender in these circumstances will ordinarily request general security over all of newco's assets and, following amalgamation with the company, over all of the amalgamated corporation's assets.

If the owner is helping to partially finance the employee acquisition by agreeing to accept payment of the purchase price in installments after the purchase transaction closes, the lender will likely require an inter-creditor agreement between the owner and the lender as a condition of the acquisition financing.

Under such an agreement, the owner often postpones all of his payments due under his take-back financing in favour of all payments due to the lender, and subordinates any security he may have to the lender's security, although the owner is usually entitled to receive any required and scheduled payments of principal and interest in the absence of any default under the lender's acquisition debt. The inter-creditor agreement usually limits the owner's rights to enforce his take-back loan security on default, often by imposing a "standstill" period during which he may not exercise his remedies so as to give the lender time to take control of the realization process. It also usually prevents the owner from assigning his take-back debt and security to any other party.

Since an inter-creditor agreement between the owner and the lender on such terms deprives the owner of the rights and remedies he would normally have as a creditor, and reduces the borrowing employees' incentive to comply with the terms of the take-back loan, the negotiation of the inter-creditor agreement can be difficult and lengthy and threaten the closing of the purchase transaction.

Yet despite the challenges in finalizing the terms of an inter-creditor agreement with the employees' lender, the owner may remain painfully aware during the negotiations that the alternative to such an agreement could be the failure of the employees to secure adequate financing, and thus the failure of the owner to sell the company.

Transfers to Other Shareholders

Should the current owner come to the conclusion that neither the members of her family nor the employees of the company's business will be the appropriate successors to the business, she may consider a succession plan involving the other shareholders of the company, if there are other shareholders. Although the other shareholders may not be considered potential buyers if they are the same age as the owner or in ill-health, or lack adequate financial resources, the familiarity of the other shareholders with the business makes them logical successors.

If a shareholder agreement is not in place, or is in place but does not contain any provisions governing the transfer of company shares from one shareholder to another, the owner may have the freedom to enter into separate negotiations with one or all of the other shareholders and plan for the sale of her shares as if it were a sale to an outside party. She might then be required to follow the procedures described later in the *Letters of Intent, Due Diligence,* and *Purchase and Sale Agreements* chapters.

As a simpler alternative, she might be able to arrange for amendments to the shareholder agreement if one is in place to set out the terms under which her shares might be bought by the others.

Although some of the following comments relate to agreement provisions which are more comprehensively described in the *Shareholder Agreements* chapter, they are intended to serve in this chapter as an overview of the process followed by the owner when selling her shares to the company's other shareholders.

EXISTING SHAREHOLDER AGREEMENT RESTRICTIONS

If the company already has a shareholder agreement in place, the owner may be constrained by its terms. The procedures to be followed in transferring the owner's shares, the price to be paid for them, and the timing of the share transfer, may all be prescribed in the agreement, although not necessarily to the owner's liking. The agreement's provisions may well be incompatible with the owner's personal succession plan.

As mentioned in the *Putting the Company in Saleable Condition* chapter, the shareholder agreement may need to be amended to accommodate the owner's wishes for business succession. Some of the restrictions mentioned in that chapter that may be in the agreement deal with the obligations of a shareholder to the other shareholders before being able to sell her shares to an outside party. Other restrictions mentioned require a shareholder to respect the rights of all of the other shareholders equally and thereby prevent her from favouring or excluding one shareholder over another.

For example, the agreement may contain rights of first refusal that require a shareholder to first offer her shares to all of the other shareholders on a pro-rata basis to their existing holdings before offering her shares to an outside party. Such a provision even prevents the owner from selling all of her shares to another shareholder as her chosen successor if any of the other shareholders want to buy as well.

AMENDING THE SHAREHOLDER AGREEMENT
Removing these kinds of restrictions may not be the only reason for the current owner to try to amend the shareholder agreement. If the owner's chosen successor is an existing shareholder, an amended shareholder agreement can be used to document how the share transfer to the successor will take place, especially if the successor is the only shareholder of the company other than the owner. If there are other shareholders, the transfer to the chosen successor can still be accomplished by way of the shareholder agreement so long as the others agree.

The proposed transfer by the current owner can be treated as a legally binding commitment in an amended shareholder agreement, or as simply an option to be exercised by the owner or successor in their discretion. If the transfer is to be entirely optional rather than mandatory, thereby allowing the owner or successor to change their minds about completing the transfer, a number of "puts" and "calls" can be used to achieve the transfer in a variety of circumstances.

PUTS AND CALLS

A put, or option to sell, generally gives a shareholder a right, but not an obligation, to sell her shares to other shareholders in certain circumstances. The owner can be given the right to put her shares to her successor, for example, in the event that she becomes disabled, dies or retires, or in accordance with a prescribed timetable, or upon the meeting of specified financial targets or business milestones. The successor is then required to buy the owner's shares once the owner decides to sell and "exercises" the put.

As the opposite of a put, a call generally gives a shareholder a right, but again not an obligation, to buy the shares of another shareholder in certain circumstances. The successor can be given the right to call for the owner's shares in the same circumstances as the owner may exercise a put, and the owner is then required to sell her shares to the successor once the call is exercised.

By inserting a put into the shareholder agreement, which she may exercise upon her "voluntary cessation of employment" with the company, the current owner may be assured of liquidity, a fair selling price and a known buyer for her shares when she retires. The other shareholders may then be assured of a smooth, pre-arranged transition of ownership without the interference of outside parties.

By inserting a call, not all of the other shareholders need to be given the opportunity to acquire the current owner's shares in proportion to their own shareholdings, or given such an opportunity at all. The shareholder who is the owner's chosen successor may be given the right to acquire all of the owner's shares in priority to the others.

Whatever puts and calls are inserted, they are still options and until they are exercised, they do not represent binding agreements of purchase and sale. They may, however, be written not as options but as obligations which must be satisfied upon the triggering event. But either way, the owner nonetheless runs the risk that the chosen successor can still become insolvent and unable to pay for the current owner's shares when required.

As an alternative to providing in the amended shareholder agreement for the mandatory or optional purchase by the owner's chosen successor, the company itself may be specified as the buyer of the owner's shares. Apart from considerations of whether the company will have the funds available to pay for the shares, a share redemption or repurchase by the company may have undesirable consequences.

For example, a company redemption or repurchase may trigger a deemed dividend to be received by the selling owner which she would not be able to shelter from tax under her available lifetime capital gains exemption.[1] Also, the proportionate voting rights of the other shareholders and voting control could be altered upon the cancellation of the current owner's shares. Furthermore, the redemption or repurchase could possibly cause the company to be in default under the negative covenants in its financing agreements, or perhaps be in contravention of the corporate laws governing the company which prohibit share redemptions or repurchases when the company is unable to meet prescribed liquidity or solvency tests.[2]

VALUATION METHODS

A shareholder agreement will often prescribe one of three methods to be used in valuing the shares being sold. The first requires that a value initially agreed upon by the parties is to be reviewed and adjusted annually by them. The second involves the application of a specific formula, such as the net book value of the company's assets or a certain multiple of its recent earnings. The third entails the retention of an independent valuator.

There are disadvantages to each of these methods. While they afford the parties a mechanism for setting a purchase price, they don't guarantee either certainty or fairness of result. Annual share value reviews usually stop after the second year. A decision to use book and not appraised asset values, or a multiple of recent earnings and not a discount of projected earnings, may appear misguided in hindsight and create resentment. Or the parties may fail to be unanimous in their choice of valuator.

Whatever method may be selected, there may still be difficulties in interpreting the actual price/value term or standard used. For example, prescribing the "fair market value" of the shares as the applicable sale price without further qualification or guidance to the valuator will give rise to the questions of whether a minority discount should be applied, or whether goodwill should be included. Some of the other questions which might arise have already been discussed in the *Valuation* chapter.

The more the current owner and the other shareholders attempt to address these questions in advance when preparing the amendment to the shareholder agreement, the less their chances of arguing over valuation when the time comes for the owner to sell her shares to the others.

CAPITAL GAINS

In the event the current owner transfers her shares in the company to other company shareholders, either pursuant to the buy–sell provisions in a shareholder agreement, or under a negotiated purchase agreement in the absence of, or independent from, any shareholder agreement, the owner will face the same issues about the taxation of capital gains as might arise upon the sale of her shares directly to an employee group or employee ownership trust. She will realize a capital gain if her proceeds of disposition exceed her adjusted cost base of the shares.

However, as discussed in the *Transfers to Employees* chapter, if payment of the purchase price for the shares is to be made in installments, the owner may be able to claim a reserve, and spread the capital gain over a maximum of 5 years.[3] In the event that the successor shareholder is a corporation "related" to the owner, perhaps controlled by a parent, sibling or child of the owner, the transfer to the successor shareholder may result in a deemed dividend taxable in the hands of the owner instead of resulting in a capital gain which the owner would otherwise have been able to shelter from tax using her lifetime capital gains exemption.[4]

DEAL PROCESS

Bearing some similarity to the procedure described in the *Transfers to Employees* chapter, the transfer of the owner's shares to another shareholder may involve considerably less documentation and due diligence than the procedures described later on in the *Letters of Intent, Due Diligence* and *Purchase and Sale Agreements* chapters. Some shareholder agreements providing for such a transfer contain only a minimum number of warranties from the owner and require nothing more than the delivery of the owner's endorsed share certificates in exchange for the successor's certified cheque in order to complete the transfer.

The need for the other shareholder as a buyer to engage in thorough due diligence is often largely reduced if she is already familiar with the assets and liabilities of the business through her ongoing inside knowledge as a shareholder and possibly as a director. She may simply confine her due diligence inquiries to the capacity of the owner to transfer good title to the shares.

Transfers to Outside Parties

If the current owner concludes that neither the members of his family nor the employees of the company's business will be appropriate successor owners, and if there are no other shareholders of the company, he may consider selling his ownership to outside parties. Even if there are other shareholders, the absence of a shareholder agreement may permit the current owner to sell directly to outside parties instead of to the other shareholders, perhaps for a higher price, though subject to any restrictions on transfer which may be contained in the company's charter documents.

But selling to an outside party can often involve a different and more complicated process. Unlike the transfer of ownership to family members, employees or other shareholders who are already known to the current owner, the transfer of ownership to outside parties often involves dealing with complete strangers. Even if they are already known to the current owner, perhaps as suppliers, customers, or even competitors, they are likely strangers to the inner workings of the business.

The owner may therefore need to spend considerable time not only in identifying which outside parties may be suitable buyers but also in familiarizing them with the business and its key selling features. In other words, the owner may have to engage in marketing the business.

MARKETING THE BUSINESS

Just as the current owner might need the help of a valuator, as suggested in the *Valuation* chapter, in determining a range of approximate values for the business, the owner might also need the help of a business broker to assist in identifying candidates as possible buyers and soliciting their interest in buying the business. The broker, often a mergers and acquisitions specialist, can perform a number of services.

For example, the broker can analyze relevant market information to arrive at a "short list" of outside parties and then approach them as possible buyers. The broker can also prepare an information memorandum setting out the strengths of the company and the opportunities facing the business, which can be given to the selected candidates for their consideration. The broker can assemble and make available the more important information and documentation about the company in a "data room" for review by the candidates. The broker can perhaps even take charge in negotiating the terms of the sale on the owner's behalf.

Potential buyers can be found in a number of different groups. They may be competitors or suppliers, or businesses looking to expand their own product lines or distribution channels. Or they may be hoping to gain access to the company's customer base, or simply wanting to buy a business which is countercyclical to their own.

While there may be many potential buyers capable of benefiting from operational synergies with the company, only a few may be willing or able to pay a premium over the others. Despite the advantages of using a "wide net" at the beginning to possibly create an auction and generate a number of expressions of interest, separate negotiations with just a few of the initial top bidders may result in the best overall deal.

SELECTION CRITERIA

Although deciding upon a family member, employee or other shareholder as the successor owner may often depend upon various personal qualities of the successor, deciding upon an outside party as the successor will ordinarily depend upon the proposed terms and conditions of the sale itself.

However, some outside parties can present certain risks not presented by others. Unlike dealing with family members and long-standing employees as possible successors, negotiating a sale to a competitor, and possibly to a supplier or customer, can involve the disclosure of highly sensitive information which can be used and abused by the recipient should the sale fail to close. Furthermore, some outside parties may entail a greater risk of default than others, whether being unable to close their purchase or to pay installments of the purchase price after closing.

In deciding which outside party should be selected as the successor, the current owner will need to ask a number of fundamental questions about each proposed deal. Is the proposed purchase price within the range of values suggested by the valuator? How much of the purchase price will be paid on closing? What warranties is the current owner expected to give and how long will they last after closing? Is the owner's liability for the sale to be unlimited or "capped"? How will the employees be treated and will any employee liabilities stay with the owner after closing? Can all of the conditions for closing be easily satisfied?

SHARES VS. ASSETS

One of the issues to be decided in the early discussions which take place between an owner and outside buyer is whether their deal should be structured as a sale of shares or a sale of assets. Outside buyers generally prefer to acquire a company by buying its assets, not shares.

In a share sale, the buyer acquires the company as a whole, with all of its liabilities as well as its assets, including those liabilities which may be unknown at the time of closing. In an asset sale, the buyer acquires only those assets, and assumes only those liabilities, of the company which are identified in the purchase agreement.

Avoiding the obligation to take on undisclosed or hidden liabilities, and the potential risks such liabilities might entail, is often the main reason why a buyer will insist that the purchase be structured as an asset sale. A failing business will usually be sold by way of assets, not shares.

A seller, by contrast, generally prefers a share sale as a way of shifting any residual liabilities of the company on to the buyer. However, as discussed under the heading "Indemnification" in the *Purchase and Sale Agreements* chapter, the seller may still be subject to certain residual liabilities for a certain period of time after the deal closes.

INCOME TAX CONSIDERATIONS

Avoiding the risk of unknown liabilities is not the only reason a buyer might have for preferring an asset sale. There are certain tax advantages to a buyer in an asset sale as well, especially when the assets being purchased have a fair market value in excess of the tax cost of such assets recorded on the company's books. The purchase price may be allocated by buyer and seller amongst the various purchased assets to provide the buyer with a higher cost base for such assets, thereby enabling the buyer to claim after closing larger capital cost allowances and eligible capital expenditures on such assets. [1]

From a tax perspective, the seller usually prefers a share sale, especially if the lifetime capital gains exemption described in the *Reorganization* chapter is still available to him. While the exemption is afforded to individuals with respect to the sale of shares of a QSBC, any gains on the sale of assets by the company would not qualify for the exemption.

Even without using the exemption, the capital gains tax liability to the seller on a share sale is likely to be less than the tax liability to the company on an asset sale, given that the company will likely have to include in its income any "recaptured" capital cost allowance when the purchase price for any depreciable assets exceeds the undepreciated capital cost of such assets as recorded on the books of the company.[2] However, a seller may prefer an asset sale over a share sale if the company has considerable loss "carryforwards" which it can use to reduce the income earned on the sale.[3]

Deciding between a sale of assets and a sale of shares affects the actual purchase price which a buyer is prepared to pay and a seller is prepared to receive. For example, a buyer in a share sale will want to discount the price because of the risks of contingent liabilities, but a seller may be prepared to accept such a discount for the share sale if it's roughly equal to the seller's available capital gains exemption.

DEAL PROCESS

Although there may be some similarities in the procedures and documentation used to transfer an owner's interest in a business to his family, employees, fellow shareholders, or to outside parties, there are nonetheless considerable differences. Transfers to family members, especially to those quite conversant with the operations of the business who are paying only nominal consideration, will be implemented quite differently from transfers to outside parties with no prior experience with the business and who are paying top value.

As generally described in earlier chapters, transferring ownership of the business may be accomplished directly from the current owner to the successor with just one transaction, or indirectly by way of a number of intervening transactions. At the outset, family members may acquire company shares under a freeze transaction, or employees may acquire shares under a stock purchase or stock option plan, or other shareholders may acquire shares under the procedures prescribed in a shareholder agreement.

An outside party, however, may acquire shares by following a different path along a "deal continuum" which usually consists of a number of stages. In attempting to document the progress of the owner and an outside buyer at each stage along this continuum, their respective legal counsel will generate certain agreements and carry out various investigations.

Counsel will usually prepare a confidentiality agreement to be signed by the parties at the initial stage of discussions, and then later on, when the parties have come to an understanding of the principal business terms of the deal, a letter of intent will be prepared. Still later on, and depending upon the results of the investigations conducted during the due diligence stage, a comprehensive purchase and sale agreement expanding upon the provisions of the letter of intent will be prepared, negotiated, and possibly signed. And eventually, if all of the conditions prescribed in the purchase and sale agreement are satisfied, including the preparation and execution of numerous other definitive agreements, the deal may be closed.

Each of these stages of the deal continuum is described in greater detail in a separate chapter later in this book.

While not every deal will follow along this continuum, current owners and prospective buyers are generally advised to enter into confidentiality agreements and letters of intent, and to engage in a certain amount of due diligence, before they immerse themselves in all of the details of a comprehensive draft purchase and sale agreement. By starting their deal this way, they are given an opportunity early on to identify the principal interests and concerns of each other, and discover any major obstacles to proceeding, before they have spent considerable time and money, and suffered a lot of aggravation, in drafting, reviewing and redrafting numerous documents which may not be used in the end.

Starting their deal this way will, in other words, increase the likelihood that the purchase and sale agreement will be signed and the deal closed because many of the potential "deal killers" will have already been addressed.

Family Trust Agreements

In the *Transfers to Family – Part 1* chapter of this book, the advantages of using a discretionary family trust in transferring ownership of the company to members of the owner's family were discussed. Although often used in estate freezes, when a family trust acquires new common shares of the company after the owner has exchanged her own common shares for preferred shares, a family trust can also be used to acquire all of the owner's common shares directly from her.[1]

Either way, a family trust allows the owner to achieve a number of tax and non-tax objectives.

As a means of reducing taxes, a family trust can be used to transfer the tax burden from the owner, who may be in a higher tax bracket, to her children, who may be in a lower tax bracket. It can also put her children in the position of eventually using their respective lifetime capital gains exemptions when company shares are sold.

Aside from the tax benefits which may result, a family trust enables the owner to give her children the benefits of property ownership without the owner giving up control over the property, as might occur upon an estate freeze allowing the owner to remain in control of the company. A trust can also allow for successive interests, as occur when children and grandchildren are provided for, and can provide a mechanism for managing property in the face of incapacity or disability. And a trust can be used to protect property from the claims of creditors.

A discretionary family trust is created when property is vested in trustees to be held for the benefit of a class of beneficiaries, such as children and grandchildren, or for specifically named persons. The trustees are given discretion over the payment of the trust's income, or capital, or both.

But the trust agreement will determine the extent of the discretionary authority which the trustees have in making decisions about the trust property. While some trust agreements may give the trustees absolute unfettered discretion to deal with the trust property as they see fit, other trust agreements may place a number of restrictions or limitations on the discretion they may exercise.

While they may be obligated to distribute all of the trust property among the class of beneficiaries, they may nonetheless have discretion as to whom payments may be made within the class and as to how much each beneficiary may receive. They may even have the discretion not to distribute any of the trust income or capital until certain events have occurred or certain conditions have been met.

Although a family trust can be established by an individual simply declaring that she holds specific property on behalf of others within her family, using what is called a "declaration of trust", a family trust is usually established by means of a trust agreement which evidences the transfer of property by the settlor to the trustees for the benefit of the beneficiaries.

This chapter will attempt to summarize many of the provisions ordinarily found in an agreement creating a discretionary family trust. It will also look at the potential conflicts faced by a trustee when serving as a director of a company whose shares are held by the trust.

However, some of the provisions which are described below, particularly those which do not relate directly to a trustee's exercise of discretion, apply to trust agreements in general.

Any trust agreement should accomplish the following three things in order to validly establish a trust. First, the trust agreement should reflect the intention of the settlor to transfer the property to the trustees for the benefit of the beneficiaries, not for the benefit of the trustees. Second, it should clearly indicate what property is being vested in the trustees to be held for the benefit of the beneficiaries. And third, it should be specific as to who is to actually benefit from the trust.

A number of the decisions which the owner may make when setting up the family trust to acquire her company shares and other property directly from her will be influenced by certain tax attribution rules.[2] Some of these rules were referenced in the *Transfers to Family – Part 1* chapter. Under these rules, the income, and possibly capital gains, arising from property transferred to the trust can be attributed back to the person making the transfer and taxed in her hands.

Specifically, deciding who should be the settlor and who should be the trustees, what powers they should have, who should be the beneficiaries and what they should receive, and how the trust will be funded, will all be affected by these rules.

THE TRUST PROPERTY

The property of the trust consists of the property first transferred to the trustees by the settlor when the trust is established, together with all other property which is subsequently acquired by the trustees and which is intended to be included in the trust property. The trust agreement usually states that all of the trust property and any accretions and additions to it shall constitute the trust fund.

Sometimes a family trust will be set up with the initial transfer to the trustees of just a single item, such as a silver dollar, gold coin or even a sentimental family heirloom. The use of such an item, which does not generate any income or capital, is designed to avoid a tax attribution rule which applies when the beneficiaries include a spouse or minor child of the settlor, or other "designated person".[3] The beneficiaries of family trusts often include designated persons related to the settlor.

Whatever property or amount is transferred by the settlor to the trust, it should not be sold or used to subscribe for income producing assets, such as the common shares created under an estate freeze. Property acquired by the trust which will produce income or capital gains should be acquired with funds which are borrowed from a financial institution or other third party.

THE SETTLOR

The selection of the settlor of the trust is also influenced by another attribution rule, which may apply when the settlor has an interest in the trust or control over it. Therefore, if the owner wishes to be the sole trustee, or one of two trustees, of the family trust, or to be a beneficiary under it, she should not be selected as the settlor in order to avoid the attribution back to her of any capital gains or income earned by the trust which would then be taxed in her hands.[4]

Even if she is one of three trustees, she may be deemed to have some control over the trust if the trust agreement requires unanimous consent of the trustees, or requires that she be part of any majority, in making decisions for the trust, thereby subjecting her to the attribution rule.

Furthermore, capital gains and income earned by the trust may also be attributed to the settlor if there is a possibility that any of the property transferred to the trust by the settlor might revert back to the settlor. Such attribution to the settlor may result if the settlor has the power to determine which beneficiaries will receive any of the trust property, or if the settlor has a right to veto a transfer of trust property to any beneficiary.

Because of this attribution rule, most family trust agreements provide that the property originally transferred by the settlor to the trustees is irrevocably transferred, and that no part of the trust fund is reserved for the settlor or reverts to the settlor.

To avoid the application of this rule, the agreement should allow the settlor as a trustee to be outvoted on any issue relating to the benefits flowing to any beneficiary or to the investment or disposition of trust property. Having a minimum of three trustees at all times with majority approval required for decision-making is generally used to accomplish this. If there are only two trustees at any time, and one of whom is the settlor, the agreement should provide that the trustees cannot make any decisions until a third trustee is appointed.

In light of this rule, if the owner is to be a trustee or beneficiary of the trust, the settlor may be a parent of the owner, if a parent is still living, or another relative or friend of the owner, but not the owner. If the owner will be neither trustee nor beneficiary, the settlor may be the owner.[5]

THE TRUSTEES

A family trust agreement is likely to provide for a number of trustees, including persons who are quite familiar with the business and personal affairs of the owner who is setting up the trust.

Each trustee is in a fiduciary position towards the trust fund and the beneficiaries. Accordingly, the trustees must exercise their discretion with regard to the interests of the beneficiaries, not the interests of the settlor or the trustees themselves.

While the trustees will be guided by the terms of the trust agreement, they still must be mindful that their overall conduct will generally be governed by the rules found in applicable provincial trust legislation[6] and case law.

The agreement usually contains a provision which allows for the substitution of trustees should any of them die, become incapacitated, or withdraw. It may also provide for their retirement or removal. Such provisions are discussed in more detail below.

Trustees are often required to automatically withdraw should they cease to be Canadian residents. This mandatory withdrawal is intended to ensure to that the family trust does not become a non-resident for tax purposes since the residence of the trust is often determined by the residence of the majority of the trustees and the trust may be deemed to have disposed of all of its property should it cease to be resident in Canada.[7]

In selecting trustees, and in order to avoid the impact of the income tax attribution rules upon the settlor discussed above, often the trustees of a family trust include the owner, her chosen successor and a third party familiar with the family's affairs.

If the owner and her spouse are the only trustees of the family trust, they will clearly have a conflict of interest in exercising their discretion to distribute trust assets to themselves as beneficiaries. Even though the trust agreement may permit such distributions to be made despite the conflict, the children may nonetheless bring legal proceedings to overturn them. It is therefore preferable for the trust to have a third trustee, thereby allowing the parents to abstain from voting on any distributions in their favour.

The trust agreement may provide for the number of trustees to be within a prescribed range, such as between three and five, and permit the appointment of additional trustees within the range from time to time, perhaps by the existing trustees or perhaps by the majority of the adult beneficiaries.

THE BENEFICIARIES

The beneficiaries of a family trust often include the owner, her spouse, and her children and grandchildren, but may also include other family members, and possibly their spouses. Even a corporation owned by any of these persons may be included as a beneficiary. While the trust agreement may describe the beneficiaries generally as a class, such as children and grandchildren, it is quite common for each beneficiary to be individually named.

If the trust agreement refers to the owner's children or grandchildren as a class instead of identifying them by name, it may contain a provision which excludes children born outside of wedlock, depending upon the wishes of the owner. If the agreement refers to a spouse, it may contain a definition of a spouse which includes not only a legally married spouse who is living with a particular beneficiary but also a person who has been cohabiting with a beneficiary in a conjugal relationship for a certain period of time.

The beneficiaries of the trust may be placed by the trust agreement into two separate categories. One group, the income beneficiaries, may be entitled to only the income generated by the trust, and the other group, the capital beneficiaries, may be entitled to only the capital of the trust. However, a beneficiary may be both an income beneficiary and a capital beneficiary.[8]

TRUSTEE POWERS GENERALLY

The main obligation of the trustees is to carry out the instructions of the settlor as contained in the terms of the trust agreement.

It is usually necessary to give the trustees certain powers to administer the trust, since the applicable trust legislation alone gives trustees only limited powers as to what they can do with the trust property. Some of the important powers ordinarily given in the trust agreement include investing cash funds, acquiring or disposing of life insurance, converting or distributing trust property, adding to the assets of the trust, dealing with stocks, bonds, and other securities and properties, investing minors' shares and using income and capital for minors, making payments on behalf of minors to parents or guardians, and lending or borrowing money. The agreement ordinarily provides that all decisions of the trustees in exercising their powers shall be made by a majority vote.

Apart from these specific powers, the trustees may be granted certain discretionary powers, including the right to distribute income and capital.

Specifically, the trustees may be given the discretion to make differential payments, or even no payments at all, to specific beneficiaries. A discretionary family trust agreement ordinarily states that the trustees may pay all or any part of the income generated by the trust fund to any one or more of the beneficiaries from time to time, and to the exclusion of any one or more of them, under such terms and conditions as the trustees may in their absolute discretion determine. Any annual net income which is not paid out in the year is to be accumulated and added to the capital of the trust fund at the end of the year. A similar discretion is given to the trustees to pay to one or more of the beneficiaries all or any part of the capital of the trust fund.

However, if the settlor believes that all of the distributions amongst the beneficiaries should be equal, the agreement may restrict the discretion of the trustees accordingly.

In the absence of discretionary powers in the agreement to make differential payments, trustees are subject to a duty of impartiality. Unless the trust agreement authorizes the disparate treatment of beneficiaries, trustees are not permitted to give preferential treatment to any single beneficiary or group of beneficiaries.[9]

This duty of impartiality leads to the "even-hand" rule which requires the trustees to be impartial and maintain an even-hand between the income beneficiaries and capital beneficiaries. In practical terms, it essentially proscribes actions that favour income beneficiaries by generating high income at the expense of capital gains, or conversely, actions that favour capital gains over income generation.

A provision in the trust agreement that one class of beneficiary is to be preferred over another may be sufficient to override the even-hand rule, as will a provision empowering the trustees to encroach on the capital for the benefit of an income beneficiary. Ordinarily, a discretionary trust which allows the trustees to determine which of the named beneficiaries shall benefit from the trust property and in what amounts is the usual way of overriding the rule.[10]

In addition to the discretion which may be exercised by the trustees in the distribution of income, or capital, or both, the trustees may also have a wide discretion over how the trust property may be invested and reinvested, or how the trust may be managed in general.

By allowing the payment of income to be discretionary, any unpaid income is accumulated, thereby permitting the trustees to avoid making payments of income to a minor child. Such payments could otherwise result in the attribution of the income to the settlor if the settlor is the parent or grandparent of the child.

However, most trust agreements provide that if any beneficiary is under the age of majority when entitled to receive a share of the trust fund's income or capital, the trustees are then empowered to keep such share invested until the beneficiary reaches majority. The trustees are also ordinarily given the discretion to pay such income or capital to the beneficiary's parent or guardian, although payment to a minor beneficiary may be permitted if circumstances so require.[11]

To allow the trustees to deal with the changing circumstances of beneficiaries in general, or to react to changing tax laws, the agreement may contain a "resettlement" provision which permits part or all of the trust fund to be transferred or resettled to another trust for the benefit of one or more of the beneficiaries. The property which is transferred then becomes subject to the provisions of the other trust and will be governed by the laws applicable to that trust.

INVESTMENT POWERS

While some trust agreements may authorize the trustees to invest only in those investments which are authorized in applicable trust legislation,[12] most trust agreements permit the trustees to invest in any investments which they deem to be advantageous to the trust fund regardless of any legislated requirements.[13]

Sometimes the trustees are specifically allowed to invest in mutual funds or other trust funds which might otherwise be regarded as an improper delegation of their investment powers, or regarded as a commingling of the trust fund with the property of other persons.

Without investment instructions in the agreement, the even-hand rule mentioned above imposes a duty on the trustees to convert any risky or unproductive assets of the trust into investments with a reasonable rate of return, as well as a duty to diversify the assets held by the trust.[14]

However, a diversified investment portfolio and the exercise of unlimited discretion by the trustees may be inconsistent with the original purpose of the trust. The duty to diversify poses a particular problem for trustees when the trust is established to hold the shares of one company and the shares are the trust's major asset, since the even-hand rule suggests that at least some of the shares be sold and the sale proceeds directed to alternative investments.

Therefore, in the case of an estate freeze when a family trust is used to hold just one asset, namely the family company, for a relatively long time, the trust agreement should deny the trustees the power to invest as they choose. If it is intended that the shares be held over the lifetime of the trust, the agreement must clearly authorize the trustees to do so.

But the trustees may be given the right to exercise any rights which are incidental to share ownership, such as pre-emptive rights or rights of first refusal which enable the trustees to acquire additional shares of a corporation in which they have already invested. They may also be allowed to participate in any reorganizations or creditor proposals under which they may exchange their current security holdings for other securities, or issue options or participate in voting trusts in connection with their holdings.

Whether or not there are any restrictions imposed on the trustees' investment powers, the agreement may still permit the trustees to appoint investment managers or advisors and delegate to them the direct management of some or all of the trust fund, including the right to acquire and dispose of investments.[15] The fees charged by such managers and advisors are normally paid out of the trust fund, with the trustees being given the discretion to decide if such fees are to be charged to the fund's income or to the fund's capital, or partly to both.

A trustee may be given the power in the agreement to purchase any assets from the trust fund or to sell any assets to the trust fund, although the agreement will likely require that the terms of any such purchase or sale are first approved by the other trustees.

BORROWING AND LENDING POWERS

The trustees may be given in the agreement the absolute discretion to borrow money on behalf of the trust fund, either with or without interest, and to mortgage or charge the income or capital of the trust fund as security for any such loans. The trustees may also be given the power to similarly mortgage or charge the trust fund as security for any guarantee they may wish to give to facilitate any borrowing by a beneficiary or by a corporation controlled by a beneficiary.

Furthermore, the trustees may be permitted under the agreement to lend money to any of the beneficiaries upon such terms as the trustees see fit, including the rate of interest, if any, and the security to be taken.

ADMINISTRATIVE POWERS

Even though all of the trustees have to be involved in making decisions for the trust, the agreement normally provides for their delegation to just one or two trustees the power to sign documents and carry out various decisions which the trustees have collectively made. For example, the trustees may appoint a particular trustee to sign stock transfers and promissory notes on behalf of all of the trustees at any time.

The trustees may be authorized to appoint a variety of professional advisors, including lawyers, accountants, valuators, and other consultants, and to delegate various powers conferred upon them in the agreement to such professionals. If a trustee is qualified and regarded as the most suitable professional to be retained to advise the trust on a specific matter, the agreement will likely allow the trust to retain and pay that trustee for professional services rendered.

The trust agreement ordinarily permits the trustees to initiate or defend lawsuits affecting the trust fund, or compromise any debt owed to the trust fund, or to settle any claims against the trust fund. It also permits the trustees to pay out of the trust fund any taxes owed by the trust fund and any expenses incurred in administering the trust fund. Unless the agreement otherwise provides, the even-hand rule generally requires that expenses of the trust should be allocated fairly between income and capital beneficiaries. For example, the cost of insurance, taxes and repairs relating to the trust property might be borne by the income beneficiaries, and the cost of major improvements might be borne by the capital beneficiaries.

The trustees may be given discretion in the agreement to maintain just one common fund for the trust, or set up instead a number of separate funds for each beneficiary or group of beneficiaries, or to re-allocate assets from one fund to another. They may also be given the discretion to carry on a business.

Although the trust agreement is unlikely to prescribe the form of accounts to be maintained by the trustees when administering the trust fund, it may provide the trustees with some discretion over how depreciation and depletion of certain assets are to be accounted for, and how certain elections and allocations for tax purposes might be exercised or perhaps avoided, even though such decisions may result in favourable tax consequences to some beneficiaries and adverse tax consequences to others.

In addition to being reimbursed for all of their expenses incurred while acting for the trust, the trustees may be entitled under the agreement to receive reasonable compensation for their time and trouble. If any of the trustees declines such compensation, the agreement often provides that the aggregate trustee compensation shall be reduced so that no trustee receives more compensation than would have been received if all the trustees had accepted compensation.

Some family trust agreements require that the activities of the trustees be recorded in almost the same manner as the activities of the directors of a corporation, with proper minutes of trustee meetings or resolutions being produced and circulated in written form.

While some trust agreements empower the trustees to purchase on behalf of the trust fund insurance or annuities on the lives of any of the beneficiaries, the trustees are ordinarily relieved of responsibility if any such insurance policy or annuity lapses or becomes unenforceable for any reason.

POWERS TO SERVE AS DIRECTOR OR PARTNER
To support the powers of the trustees to make various kinds of investments, the agreement ordinarily permits the trustees to serve as directors, officers or employees of any corporation in which they may have invested on behalf of the trust fund, and allows them to keep for themselves any remuneration they may receive from the corporations involved for performing such roles. A similar provision may allow the trustees to act as partners in any partnership with which the trust has business dealings, again without any duty to pay over to the trust fund any remuneration they may receive from the partnership.

Conversely, the agreement may state that no trustee is under any obligation to become a director, officer or employee of any corporation, or a partner or employee of any partnership, the trust fund may have invested in.

Although the trustees will likely be authorized in the agreement to appoint any person they feel is suitable to serve as a director of a corporation in which the trust fund has invested, they will likely be relieved of any obligation to oversee the performance of any person they have appointed as a director.

RETIREMENT AND REMOVAL OF TRUSTEES
Since a discretionary family trust usually has more than one trustee, the agreement ordinarily provides that any trustee may retire after giving a certain amount of notice of the retirement to the other trustees and the beneficiaries (or the adult beneficiaries if some of the beneficiaries are

minors). The agreement may also provide that any trustee who becomes incapable of managing property will cease to be a trustee and be deemed to have retired. If there is only one trustee, the agreement will likely state that a court order permitting the trustee to resign will be required.

Although some trust agreements allow the settlor while a trustee to remove another trustee,[16] the agreement is more likely to provide when there are at least three trustees that any trustee who is incapable of properly serving as a trustee may be removed by the others. The agreement may stipulate that a trustee may not be removed unless a court has ruled that the trustee is incapable of managing property or unless the other trustees have received letters from at least two physicians stating that the trustee is incapable.

LIABILITY OF TRUSTEES

The liability of a trustee for any losses incurred by the trust fund is usually limited in the trust agreement to losses caused by the trustee's own dishonesty or fraud, gross negligence or willful breach of the trust. The agreement will often specifically presume that a trustee has acted honestly and in good faith, and will relieve a trustee from liability for any losses resulting from the exercise of discretion or the refusal to exercise discretion. It will also relieve a trustee from any liability for the acts or omissions of any other trustee.

The agreement ordinarily provides that each trustee is entitled to be indemnified out of the trust fund for any liability incurred by the trustee in exercising the duties and discretion prescribed in the agreement, even if such duties are improperly performed or not performed at all, unless the liability is brought about by the trustee's fraud, gross negligence or willful breach.

If the agreement doesn't absolve the trustee from liability for breaching certain duties, it may well remove the requirement to perform the duty in the first place. For example, as mentioned above, trustees are often excused from exercising an even-hand between the income beneficiaries and capital beneficiaries.

However, these exemptions from liability clauses do not always afford a trustee complete protection for the breach of fiduciary duties. While the courts have usually respected a trustee's right to exercise absolute discretion, the discretion must not be exercised in bad faith.[17] Even in the absence of bad faith, which is often taken to include personal dishonesty and fraud, the courts will intervene in the exercise of trustee discretion when the discretion is exercised for an improper purpose,[18] or when the trustee has failed to consider whether to even exercise the discretion,[19] or when the discretion is exercised in an unreasonable or arbitrary manner.[20]

TERM OF THE TRUST

As mentioned in the *Transfers to Family – Part 1* chapter, the property of a family trust is deemed to be disposed every 21 years for tax purposes in order to prevent a trust from deferring the payment of capital gains tax indefinitely.[21] Because of this tax rule, some family trust agreements provide for the termination of the trust, and the distribution of all of the trust property to the beneficiaries, before the 21st anniversary of the creation of the trust.

Alternatively, the agreement may provide that unless the trustees pick an earlier date to terminate the trust, all of the trust property shall be distributed on a date which is before the 21st anniversary of the death of the last to die of the settlor's children and grandchildren who are alive when the trust agreement is signed. This is intended to reflect the applicable perpetuity period under provincial legislation.[22]

CONFLICTING ROLES: TRUSTEE VS. COMPANY DIRECTOR

Even though the trust agreement may allow a trustee to serve as a director of a corporation in which the trust has invested as mentioned above, serving as a director can create conflict for the trustee. While the trust agreement may permit the trustee to keep any remuneration received from the corporation for performing the role of director, the agreement is limited in reconciling a trustee's duties under trust law with a director's duties under corporate law.

While previous chapters of this book have discussed the use of a discretionary family trust in holding the shares of the company as part of the owner's business succession plan, the use of a trust can frustrate the owner's wishes for a smooth and amicable succession if the trustees are also the directors of the company.

For example, if one of the owner's children is a trustee of the family trust as well as a director of the company, that child may find herself in the uncomfortable position of having to balance competing interests when playing these different roles, particularly when company dividends are about to be declared, or when compensation and other perks for company directors and officers are being considered.

The beneficiaries of the trust which holds all or most of the company's shares may not be content with the way the company is being managed and, more likely, the way the company's profits are being spent or distributed.

Although a trustee's powers and duties are generally prescribed in the applicable provincial trust statute[23] as well as in the common law, those powers and duties are often modified by the trust agreement. Additional powers are given, and some duties are limited or removed entirely, in the trust agreement. Yet despite the trustee's first duty to adhere to the trust agreement, the trustee must still adhere to the duties imposed under trust law which are not in conflict with the provisions of the trust agreement.

The law imposes three fundamental duties upon all trustees. The first is the duty of the trustee not to delegate her office to others, so that she acts personally when acting in the best interests of the beneficiaries. Her second duty is to avoid profiting personally when dealing with the trust property, so that her own interests do not conflict with the interests of any of the beneficiaries. Her third duty is a duty of care, to act honestly with the level of skill and prudence expected of a reasonable business person managing her own affairs.[24] These three fundamental duties, however, are far from all of the duties imposed by law upon trustees.

Trust Law vs. Corporate Law

While these fundamental duties of trustees may appear consistent with the fundamental duties of company directors, the trustee of a trust that holds shares of a company of which she is a director may be placed in a very uncomfortable situation when trust law and corporate law are applied to her actions at the same time.

Under corporate law, a company director is under a statutory duty to "act honestly and in good faith with a view to the best interests of the corporation" and to "exercise the care, diligence and skill that a reasonably prudent person would exercise in comparable circumstances."[25]

Given this corporate law duty to act in the best interests of the company, in contrast to the trust law duty to act in the best interests of the beneficiaries and in accordance with the terms of the trust, certain actions to be undertaken by those directors who are also trustees may not comply with both duties at the same time.

While it is not necessary that the trustees of a trust holding a majority interest in a company appoint at least one of their number to the board or at least a nominee to the board, doing so is certainly consistent with their duty of care to act as reasonably prudent business persons in handling their own affairs After all, serving as a director is a good way to know what is going on with the company and to make informed decisions about what actions are necessary to protect the main asset of the trust.

By refusing to serve as a director, and thereby receiving only the financial statements and reports handed out at the company's annual meeting of shareholders, a trustee might be viewed by the trust's beneficiaries as breaching her duty of care. It is for this reason, and in order to protect the trustees, that most trust agreements state that a trustee is under no obligation to become a director, officer or employee of any corporation in which the trust fund may have invested, as described above.

But even though trustees are usually expected to become company directors as nominees of the trust holding the company's shares, they should nonetheless be aware that the corporate law requires them to exercise their discretion as a director and that they may not fetter their discretion by acting only in accordance with the instructions of the other trustees or the trust agreement. Despite a provision in the trust agreement requiring the actions of the trustees to be approved by a majority of them, any trustee who is a director must exercise her discretion as a director independently.[26]

Directors are also required to keep company information confidential. Under trust law, beneficiaries have the right to information available to trustees in their capacity as shareholders. But under corporate law, if the trustees also act as directors or officers, the trustees have an obligation to keep the affairs of the company confidential and this obligation takes priority over the rights of the beneficiaries to information.[27]

Certain matters, as discussed below, are prescribed under corporate law as being within the control of the directors and not the shareholders. Although the trustees who are not directors, along with the trust beneficiaries, may be extremely interested or concerned over how these matters are handled, they may not have any right to interfere with the board's actions. They may not even know what the board is doing at all.

Declaring Dividends

Only the directors have the right to declare that dividends be paid by the company.[28] If a trust is dependent upon the income generated by the company, then one or more of its trustees should become directors of the company to ensure that the timing and amounts of company distributions satisfy the needs of the trust.

The nature of the company's business will affect the board's dividend policy, since an operating company with an erratic earnings history or need for large capital expenditures may be more inclined to retain its earnings than a holding company with mainly recurring investment income. But the board's desire to hold funds in reserve may well conflict with the trust's desire for a maximum distributions.

Dividends come in many different forms. They may be in cash, or in company shares, or in other company property. They may be distributions on a winding-up of the company, or on a redemption of company shares, or on the authorized reduction of the company's paid up capital. When a trust holds the shares of a family company, it is not always clear how the trustees should determine whether a company dividend is income or capital to the trust.

In the absence of any guidance in the trust agreement, the trustees may be inclined to assume that the dividends constitute payments of the company's profits and are trust income for the benefit of the income beneficiaries. However, the trustees should be guided by the "form rule"[29] which determines whether the dividends should be treated as either trust income or capital. In short, for those dividends received in cash, they should be treated by the trustees as income of the trust, and for those dividends not in the form of cash, they should be treated as capital received by the trust.

This is where the conflict facing trustees who are also directors of the company then becomes apparent, since the directors determine the form in which a company dividend is paid. They are then in the position of deciding whether a company distribution to the trust should be characterized as income or capital, and thereby belongs to either the income beneficiaries or capital beneficiaries.

While it is difficult to foresee all possible kinds of distributions, the trust agreement should therefore specify an alternative to the form rule, giving trustees the discretion under the agreement to decide between income and capital.

Borrowing

Without the authorization of the shareholders but subject to the company's articles, by-laws or unanimous shareholder agreement, the directors may borrow money on the credit of the company, issue or pledge debt obligations of the company, give company guarantees, and mortgage or pledge the company's property to secure any company obligations.[30]

Depending upon the amount borrowed, how the borrowed funds are used, and the extent of any security given, the value of the company as the trust's main asset can be significantly impaired or reduced. Should the directors borrow for the purposes of a risky or highly speculative investment, their actions may be seen as contrary to the more conservative investment approach followed by the trustees for the trust.

The power of the directors to give company guarantees can become problematic for the trust and its beneficiaries, particularly when the company's financial statements may not reveal the existence of such guarantees. The company's guarantee of the debts or obligations of others can not only put the trust's main asset at risk, it can also invite self dealing on the part of the directors.

Director and Officer Compensation

The level of compensation payable by the company to the directors and senior officers is ordinarily set by the board. It is not unusual for a closely-held family company to compensate its directors and officers at above market rates, or at higher levels than such individuals might earn elsewhere.

The board may also be prompted to pay generous annual or special bonuses in an effort to reduce the company's income to the limit which allows the company to qualify for the "small business deduction" when paying its income taxes.[31]

However, such company salaries and bonuses may be viewed by the beneficiaries of the trust controlling the company as being excessive or unwarranted.

A further concern facing trustees of a trust which holds company shares is whether they are allowed to personally retain the fees they may receive as directors of that company. As mentioned above, trustees are generally prohibited from making a profit out of the trust unless the trust instrument expressly allows them to receive a fee for additional services rendered over and above their normal trustee compensation. Since the opportunity to earn that additional compensation results from their discretion as trustees to serve as directors, they would be required to pay such fees to the trust unless the trust agreement provides to the contrary.[32]

Recourse by Beneficiaries and the Oppression Remedy

Although a trustee serving as a director may feel that she is protected by the various exemptions from liability clauses in the trust agreement, or may feel that she has exercised her discretion in the absence of bad faith, or at least in a satisfactory manner, she may nonetheless be held accountable to the beneficiaries if she acted toward them oppressively as a director.

Under trust law, a beneficiary will ordinarily be without recourse against a trustee who has not been in breach of any trust or has not exercised her discretion in an improper fashion. Furthermore, while a beneficiary has rights to the due administration of the trust, the beneficiary has no rights in and to the trust property. It is this lack of a direct interest in such property which is often an obstacle to a beneficiary seeking recourse under trust law.

However, the corporate law provides recourse for beneficiaries under what is called the "oppression remedy" when the trust holds company shares. While beneficiaries may be denied an adequate remedy against a trustee under trust law, they may still have a remedy under corporate law against a trustee who serves as a company director, or against the company itself.

An oppression remedy may be sought by any person having a beneficial interest in the shares of a company, which includes any person holding an interest through a trust or nominee.[33]

The CBCA and its provincial counterparts provide that a court may make an order to rectify the results of certain "oppressive" conduct. The conduct may be a specific act or omission of the company, or the manner in which the company has carried on business, or the manner in which the directors have exercised their powers. Conduct that is not oppressive but is still unfairly prejudicial or that unfairly disregards the interests of any security holder, creditor, director, or officer can give rise to a remedy. Rectification can also be ordered in respect of similar conduct involving the company's affiliates.[34]

The court is empowered to make any order it thinks fit. It may order, for example, the appointment of a receiver, the amendment of the company's articles, by-laws or unanimous shareholder agreement, the issue, exchange or purchase of securities, or the appointment or replacement of directors. It may also order the setting aside of a company transaction, provide for the compensation of aggrieved persons, or even require the liquidation and dissolution of the company.[35]

In examining the conduct complained of, the court generally first assesses whether the conduct breached the complainant's reasonable expectations, and then goes on to determine whether the conduct amounted to oppression, unfair prejudice or unfair disregard. Because an oppression action is regarded as an "equitable" remedy, the court looks at business realities, not simply narrow legalities, and attempts to enforce not what is just legal but also what is fair.

While the oppression remedy has been used to rectify the results of many different kinds of oppressive conduct, it has been specifically used to fashion a remedy for those complainants who had a reasonable expectation of receiving company dividends which were not forthcoming, even when the declaration of dividends was left to the discretion of the company's directors.[36] For those income beneficiaries of a trust who expect and rely upon dividends from the company which the trust owns or controls, they may have an oppression claim against the company and its directors in certain circumstances.

In short, despite the broad discretionary powers which may be granted to a trustee in a trust agreement, along with the agreement's broad exemption from liability clauses, a trustee must still be aware of her accountability to the trust's beneficiaries under corporate law when the trust holds company shares.

Shareholder Agreements

Previous chapters of this book have briefly referred to the role played by a shareholder agreement in setting out certain rights and responsibilities of the company's shareholders and in providing for the ongoing governance of the company's business. Some of these references cited the advantages to the owner of having such an agreement in place, whereas other references cited specific disadvantages and suggested that amendments to an existing agreement might have to be made.

There are a number of different circumstances which make a shareholder agreement quite useful to the parties involved. The preparation and execution of a shareholder agreement or agreement amendment is often an essential condition to be satisfied in order for each of the various share transfers described in this book to be completed.

In those circumstances where the owner has decided that members of his family should hold shares in the company, either by direct gift or sale from him of his own shares, or by way of an estate freeze, a shareholder agreement can be used to provide him with continuing control of the company even though the others have acquired voting power through the shares issued to them. The agreement may reinforce the owner's control by giving him the right to appoint a majority of the company's directors or to veto certain company decisions, such as the declaration of dividends or issuance of shares.

A shareholder agreement can also be used to impose various restrictions upon the children who have acquired company shares under an estate freeze. To ensure that the company stays in "good hands" by remaining under family ownership, the agreement might provide for rights of first refusal and various buy-sell rights which are described below, including call rights which might give those children who are actively involved in the company a right to buy the shares of those children who aren't. It might require instead that a child's shares are to be sold to the company if the child ceases to work for the company on a full-time basis.

In order to provide the owner with sufficient funds to retire on, a shareholder agreement can be used to require the other shareholders or the company to purchase or redeem the owner's shares over time in accordance with a series of prescribed dates or milestones.

If the owner decides that company employees should become shareholders, perhaps pursuant to an employee stock purchase or option plan, a shareholder agreement can be used to address what happens to their shares in the event that they cease to be company employees, or they die or become disabled. They may be required, for example, to sell their shares back to the company, or alternatively, sell to the owner at a specified price.

They may also be restricted in the agreement from having any rights to veto a major transaction or otherwise block any company action which is supported by the owner. In the event that the owner receives an offer to purchase all of his shares from an outside party, the agreement may allow the owner to "drag along" the shares of the employees when selling to the outsider, as discussed below. On the other hand, the employees may be given in the agreement the right to buy the owner's shares at a set price upon the owner's death.

In those circumstances where the owner's chosen successor is an existing shareholder, an amended shareholder agreement can be used to document how the share transfer to the successor will take place, especially if the successor is the only shareholder of the company other than the owner. If there are other shareholders, the transfer to the chosen successor can still be accomplished by way of the shareholder agreement so long as the others agree. The proposed transfer by the owner can be treated as a legally binding commitment in the amended agreement or as simply an option to be exercised by the either the owner or successor in their respective discretion.

If the owner has chosen to sell his shares to an outside party but is able to accomplish such a sale only in a series of installments or tranches which leave him holding a portion of his company shares pending final payment from the purchaser, a shareholder agreement may be used in such circumstances to govern his rights as a continuing shareholder in the meantime. Being reduced to a minority shareholder, he may still want to ensure that he has a seat on the company's board of directors in order to have access to inside information and be able to participate in important decisions in the same way as the purchaser.

Alternatively, if he sells his company shares to another corporation which wants to pay the purchase price not in cash but in its own shares, the owner may have to enter into a shareholder agreement as a shareholder of the purchasing corporation. As a condition of his sale, however, he may be able to negotiate additional rights to be included in the shareholder agreement which are beyond what he might enjoy as a minority shareholder under the CBCA.

Regardless of the many different circumstances in which the owner might encounter a shareholder agreement in carrying out the share transfers described in this book, a shareholder agreement usually exists because the shareholders anticipate problems which might arise in the future. They generally use a shareholder agreement to implement certain practices to deter such problems from arising at all. Some of these problems relate to control and management, others relate to financing and conflicts of interest, while others relate to the possible abuse of power by the majority shareholder.

The remainder of this chapter attempts to describe some of the provisions commonly found in shareholder agreements which are used to address such problems. Unlike other parts of this book which look at various issues from the perspective of the company owner who is in the process of transferring his shares to his successor, this chapter will look at shareholder agreements from the perspective of a shareholder, whether the shareholder is a member of the owner's family, a company employee, an existing company shareholder, an outside purchaser, or the owner himself.

While these shareholders are most commonly individuals, they may well be corporations, partnerships or trusts in the case of other company shareholders or outside purchasers, such as venture capital firms and institutional investors, and therefore some of the comments appearing below may relate more to these kinds of shareholder than to individuals.

Furthermore, while some company shareholders such as the owner's intended successor, members of his family or long serving employees may expect their shareholding to continue for some time, other shareholders, particularly financial investors, may view their holding only on a short-term basis as a means of achieving a certain financial return. Consequently, a number of the agreement provisions outlined below address the possible short-term goals of a shareholder who may prefer an early exit from the company.

But at the outset, a brief explanation of "unanimous shareholder agreements" may be helpful.

UNANIMOUS SHAREHOLDER AGREEMENTS

A unanimous shareholder agreement is an agreement among all of the company's shareholders, both voting and non-voting, which restricts the powers of the directors. It is specifically authorized by the CBCA[1] and is often used to allow a private company to operate much like a partnership but with limited liability. The shareholders can be empowered to run the company in the same way as partners run a partnership.

To qualify as a unanimous shareholder agreement, it must to some extent restrict the powers of the directors to manage, or supervise the management of, the business and affairs of the company. It thereby effectively transfers to the shareholders some or all of the rights, duties and liabilities of the directors. Although agreements to fetter the discretion of company directors have traditionally not been permitted under common law,[2] the CBCA allows the shareholders to take away that discretion by means of a unanimous shareholder agreement.

In the absence of a unanimous shareholder agreement, the ability of shareholders to control a private company is generally limited in practice to their power to elect and dismiss directors. It is the directors who have the fundamental power and duty[3] to manage the company unless restricted by a unanimous shareholder agreement.

Sometimes viewed as a hybrid concept[4] under corporate law, a unanimous shareholder agreement is part contractual and part constitutional in nature. It must be a written agreement among all of the shareholders of the company, or among all of the shareholders and other parties.[5] As a contract, it governs the personal rights of the shareholders. As a component of the company's constitution, it governs the overall management of the company, including the issuing of shares, passing of by-laws, and appointment of officers. It can also set higher standards than those required under the CBCA, such as the number of votes of directors or shareholders needed to approve any action.[6]

If a unanimous shareholder agreement is in place for a private company, any person acquiring the company's shares is deemed to be a party to it. If certificates are issued for the company's shares and do not conspicuously note or refer to the agreement, the agreement may be ineffective against a share transferee who has no actual knowledge of it.[7]

A declaration by the only shareholder of a company which restricts the powers of the company's directors to manage is deemed to be a unanimous shareholder agreement.[8] Such a declaration is often used by foreign corporations wishing to maintain managerial control over their wholly-owned Canadian subsidiaries.

While a shareholder who is a party to a unanimous shareholder agreement acquires some or all of the rights, powers, duties and liabilities of the directors, including any defences available to the directors, the directors are relieved of their rights, powers, duties and liabilities to the same extent.[9] However, while the directors may be relieved of their liabilities under the CBCA, including their obligation[10] for six months wages remaining unpaid to the company's employees, such relief may not extend to all liabilities, including those imposed on directors by provincial legislation (even though it is unlikely a court will make a director liable for a company's conduct over which he has no control).

This rest of this chapter discusses some of the rights, powers and duties otherwise performed by directors which are often assumed by shareholders pursuant to a unanimous shareholder agreement. It also discusses some of the restrictions which are often imposed upon shareholders and some of the rules for governance and financing of the company's business which are normally found in such an agreement. Also discussed are the provisions of the agreement relating to the issuance of company shares and the transfer of company shares.

All of these provisions in the agreement that represent something other than restrictions on the directors' powers can sometimes cause confusion over whether the agreement actually qualifies as a unanimous shareholder agreement. But so long as the agreement is signed by all of the company's shareholders and restricts the powers of the directors to some extent, its inclusion of other items such as the rights of shareholders to acquire each other's shares or their obligations to finance company operations does not disqualify the agreement as a unanimous shareholder agreement.

BOARD AND MANAGEMENT REPRESENTATION

The shareholders may be quite prepared to leave the directors and officers free to operate the company on a day-to-day basis so long as the company is complying with its budgets and business plans and meeting any specific objectives or milestones that have been agreed upon. However, a shareholder may be given the right to nominate one or more directors to the company's board, or at least be given the right to have a nominee attend board meetings as an observer.

Observers are usually entitled to receive notice of and to attend meetings of the board of directors, but are not entitled to vote. Shareholders comprised of venture capital and private equity firms often prefer to limit the involvement of their nominees to observer status if the board already consists of nominees of other professional investors, or as a way of avoiding director liability or the policies of certain stock exchanges which place escrow requirements during an initial public offering on shareholders having board representation.

Although the right to appoint observers to the board may be appropriate in certain circumstances, most minority shareholders try to assert greater control over the management of the company by insisting upon guaranteed board representation. The shareholder agreement may provide that each shareholder, or related group of shareholders, has the right to nominate a number of directors which is roughly proportional to their shareholdings. This may allow a group with similar interests, perhaps a group of individual employees or financial investors, to have their respective representatives appointed to the board. The agreement may also provide that when the percentage shareholdings of the group changes, their right to board representation correspondingly changes.

The agreement will usually require that all of the shareholders vote in favour of the election of the prescribed nominees to the board of directors and to fill any vacancy on the board with the nominee of the shareholder who was represented by a vacating director. The shareholders will also be required to remove any nominee director who contravenes or votes against the wishes of the shareholder nominating him. A related provision may limit the number of directors so that the right to nominate directors is equal to the right to control a specified portion of the board.

The agreement may require that audit and compensation committees of the board be established, comprised solely of directors unrelated to a majority shareholder or current management, and that directors' and officers' liability insurance be put into place. It may also require that board meetings be held quarterly, if not more frequently, and that the board's quorum rules not allow such meetings to proceed in the absence of certain nominee directors.

To ensure that the company's key management positions are filled by people with suitable skills and experience, the shareholder agreement may specifically name certain individuals to serve, for example, as the chief financial officer or chief marketing officer of the company.

The agreement may even require that all of the company's top managers enter into comprehensive employment agreements not only setting out their respective duties, compensation (including bonus entitlement and participation in stock purchase and option plans), and rights on termination, but also their assignment of intellectual property rights and their non-disclosure, non-competition and no "moonlighting" obligations. The need to maintain "key person" insurance for them may also be stipulated.

To provide a shareholder with the right to become more involved with the company should the company's financial position deteriorate, the agreement may contain "voting switch" provisions. These provisions give the shareholder the right to elect more directors, even a majority of the company's board, upon the occurrence of certain materially adverse events, such as the failure by the company to meet certain objectives or milestones specified in the agreement or the breach by the company of any covenant in the agreement. Sometimes these provisions even include the right of the shareholder to relieve any of the managers from their management duties upon relatively short notice without cause, but subject to an obligation to pay appropriate severance and to buy back any company shares which the managers may hold.

For those companies with just two shareholders having equal or almost equal holdings, the prescribed number of their respective representatives on the board will likely be equal, leaving open the possibility of a deadlocked board on the more contentious issues. Repeated tie votes may result in the company being unable to take necessary action on a number of important matters, much like a partnership with feuding partners being unable to function.

One solution to breaking these possible tie votes is providing in the agreement for a right of the company's chairman to have a second or casting vote on the matter creating the tie. If such a right is included, the parties may insist that the agreement also include a rotation of the chairman position between the two shareholders at certain intervals, since the shareholder with the right to appoint the chairman effectively controls the board.

Each of these rights to appoint board and management representatives must be considered in the context of the company's overall governance and its need for directors and officers who have the skills and experience to properly manage the company's business.

A nominee director or officer still owes a fiduciary duty[11] to the company, not to any particular shareholder. Regardless of being appointed by that shareholder pursuant to a shareholder agreement, the director or officer may not subordinate the interests of the company while preferring the interests of the nominating shareholder. Individuals who are appointed to key company positions because of their loyalty to their nominating shareholder may soon be unable to reconcile the conflicts between the interests of the company and the interests of the shareholder nominating them.

INFORMATION RIGHTS

A shareholder may be entitled under a shareholder agreement to receive ongoing financial information directly from the company on a regular basis and not simply by way of his nominee director at board meetings, if he is entitled to nominate a director at all. The information to be provided usually includes monthly or quarterly management financial statements and audited annual financial statements. Other information generally to be provided includes management budgets, forecasts and variance reports, along with research and development reports and certificates from the chief financial officer that all statutory deductions have been appropriately withheld and remitted.

The shareholder may also be granted ongoing inspection and audit rights which permit him to visit and inspect the company's properties, examine the company's accounts and records, and discuss the company's affairs and finances with company officers. The company may, however, qualify such rights by excluding the provision of any information which it reasonably believes to be trade secrets or other confidential information unless it is satisfied with the confidentiality arrangements made with the inspecting parties.

MAJOR DECISIONS

Most shareholder agreements impose higher approval thresholds for major decisions. While some agreements simply require a higher than normal percentage for director approval, most agreements require the approval of the shareholders, and often specify a percentage well above a simple majority. It is not uncommon for an agreement to require the approval of three-quarters or four-fifths of the shareholders in order for a major decision to proceed. This need for shareholder approval is an example of the kinds of restrictions on director powers which unanimous shareholder agreements contain.

A list of the various company actions which comprise major decisions is often lengthy and is usually attached as a schedule to the agreement. While it sets out a number of actions which can result in an increase in the company's liabilities or a dilution of the current shareholders' percentage interests, many of these actions are qualified or limited by certain exceptions when taken in the normal course of the company's business or which entail only minor or immaterial liabilities. The list is intended to include any action with the potential to have a material adverse effect on the company or its business.

The list ordinarily includes any changes to the company's articles or by-laws, the issuance of additional shares or securities convertible into shares (other than under an employee share ownership plan or option plan, or as may be required to obtain working capital financing), the redemption or repurchase of company shares, and the payment of any dividends.

Also included are any amalgamation agreement, any asset or share purchase agreement, any partnership or joint venture agreement, and any loan, guarantee or security agreement between the company and any other party. However, borrowing for working capital purposes, whether on a secured or unsecured basis, is generally a permitted exception.

Any proposal or assignment made by the company under applicable insolvency legislation, any attempt to dissolve or liquidate the company, and any prepayment by the company of any shareholder loans, are other actions likely to appear on the list.

Although the list may stay the same for some time, the percentage approval thresholds may have to change to reflect changes in the percentage holdings of the various shareholders. A current shareholder may not be prepared to invest more money in the company when the other shareholders decline to do so unless the approval thresholds are lowered. The agreement may specify that a lower threshold will apply in the event that the holdings of any shareholder rise above a prescribed percentage.

For example, a three-quarters threshold might be reduced to two-thirds when a shareholder ends up with two-thirds of the outstanding shares.

USE OF PROFITS

Shareholders may have different expectations on how and when they will realize a return on their investment in the company. Some may be looking to dividends, while others may be anticipating a large increase in the value of their investment which they will receive when they eventually sell their shares. Some may have a more immediate, short-term view, whereas others, often called "patient capital", may be investing for a longer term.

Since the shareholders are unlikely to have a common view over how often and how much the company should pay them as dividends, the agreement may set out a desired dividend policy for the company to follow when profits permit. The agreement may specify the percentage of the company's earnings, over the amounts needed for operating purposes and required capital expenditures, which is to be distributed to the shareholders as dividends.

Instead of providing guidance for the payment of dividends, the agreement may require that the company's profits first be used to expand the company's operations, or pay down outstanding bank indebtedness, redeem company shares or repay shareholder loans.

BANK FINANCING AND GUARANTEES

Just as the shareholders may have different preferences for the use of the company's profits, they may also have different preferences for how the company raises funds to satisfy its ongoing capital requirements. Some companies have more financing alternatives than others. Those with consistent earnings and substantial assets may be able to choose from a number of sources. Seed stage and start-up stage companies usually cannot secure debt financing and may have to resort to equity capital to fund their growth.

For those companies able to raise money from outside sources, the shareholders may want the agreement to stipulate that the company should first try to obtain new financing from the chartered banks or other financial institutions before calling upon the shareholders for additional funds.

To obtain such financing on reasonable terms, especially in the earlier stages of the company's life cycle, it may be necessary for one or more of the shareholders to personally guarantee the repayment of all amounts the company may borrow.

The agreement usually addresses this requirement by stipulating that the shareholders provide their personal guarantees to support any bank borrowing so long as their guarantees are limited to a percentage of the amount borrowed which is equal to their percentage shareholding in the company. It may also require the shareholders to indemnify one another if any shareholder becomes liable under his guarantee for more than his percentage interest in the company.

PRE-EMPTIVE RIGHTS

The agreement may also address the company's need to raise equity capital by allowing for voluntary share subscriptions by the current shareholders while providing them with some protection against the dilution of their current percentage holdings. This may be accomplished by giving them pre-emptive rights.

These rights apply when the company intends to issue additional shares, which must first be offered to all of the shareholders in proportion to their current holdings at the same price and on the same terms. While pre-emptive rights provide the shareholders with some protection against dilution of their equity interest in the company, such rights may hinder the company's ability to raise additional capital and may not be appropriate in every circumstance.

Notice of the proposed share issuance is to be given by the company to the shareholders, who then have a certain amount of time in which to reply that they want to buy their portion of the offered shares. Each shareholder is usually then given the right to buy more or less than the portion they are offered. If any shareholder subscribes for less than he is entitled to, the balance of the shares he is offered then becomes available for possible issuance to those other shareholders who subscribed for more than the portion they were entitled to, ordinarily in proportion to their own percentage holdings in the company.

Some agreements may alternatively prevent shareholders from subscribing for more shares than they are offered in the first round. Any unsubscribed shares are to then be re-offered to all participating shareholders based upon their respective percentage holdings until there are no shares left for subscription, or until there are no shareholders left who are willing to subscribe for more shares. If the company has a large number of shareholders, this process of providing notice of each successive offer may be quite time consuming to follow.

The agreement usually provides exemptions from pre-emptive rights for shares issued to employees, officers, directors and consultants pursuant to incentive compensation arrangements, or for shares issued upon conversion of other company securities or in connection with stock dividends or stock splits. Exemptions may also be available for shares issued to commercial lenders and equipment lessors in the ordinary course of business, and shares issued as consideration for the company's acquisition of another business.

MANDATORY SHAREHOLDER FUNDING

In addition to providing for voluntary share subscriptions by the current shareholders through pre-emptive rights, the agreement may impose mandatory subscriptions upon the shareholders as well. The agreement may require the shareholders to invest in additional shares within a certain amount of time after a "capital call" is made upon them. As with pre-emptive rights, capital calls are usually made upon shareholders in proportion to their respective percentage holdings of company shares.

Instead of calling for additional equity investment, the company may require the shareholders to provide additional capital by way of shareholder loans. The shareholders may prefer to advance funds as loans rather than as equity because of the possibility of receiving some security from the company for such loans. Even if their loans are unsecured, they will still rank as creditors in any insolvency or bankruptcy of the company.

While the agreement will likely require them to postpone payment of their loans and subordinate their security in favour of any bank or other financial institution which has provided financing to the company, lending funds to the company may still be preferred over investing in additional equity.

Any decision to include mandatory funding in an agreement should not be made lightly. The relative financial resources of each shareholder need to be considered, especially when such resources could be significantly reduced by the time a call is made. It may be appropriate for capital calls to be made only with the approval of a very high percentage of shareholder votes.

If the agreement does include mandatory funding provisions, it will likely also include a provision specifying what happens if a shareholder is unable or unwilling to satisfy any capital call.

Ordinarily those shareholders who meet their capital calls are given the right to subscribe for the shares or make the loans that a defaulting shareholder was called for. Their exercise of such right in the case of an equity funding call will result in the dilution of the defaulting shareholder's percentage interest. They may also be given an option upon such default to acquire the defaulting shareholder's shares at less than fair market value, resulting in the further dilution or complete transfer of the defaulting shareholder's interest if the option is exercised. In the case of a debt funding call, their additional loans may be set at a higher rate of interest and given a preference to be paid in priority to the company's ordinary shareholder loans.

FIRST REFUSAL RIGHTS

A shareholder may be given a right of first refusal on the transfer of any company shares proposed by any other shareholders in the future. In contrast to pre-emptive rights which are intended to maintain a shareholder's percentage of equity ownership in the company, rights of first refusal are intended to increase his equity ownership in the company in the event that any of the other shareholders decides to sell. As with pre-emptive rights, rights of first refusal often apply to any shares, or securities exchangeable or convertible into shares, including rights, options or warrants, and not just to shares of the same class as are already held by the shareholder.

Exemptions from rights of first refusal are ordinarily given for transfers to a registered retirement savings plan or other trust of which the shareholder is the beneficial owner, or to a shareholder's spouse, or to a shareholder's personal holding corporation provided that the shareholders of the holding corporation agree not to transfer their shares in the holding corporation unless they concurrently transfer the shares of the company to another exempt party.

In the case of corporate shareholders, exemptions from rights of first refusal may be available to cover transfers to affiliates. In the case of shareholders who are investment managers, exempt transfers might include transfers to other funds or corporations which they manage.

The events which specifically trigger the right of first refusal often vary. Some shareholder agreements require that a "bona fide offer" must be received by the selling shareholder for all of his shares from a third party before notice is to be given to the other shareholders of their rights to purchase such shares. They are then entitled to purchase a percentage of the shares equal to their percentage ownership of the company, at the same price and on the same terms as the third party offer. If the other shareholders do not take up all of the shares, the selling shareholder may then sell all of his shares to the third party at the price and on the terms of the original offer. In order to prevent any disputes over the value of non-cash consideration, the agreement usually provides that the price in the original offer be paid in cash on closing. It also usually provides that upon closing, the third party purchaser must become a party to the agreement.

Obviously this requirement deters potential third party purchasers from incurring the time and expense involved in preparing a serious offer which may be ignored if any one of the other shareholders elects to exercise his purchase rights. It does, however, benefit the existing shareholders by letting them know the identity of their prospective fellow shareholder and effectively giving them a veto over him. Perhaps more significantly, it gives them some indication of the fair value of the shares being offered to them, assuming the third party is acting at arm's length with the selling shareholder.

As an alternative, the agreement may provide what is commonly called a "right of first offer", which permits the selling shareholder to simply give notice to the other shareholders of his intention to sell at a price and on such terms as he chooses. They are then entitled to purchase a percentage of his shares equal to their percentage ownership of the company, but if they don't, he may then sell his shares to a third party provided the price and terms are no more favourable than those originally offered to the other shareholders.

While this alternative helps the selling shareholder to set a minimum price which he can then use in subsequently negotiating with third parties, it may encourage the selling shareholder to specify an inflated price with the expectation that the other shareholders will elect to purchase at that price rather than risk a third party becoming a shareholder. Furthermore, if the other shareholders have decided not to purchase the offered shares, it affords them no opportunity to prevent the selling shareholder from selling to a third party who they might regard as an undesirable shareholder. This latter concern, however, may be addressed by incorporating into the agreement a list of prohibited third party purchasers, which might include any competitors of the company or of the current shareholders.

Deciding which of these two alternatives is preferable for inclusion in the shareholder agreement requires the shareholders to weigh their desire for the potential liquidity of their shares against their desire to control who may become a new shareholder.

Despite the inclusion of any first refusal rights, the agreement may contain a prohibition against any share transfers to third parties for a certain period of time. Sometimes referred to as a "standstill" provision, it can be used to keep all of the current shareholders working together to promote the success of the company's business, perhaps during the crucial start-up or growth stages of the company's life cycle.

Under most rights of first refusal, the selling shareholder is required to offer all, but not less than all, of his shares to the other shareholders. Furthermore, once the other shareholders have declined to buy all of his shares, the selling shareholder is usually required to close his sale to the third party within a certain period of time, failing which the first refusal process has to start all over again. Rights of first offer may permit a longer time period, since the third party negotiations may not start until after all of the current shareholders have declined. However, the longer the time period, the greater the chance that the offer price will cease to reflect the current value of the shares because of intervening material changes to the company's business.

PIGGYBACK RIGHTS

A shareholder may be entitled under the agreement to participate in another shareholder's proposed sale of company shares, usually when the sale results in a change of control of the company or involves a substantial percentage of outstanding shares. Intended to enhance the liquidity of minority shareholdings, many shareholder agreements allow a shareholder to "piggyback" on a third party offer made to a majority shareholder.

A piggyback provision often applies when a shareholder or group of shareholders with a majority of the company's shares has complied with the rights of first refusal requirements and proposes to sell to a third party.

He may proceed to sell his shares to the third party so long as he has caused the third party to offer to purchase the shares of the other shareholders at the same price and on the same terms. The piggyback provision effectively provides minority shareholders who can't afford to exercise their rights of first refusal with a possible exit from the company should they wish to avoid dealing with a new majority shareholder in the future.

The agreement may provide "co-sale" rights instead. Unlike piggyback rights which allow minority shareholders to have all of their shares included in a third party purchase offer, co-sale rights provide for the inclusion of only such portion of their shares which, when added to the portion held by the majority shareholders, equals the number of shares which the third party wishes to purchase. The number of shares that the majority can sell is effectively reduced and replaced by the number of shares that the minority shareholders elect to sell to the third party. In the event that the third party wishes to purchase all of the company's outstanding shares, the difference between piggyback rights and co-sale rights disappears in practice.

While rights of first refusal generally prohibit third party offers from consisting of non-cash consideration, piggyback rights and drag-along rights discussed below, often permit non-cash consideration to be part of third party offers.

DRAG-ALONG RIGHTS

A minority shareholder may also be required to participate in a sale of company shares by a majority shareholder. His own shares may be "dragged along" as a way of increasing the marketability of the majority shareholder's shares since a third party purchaser may be more likely to want all of the shares of the company rather than have to deal with other company shareholders after the purchase. The drag-along provision is also viewed as an effective way to eliminate minority positions in a private company.

A drag-along provision is effectively the reverse of a piggyback provision. It provides that if a third party makes an offer to purchase all of the shares of the company, those shareholders holding a majority or perhaps higher percentage of the company's shares who wish to accept the offer may require the other shareholders to sell their shares to the third party at the same price and on the same terms, so long as the right of first refusal provisions have first been complied with.

This provision allows the majority shareholder to market 100 per cent of the company's shares and obtain the maximum sale price from a purchaser prepared to pay a higher price for all of the shares than it would pay for just majority control.

TRANSFER RIGHTS UPON CERTAIN EVENTS

A shareholder may be able to require the other shareholders to buy his shares upon the occurrence of certain events. Alternatively, the shareholder may be required to sell his shares to the others upon the occurrence of the same events. The death of the shareholder, if the shareholder is an individual, is the event specified in most shareholder agreements as requiring a share transfer. Other events triggering such a requirement include the termination of a shareholder's employment with the company, whether voluntary or involuntary, the shareholder's disability, bankruptcy or insolvency, or a breach of a material provision of the agreement.

These requirements usually appear as a number of "puts" and "calls" in the agreement. A put, or option to sell, gives a shareholder a right, but not an obligation, to sell his shares either to the company or to other shareholders upon the prescribed events. As the opposite of a put, a call gives a shareholder or the company a right, but again not an obligation, to buy the shares of another shareholder.

However, instead of structuring the requirements as a series of puts and calls, some agreements provide for mandatory, not optional, purchases. This approach is often thought to be desirable in the event of death or disability of the shareholder since the shares will have a ready buyer.

Most agreements require a shareholder to sell his shares when a call is exercised after a prescribed event. Yet they often vary over which party may exercise the call and purchase his shares. Some agreements give call rights to the company, some give them to just a majority shareholder or group of shareholders, while others give them to all of the shareholders based upon their percentage holdings of company shares.

Although selecting the company as the buyer may appear to be the easiest approach to take, it may result in undesirable consequences, apart from considerations of whether the company will have the funds available to pay for the shares.

For example, a company redemption or repurchase may well have negative tax implications for the selling shareholder.[12] Also, the proportionate voting rights of the other shareholders and voting control could be altered upon the cancellation of that shareholder's shares. Furthermore, the redemption or repurchase could possibly cause the company to be in default under the negative covenants in its financing agreements, or perhaps be in contravention of the statutory solvency test for the redemption or purchase of its shares.

Under this solvency test, the directors of the company are prohibited from repurchasing the company's shares if there are reasonable grounds for believing the company is, or after payment for the shares will be, unable to pay its liabilities as they become due, or if the realizable value of the company's assets will then be less than the aggregate of its liabilities and stated capital of all classes. A similar prohibition applies to the redemption of the company's shares, although the realizable value of the company's assets must not be less than the aggregate of its liabilities and the amount it has to pay to the holders of other shares before or rateably with the holders of the shares being redeemed.[13]

In light of these possible consequences, the agreement may provide that if the company is unable to buy the shares, then another shareholder or group of shareholders shall buy the shares instead.

The treatment of an employee's shares upon termination of employment often depends upon how and why the termination takes place. If it is "for cause", the company is likely to be given a call option to purchase the employee's shares, whereas the employee is likely to be given a put option to sell his shares if he is terminated without cause. If the employee simply resigns, the company can usually call the employee's shares.

VALUATION OF TRANSFERRED SHARES

Even though the shareholders may be able to agree upon the various puts and calls to be exercised in respect of their shares, they may have some difficulty in deciding which method should be used to value their shares when these options are exercised. Since there is no readily available market for determining their value, the shareholder agreement must provide some valuation guidance. Whether a share purchase is mandatory or optional, the agreement usually specifies one of three ways, previously mentioned in the *Transfers to Other Shareholders* chapter, to arrive at a purchase price for the shares being purchased.

One approach requires the shareholders to review and annually adjust an initially agreed upon value. The second approach entails the application of a particular formula. As described in greater detail in the *Valuation* chapter, there are different formulas to choose from. The agreement may select an asset-based method, such as net book value or appraised asset value. Or it may select an earnings based or cash flow based method, perhaps using discounted cash flow or a multiple of earnings. Or it may select a specific industry rule of thumb, such as a dollar value per existing customer.

The third approach involves the retention of a professional business valuator to determine the value of the shares to be sold. The agreement will often specify who the valuator should be and who should pay the valuator's fees. It may also provide some general rules for the valuator regarding which valuation methods should be used or avoided, and which assumptions and adjustments ought to be made. For example, it may stipulate that no control premium or minority discount is to be considered, but that the goodwill associated with a departing shareholder may be taken into account.

Each approach has its advantages and disadvantages. But while all three afford the parties a mechanism for valuation, they don't guarantee either certainty or fairness of result. The annual share value review usually stops after the second year. The formula approach tends to be easier and faster than the valuator approach, but may not be suitable for every company. For example, a decision to use book and not appraised asset values, or a multiple of recent earnings and not a discount of projected earnings, may appear misguided in hindsight and create resentment.

By taking the valuator approach, assuming that all the parties can agree upon a choice of valuator, the valuator chosen may turn out to be more expensive and take much longer to perform the valuation than the parties originally expected. Often the closing date prescribed in the agreement becomes unworkable because of delays in receiving the valuator's report. If the agreement names the company's auditor as the valuator, the auditor may have difficulty reconciling the conflicts between audit and valuation duties. It's usually preferable for an independent party to be named as valuator, and for any closing date to be a specified number of days following delivery of the valuation.

Sometimes the agreement will prescribe a different method for the valuation of shares which can be "called" in the event that the holder becomes insolvent or bankrupt in order to arrive at a value which is lower than the value which would apply upon the occurrence of the other events triggering a call under the agreement. Net book value or the original subscription price for the shares might be the method chosen in these circumstances so that a lower price will be paid by the company or other shareholders when exercising their rights to redeem or purchase the shares, since the holder will not personally benefit from the proceeds actually paid.

SHOTGUN RIGHTS

Another provision involving the transfer of shares between shareholders is the "shotgun", which has its own particular valuation mechanism. Some shareholder agreements, normally between just two shareholders, will contain a shotgun provision to provide a means of resolving a possible deadlock between the two shareholders.

A shotgun essentially permits one shareholder to set a price at which he is willing to either sell his shares to the other shareholder, or buy the shares of the other shareholder. Once the shareholder has given notice of the shotgun price, the other shareholder then has to decide which of the two alternatives to accept. Many shotguns require the other shareholder to decide within a relatively short time period, often less than 30 days, and his failure to do so requires him to sell his shares at the price set.

While some shotguns then require payment of the entire purchase price after another relatively short period, again often less than 30 days, some provide for payment in regular installments over as long as 3 or 5 years. The tight time frames dictated by the agreement can certainly work to the disadvantage of the other shareholder, who may have great difficulty in arranging suitable financing within the permitted time should he wish to buy. His ability to pay on time effectively determines whether he buys or sells.

For this reason, shotguns are often only used when there are just two equal shareholders with roughly comparable financial resources. Although shotguns impose an obvious deterrent on the offering shareholder against setting a price that is too high or too low, such deterrence breaks down when the other shareholder lacks financial strength. When that is the case, the attempt to give some certainty to the exit process by adding a shotgun clause is then made at the expense of fairness, because a low-ball price becomes inevitable. The financially stronger shareholder will simply take advantage of the other.

Consequently, shotguns may be inappropriate for many companies and shareholders. For earlier stage companies that need to keep their shareholders committed, as well as patient for a payback on whatever time and effort has been invested, shotguns are often exercisable only after a period of two years or more has elapsed.

For those companies with shotgun provisions in their shareholder agreements, such provisions are infrequently exercised. Since shareholders appear reluctant to risk the consequences in practice, shotguns may reflect mutual deterrence. They may actually motivate deadlocked shareholders to negotiate a resolution to a problem rather than pull the trigger. In other words, the main benefit to having a shotgun in place is the threat of its use, not the use itself.

AUCTION RIGHTS

Although not commonly found in shareholder agreements, shareholders may be given the right to initiate an auction for the company's outstanding shares. The right to hold an auction is usually provided as additional to, and sometimes as an alternative to, some of the rights described in this chapter.

As an alternative to the rights of first refusal, an auction may be chosen by the shareholders as providing the means for the sale of one shareholder's shares to the other shareholders. The auction gives the other shareholders an opportunity to buy a shareholder's shares but does not ensure that they will pay no more than a third party will pay. The auction procedures may require that all of the interested bidders attend at a certain location at a specified time and that a named auctioneer will conduct the auction in accordance with the rules set out in the agreement, with the highest bidder winning.

An auction may also be used instead of the right to exercise a shotgun. The shareholders, especially if there are more than two, may have the right under a shareholder agreement to initiate an auction for the company's outstanding shares. In this case, the auction procedures may prescribe that each shareholder is to make a sealed bid to buy all of the shares of the company and that the shareholder with the highest bid wins.

NEGATIVE COVENANTS

In addition to placing restrictions on the powers of the directors and on the type of business the company may carry on, the agreement may impose restrictions on the shareholders themselves, particularly on their conduct which may not be in the best interests of the company.

Although the directors are under a statutory duty to act in the best interests of the company, as mentioned above under *BOARD AND MANAGEMENT REPRESENTATION*, the shareholders are not. If the shareholders collectively decide that certain contractual duties should be placed upon their fellow shareholders to make up for the absence of certain statutory duties, a shareholder agreement may also be used for such a purpose.

The agreement may set out various shareholder duties, or "positive covenants", to do certain things. Examples of such covenants appear elsewhere in this chapter, such as a shareholder's obligation to give notice to the other shareholders of his desire to sell his company shares to an outside party so that they may exercise their rights of first refusal.

But the agreement is just as likely to set out various duties, or "negative covenants", not to do certain things. Examples of these covenants also appear elsewhere in this chapter, including the companion covenant to the right of first refusal which prohibits a shareholder from transferring his shares to an outside party.

Three negative covenants which ordinarily appear in the agreement to address possible conflicts of interest between a shareholder and the company are the non-disclosure covenant, the non-solicitation covenant and the non-competition covenant.

Non-disclosure Covenant

A shareholder of a private company is usually required under the agreement not to disclose to anyone outside the company any confidential or proprietary company information, including any intellectual property, trade secrets, sales and market data, and any other confidential information relating to the company and its business. This covenant is a companion covenant to the information rights discussed above, and generally applies whether the shareholder continues or ceases to be a shareholder.

The agreement ordinarily provides certain exceptions to this restriction. It does not apply to information which is known to the public, or information which the shareholder knew before becoming a shareholder, or information which the shareholder received from outside parties.

Non-solicitation Covenant

The non-solicitation covenant generally prevents a shareholder from soliciting any employees of the company to become employees of the shareholder, or any customers of the company to become customers of the shareholder, so long as the shareholder remains a shareholder of the company and for a certain period of time afterwards. The survival or continuing enforceability of this covenant generally lasts for a period of between six months and two years after the shareholder disposes of his shares, but longer terms are not unusual.

This provision is usually worded to prohibit only the active solicitation or inducement of company employees or customers by a departing shareholder, and is not intended to cover those employees or customers who approach the shareholder on their own. However, it can lead to a dispute between the company and a departing shareholder who subsequently employs company employees or supplies company customers, since the shareholder's subtle encouragement of the employees and customers is often inferred from the particular circumstances. The shareholder's protest that the employees or customers came on their own accord is not always credible.

Non-competition Covenant

In addition to preventing a shareholder from soliciting company employees or customers, the agreement may also try to prevent the shareholder from competing against the company or its affiliates, either directly or indirectly. A non-competition covenant is usually limited to a certain geographical territory or market and to a certain length of time. It may last as long as a non-solicitation covenant but is sometimes for a slightly shorter period. It represents a much broader restriction than a non-solicitation covenant since a shareholder bound only by the latter may continue to participate and invest in the same business as the company.

Its prohibition against both direct and indirect competition ordinarily covers a very broad range of activities. It applies to acting as an employee, officer, director, shareholder, consultant or agent for a competing business, regardless of whether such business is carried on through a partnership, joint venture, trust, other corporation, or even a governmental agency.

Furthermore, the covenant usually prevents the shareholder from lending to, investing in, or otherwise having a financial interest in any business which is the same or substantially similar to the business being carried on by the company or its affiliates. An exception is often made for any investment in publicly traded securities provided such investment represents not more than 5 per cent of the total securities outstanding of any particular issuer.

Enforcement of Negative Covenants

As monetary damages may not be easily or expeditiously proven before a court or even obtained through the enforcement of a court judgment for a breach of any of these three covenants, the agreement is likely to provide that the company may also ask a court to award an injunction to prevent any continuing breach of them.

Efforts to enforce a non-solicitation or non-competition covenant can face an additional challenge since most courts are reluctant to award a remedy for breach of either covenant if it covers too broad a geographical territory or too long a time period.[14]

The courts have traditionally viewed these two kinds of restrictive covenants as restraints of trade and have needed to be convinced that the covenants are reasonably necessary to protect the company's legitimate proprietary interest before enforcing them. However, customer lists, trade secrets, business connections with customers and goodwill are all legitimate interests worthy of the court's protection.

Often a non–solicitation covenant will be enforced by a court but not a non-competition covenant on the basis that the non-solicitation covenant is all that is necessary to protect a company's interest, provided that it has reasonable territorial and time restrictions.

However, should the company or another shareholder have either a right or obligation to redeem or purchase a shareholder's shares under the agreement as discussed above, there is a greater chance that the non-competition covenant will be enforced by the court, especially if the agreement prescribes the purchase price to be paid for the shares.

Unlike non-competition covenants contained in employment agreements which are seldom enforced, non-competition covenants in share purchase agreements are frequently enforced, due in some part to the equality of bargaining power which ordinarily exists between a purchaser and seller, but not between an employer and employee. Also, a sale of a business often involves a payment for goodwill whereas no similar payment is made to an employee upon leaving employment. Yet in order for the non-competition covenant to be enforceable, it must still contain reasonable territorial and time restrictions.

FAMILY LAW COVENANTS

As described earlier in the *Transfers to Family – Part I* chapter, the family laws applicable in many Canadian provinces generally provide a community of property regime which allows for the equalization of family property acquired by spouses during their marriage upon their marriage breakdown. Consequently, a shareholder agreement may contain a provision dealing with the implications of such laws upon a shareholder.

Under these laws, a court might order that company shares owned by one spouse be transferred to the other spouse, or that one spouse pay to the other a part of the profits earned by the company. Such orders can lead to a number of undesirable consequences for the company and its shareholders. Control of the company might change, covenants in the company's credit agreements might be breached and adverse tax effects might result. The provisions in the agreement dealing with board representation and the approval of major decisions may cease to be acceptable to certain shareholders.

Furthermore, such legal proceedings may threaten the confidentiality of sensitive company information, since its financial statements and other records may have to be produced and various details of its business described in a court judgment.

To address some of these potential concerns, the agreement may provide that any shareholder has the right to acquire for a prescribed price the shares of another shareholder who is facing a family law claim for property equalization. This call right, however, has disadvantages for both parties, since it requires the buyer to come up with the purchase funds which may be difficult to find, and may place an untimely tax liability upon the seller. A court may also be unprepared to accept the prescribed price as the correct value of the shares and wish to undertake its own assessment, thereby again threatening the confidentiality of the company's business information.

A preferred alternative is for the agreement to require the shareholders to have in place separate marriage contracts with their respective spouses which exclude their shares from any property equalization and which prevent their spouse from looking to the company to satisfy any equalization payment owing. These marriage contracts would be required immediately from shareholders who are married and upon any subsequent marriage or remarriage of a shareholder. Any proposed amendment to those contracts which conflicts with the provisions of the shareholder agreement would have to be approved by all of the shareholders.

Whichever approach is taken, the agreement will still include a provision requiring a shareholder to notify the company and all of the other shareholders if he becomes involved in equalization proceedings.

MISCELLANEOUS MATTERS

In addition to the foregoing items, a shareholder agreement may set out a number of other items which are more procedural in nature or which address the day-to-day operations of the company, whether or not they are also contained in the company's by-laws.

For example, the agreement may specify the company's bankers, lawyers and accountants, its financial year-end, and those persons who are authorized to make bank deposits and sign contracts and cheques. It may also include any special notice and voting rules for directors' meetings and the process for preparing and approving operating and capital budgets and the company's business plan.

Since the circumstances facing the company or its shareholders are likely to change during the term of the agreement, the procedure for its amendment is usually set out. Unless there are just a few shareholders, requiring the consent of all of the shareholders to any amendment may not be practicable. Normally the consent of a relatively high percentage of shareholders, perhaps 80 per cent, is all that is required to effect an amendment binding upon all of the shareholders.

While the agreement may well have an indefinite term, it may stipulate instead that it is to remain in effect for only a fixed term. The termination of the agreement may occur upon a certain date, upon a certain event taking place and result being achieved, or perhaps in the absence of such event or result by a particular date. Upon termination, the agreement may provide for the company to be liquidated and dissolved, unless the agreement has been terminated to facilitate a public offering of the company's shares.

Confidentiality Agreements

Before the current owner begins to exchange specific information about the business to a prospective buyer in an effort to determine whether a deal between them might be possible, they will often enter into a confidentiality or non-disclosure agreement as the first step in the deal continuum. If a considerable part of the value of the business is attributable to its trade secrets, a confidentiality agreement will be essential.

Some parties, particularly financial investors such as venture capital firms considering a share purchase, initially refuse to sign confidentiality agreements when requested, simply on the grounds that they receive so many business plans to look at which are all so similar, that they can't keep them all straight. Ordinarily, however, the parties entering into negotiations for the purchase and sale of a business aren't so reluctant.

Confidentiality agreements can be either "one-way", when only one party is disclosing confidential information to the other, or "two-way", when both parties are exchanging confidential information with each other. Although a confidentiality agreement covering the purchase and sale of a business may be just one-way when only the seller is disclosing information to the buyer, it is ordinarily two-way if disclosure is also being made by the buyer

If the current owner is concerned about a prospective buyer's ability to actually close the deal or to pay any installments of the purchase price which may be due after closing, the owner should attempt to obtain sufficient information from the buyer to decide upon the buyer's creditworthiness. A two-way confidentiality agreement would then be appropriate for use.

Although many confidentiality agreements are quite brief and merely recite the duty of each party to keep confidential any information disclosed by one to the other, the provisions discussed below are often found in confidentiality agreements for the purchase and sale of a business. The current owner might consider the following provisions as being necessary for the protection of all personal and business information she might be expected to disclose to a prospective buyer.

However, despite the existence of a signed confidentiality agreement between the parties, the current owner must still be aware of the risks of disclosing extremely confidential information to a potential buyer, especially a business competitor. In the event that the owner and buyer fail to close a deal, the information could then be wrongfully used by the buyer against the owner and the business. Although the owner may have recourse to the courts seeking compensation for any breach of the confidentiality agreement, sufficient damage may have already been done.

In light of this risk, the current owner may prefer to adopt a more cautious approach by using a phased disclosure schedule. The less sensitive the information, the earlier in the deal continuum such information may be disclosed to the buyer. Disclosure of specific customer information, including pricing, trade terms and profit margins, might be withheld by the current owner until the purchase and sale agreement has been signed.

DEFINITION OF CONFIDENTIAL INFORMATION

A comprehensive definition of what is regarded as confidential information and what is not confidential information should be set out in the confidentiality agreement. Information which is already in the public domain, or becomes known to the receiving party through other sources, or has been independently developed by the receiving party, is usually exempted.

In order to provide certainty, some agreements require that each document to be disclosed by one party to the other be marked "confidential" in order for it to be caught by the agreement as "confidential". However, in practice, such a marking rule is observed more often in the breach and places an extremely high standard on the seller who is required to produce the vast majority of documents relating to the deal.

SCOPE OF USE AND FURTHER DISCLOSURE TO OTHERS

The extent of the permission granted to use the confidential information should be clearly set out. Ordinarily confidential information is disclosed only for the purposes of evaluating the deal during a prescribed period of time, and the information is not to be used by the recipient for any other purpose nor disclosed to any other party.

However, further disclosure is usually permissible to employees and certain outside advisers such as lawyers and accountants provided they have a need to know the information in order to assist them in evaluating the deal. Disclosure to any advisers should only be permitted if satisfactory confidentiality arrangements are in place with them, and any confidential information disclosed to them should be clearly marked as being confidential.

A further exception for disclosure to others is generally made for disclosure required under court order or pursuant to applicable statutory or regulatory authority. However, some confidentiality agreements provide that if the recipient is required to disclose confidential information to third parties, the party originally disclosing the information to the recipient must first be given notice of the requirement. That party then has the right to review and approve, often within a very short time frame, the contents of any statement that is to be released or filed by the recipient with the applicable authority.

ERRORS AND OMISSIONS EXCEPTED

The confidentiality agreement should provide that the disclosing party should not be held responsible for any loss incurred by the receiving party in the event that the disclosed information turns out to be incomplete or inaccurate. Such a duty of care during negotiations is not ordinarily imposed upon negotiating parties under common law.[1]

Such a duty is usually imposed, however, by way of the representations and warranties contained in the purchase and sale agreement. The parties are usually given ample opportunity during the preparation of that agreement and the various schedules to it to ensure the accuracy and completeness of the information provided.

REMEDIES FOR BREACH

Each party ordinarily agrees in the confidentiality agreement to indemnify the other for any damages incurred by the other resulting from disclosure in breach of the agreement. However, such a remedy, as mentioned above, may appear inadequate to the current owner if her highly sensitive business information has been abused by a competitor posing as a prospective buyer.

Consequently, in addition to the right to sue for damages under the indemnity in the event that the confidentiality agreement is breached by one party, the other party should also be given the right to apply to the courts for an injunction. Many confidentiality agreements state that breach will cause irreparable harm to the innocent party which cannot be adequately compensated by damages alone, and that injunctive relief should be permitted.

NO PROPERTY RIGHTS GRANTED

A specific statement should be added in the confidentiality agreement that the disclosing party is and will remain the owner of the information being disclosed, and that no property rights in the disclosed information are being granted by the disclosing party to the receiving party.

This provision may prove to be helpful to the current owner should a potential buyer later claim a licence or other right in any of the intellectual property of the business which may be provided to the buyer for inspection during the due diligence stage.

TERM

Although some confidentiality agreements contain an expiry date, somewhere between two and five years from the date of the agreement, other confidentiality agreements will impose an indefinite term, especially if the disclosed information will remain confidential and proprietary to the disclosing party.

While the provisions of the confidentiality agreement may be incorporated by reference into the letter of intent between the parties, it is often replaced by the confidentiality provisions contained in the purchase and sale agreement which are usually specified to survive indefinitely, whether the deal closes or not.

DUTY TO RETURN INFORMATION

The confidentiality agreement should provide that the disclosed information is to be returned to the disclosing party by the receiving party when the purpose for the original disclosure has been accomplished. Such return is normally required when the deal is terminated by the actions of the parties or upon a specified date or the occurrence of a specified event.

Alternatively, some confidentiality agreements provide for the destruction by the receiving party of all unreturned confidential information remaining in her possession when the deal is terminated, along with the requirement to deliver a certificate to the disclosing party attesting to such destruction.

Letters of Intent

Once the current owner and prospective buyer have arrived at a stage in their discussions where they feel that they have the basis of a deal, they may then decide to confirm in writing what they have agreed upon. They will likely set out the basic terms of their proposed purchase and sale in a preliminary document variously described as a letter of intent, term sheet, memorandum of understanding, or heads of agreement.

Whatever such a document is called, and for the purposes of this chapter it will be referred to as a letter of intent, the terms set out in it will eventually be repeated and expanded upon in a definitive purchase and sale agreement, if the parties get that far in their negotiations. The definitive agreement is ordinarily intended to replace the letter of intent.

However, the letter of intent can become quite a detailed and comprehensive document. Some letters of intent are not legally binding at all. Others are fully binding, although they are often so loaded with various conditions that the obligations which they set out may be difficult to enforce.

The "hybrid" form of letter of intent, part of which is non-binding and part of which is binding, is becoming more commonplace in practice. The non-binding part usually contains the principal business terms of the deal. The binding part usually sets out the rights of the parties and the process to be followed up to the signing of the definitive purchase and sale agreement, or to the termination of the deal in the absence of such a signing.

The letter of intent provisions discussed below may be used either in binding or non-binding formats, although the expense reimbursement, deposit, exclusivity and confidentiality provisions are almost always made binding. The provisions discussed below can take on many possible variations, and should not be taken as reflecting a "best practice" or as favouring one party over the other.

Some letters of intent are considerably more detailed than others, even though they may all cover the same basic terms. Though some may simply refer to such other "standard" terms and conditions as are used in "generally comparable transactions", others may be quite specific, sometimes attaching certain portions of the definitive agreements as schedules to the letter of intent. They may actually prescribe specific definitive agreements to be produced, which may include, in addition to the purchase and sale agreement, a shareholder agreement, employment and consulting agreements, non-competition agreements, option agreements, and possibly many more.

Where the proposed deal presents any concern which is particularly important to the current owner, it should be specifically addressed in the letter of intent. By addressing his concerns at this stage of the deal continuum, he will have an opportunity to determine early on, before both parties have incurred considerable time and expense, whether the prospective buyer takes a strongly opposite position as to how such concern might be resolved. In other words, the "deal killers" should be identified and resolved in the letter of intent.

The comprehensiveness of the letter of intent depends to some extent upon the relative bargaining power of the parties involved, the importance of the deal to each party, and how quickly each of the parties wants or needs the deal to be closed. Whether the business being sold is profitable or unprofitable whether the current owner has "deep pockets" or is selling off assets to stave off bankruptcy or whether the prospective buyer needs to add the business to its existing product lines to match its closest competitor, can all affect the level of detail found in the letter of intent.

THE NON-BINDING PROVISIONS

In the non-binding part of the letter of intent, the parties acknowledge that they are not legally bound by these provisions but intend to proceed to negotiate and execute a definitive purchase and sale agreement which may contain many of these provisions. The words used in these provisions often suggest a less than binding obligation, such as "may" and "would", or "possible" and "proposed", in contrast to the wording used in the binding provisions, such as "shall" and "agree".

IDENTITY OF THE PARTIES

All of the parties expected to eventually sign the purchase and sale agreement should be made a party to the letter of intent. If the parties signing the letter of intent will not, or may not, be the parties signing the purchase and sale agreement and the other definitive agreements for closing, the letter of intent should allow for substitute parties.

Many letters of intent provide for other members of a party's corporate group to acquire the shares or assets involved, often to achieve the most tax-effective structure. Sometimes a special purpose entity will be incorporated by the buyer to carry out the acquisition, or a seller will incorporate a new company to hold only the assets and liabilities desired by the buyer and proceed to sell the shares of such new company to the buyer.

Either way, the other party may insist that the covenants and indemnities to be contained in the purchase and sale agreement and the other definitive agreements should be given by, or at least guaranteed by, the original party signing the letter of intent.

In other circumstances, it may be intended that certain parties be bound only by a few, selected provisions, such as the confidentiality or exclusivity provisions, or have their liability restricted to only a few warranties. Other parties may be intended to guarantee only certain financial obligations. However restricted the role certain parties may play in the deal, those who are intended to be liable for any part of it should be made parties to the letter of intent.

INCLUDED AND EXCLUDED ASSETS

If the parties agree that the deal is to be an asset sale, the main assets desired by the prospective buyer, especially the "jewels in the crown", should be specifically set out in the letter of intent as included assets. Those which the buyer wants to reject should be specifically set out as excluded assets.

However, many letters of intent identify the assets being sold as simply all of the assets used in the purchased business, and thereby lead to the conveyance to the buyer of many things which aren't necessary for carrying on the business. Stale accounts receivable, unmarketable inventory, obsolete technology, malfunctioning equipment, personal use vehicles and undesirable leasehold premises are all examples of the kinds of assets which may be used in the purchased business but are often specifically excluded from the deal.

If the parties decide that the deal should be structured as a share sale instead of an asset sale, the assets desired by the prospective buyer might first be transferred to a newly incorporated company, the shares of which are then made the subject of the share sale. Alternatively, the assets which the prospective buyer wants to exclude might be transferred to another company before the shares of the transferring company are to be sold to the buyer. Either way, those assets to be transferred should be itemized in the letter of intent, and the proper completion of such transfer made a condition to the closing of the share sale.

INCLUDED AND EXCLUDED LIABILITIES

Just as the assets being included or excluded from the sale should be itemized in the letter of intent, those liabilities of the purchased business which are to be assumed by the prospective buyer should also be set out. Any material liabilities which have been incurred outside of the ordinary course of business, particularly those which represent long-term commitments, should be identified as being either included or excluded.

Identifying such liabilities early on in the deal process serves to address which mortgages, security interests, leases and other charges will be "permitted encumbrances" when the purchase and sale agreement is eventually prepared, or alternatively will have to be discharged on or before closing. Knowing well in advance which liabilities will have to be paid off before closing should accelerate arrangements with the financial institutions or other third parties involved and reduce the need for closing on the basis of an undertaking by the current owner to obtain the required discharges.

In the letter of intent for an asset sale, it may be desirable to identify whether provision will be made for the payment of the company's trade creditors in general immediately after the sale, or otherwise address how any bulk sales legislation, if applicable, might be complied with on closing.[1] If compliance with such legislation is to be waived and an indemnity of the company and current owner in favour of the prospective buyer is to be given instead, the letter of intent should clearly set this out.

PURCHASE PRICE, PAYMENT HOLDBACKS AND SECURITY

The amount of the purchase price, whether it is to be paid in one lump sum or in a number of installments, and whether security for the unpaid installments is to be given, should be set out in the letter of intent. Furthermore, whether the purchase price is to be adjusted following a post-closing audit, and whether it is to be calculated upon reference to post-closing earnings of the purchased business, should also be set out.

The applicable formula to be used in any such adjustment needs to be specified. For example, the letter of intent may provide that the purchase price is to be adjusted to reflect the financial position of the company indicated in audited financial statements prepared as of the closing date. Adjustments are often provided for in the event that the receivables or inventory, or the net book value, or perhaps the earnings for the latest period, fall outside of an agreed upon range.

If any part of the purchase price is to be paid to a third party to be held in escrow pending determination of certain conditions, such escrow requirements should be identified in the letter of intent. For example, the letter of intent may provide that funds are to be held by an escrow agent for a specified time as security for any undisclosed liabilities and breaches of representations, warranties and covenants, with the cost of such escrow being shared by the parties equally.

REPRESENTATIONS AND WARRANTIES

While many letters of intent simply describe the representations and warranties applying to the deal as those which are generally used in comparable transactions, mention should be made of those representations and warranties which either party is particularly concerned about or feels may be too contentious to defer until the purchase and sale agreement is being prepared.

If the prospective buyer is likely to want the current owner to make certain representations and warranties that the owner will not be in a position to give on closing, the limitations or qualifications the owner will need in order to make such representations and warranties should be described in the letter of intent.

For example, if the business being purchased consists almost entirely of intellectual property, the representations and warranties regarding intellectual property ownership and non-infringement might be settled at the time the letter of intent is being prepared and made a schedule to it. Also, if the current owner knows at that time that certain representations and warranties will have to be restricted to the actual knowledge of certain people, or made subject to materiality thresholds, those people or thresholds should be specified.

INDEMNITIES AND SURVIVAL PERIODS

Since the remedy for a false representation is ordinarily provided by way of a claim under the indemnity sections of the purchase and sale agreement, the basic scope of such indemnities and any general limitations of liability should be addressed in the letter of intent.

The length of time after closing or "survival period" during which an indemnity claim can be made for a misrepresentation, and whether the liability under the indemnities is unlimited or is to be capped at a specified dollar amount, should be clearly described in the letter of intent. It may also be desirable to even set out any minimums or deductible levels for an indemnity claim.

JOINT AND SEVERAL LIABILITY AND GUARANTORS

If liability under the non-binding provisions of the letter of intent is intended to be jointly instead of just separately or "severally" imposed upon any parties when incorporated in the purchase and sale agreement, the letter of intent should state so.

Furthermore, if one of the parties expects a third party to guarantee the performance of the other party's obligations under the transaction, the letter of intent should clearly refer to the guarantee and, as mentioned above, provide for signature by the guarantor.

EMPLOYEES

While employee issues aren't ordinarily mentioned in a letter of intent for the purchase and sale of shares, except perhaps for certain employment or consulting contracts which may be conditions of closing, a letter of intent for the sale of the company's assets should describe how the employees of the company are to be treated in light of the sale, given that the prospective buyer may have various liabilities as a successor employer under applicable employment legislation.[2]

If it is foreseeable that any employees are to be terminated, the letter of intent should address the extent to which each party is to be responsible for compensating the employees terminated. The company's obligations for employee compensation are usually coupled with an indemnity from the current owner and the company in favour of the prospective buyer, and can be subject to a survival period and monetary cap in the same way as other indemnities referenced in the letter of intent.

Often a letter of intent for an asset sale simply provides that the seller shall terminate all of the employees, and that the seller shall be responsible for all severance costs associated with those employees who are not re-hired by the buyer upon closing.

NON-COMPETITION AND NON-SOLICITATION COVENANTS

The prospective buyer is likely to insist that the current owner covenant not to compete with the buyer, or not to solicit the employees and customers of the purchased business, after the deal closes. If the current owner truly intends to retire, providing such covenants should not pose a problem. However, problems will arise if the current owner intends to retain a related business or is reasonably expected to establish a new business similar to the purchased business.

Since such covenants are usually more contentious than other matters which are discussed between the parties during the preparation of the purchase and sale agreement, the letter of intent should at least describe how long such covenants should remain with the current owner and in which geographical areas they should apply.

These covenants are in contrast to the covenant of the prospective buyer not to solicit the employees and customers of the business which ordinarily appears in the letter of intent as a binding provision, as discussed below.

CONDITIONS OF CLOSING

Because the numerous conditions for closing the sale of a business are set out in considerable detail in the purchase and sale agreement, they are usually glossed over in the letter of intent unless they are expected to be quite difficult and time consuming to satisfy, or are of such specific importance to one of the parties who wouldn't consider doing the deal unless such conditions are first satisfied.

These stated conditions often relate, as with the identification of the included assets, to the "jewels in the crown" of the purchased business. They might cover the re-issuance of an essential government permit, or the receipt of a favourable environmental report, or the extension of the term of a crucial customer contract. Or they might just require the execution of employment contracts with certain key executives currently employed by the company, or require the consent of a landlord to waive the "non-assignment" or "change of control" prohibitions found in the company's lease which is for a particularly valuable location at below market rental. Such essential conditions, therefore, should be included in the letter of intent.

THE BINDING PROVISIONS

In the binding part of the letter of intent, the parties acknowledge that they are legally bound by these provisions even though they intend to proceed to negotiate and execute a definitive purchase and sale agreement which may expand upon many of these provisions and which will generally replace them. The words used in these provisions, such as "shall" and "agree", suggest binding obligations. This part should clearly indicate if liability is being imposed jointly and not just severally on any of the parties.

CONFIDENTIALITY AND NON-DISCLOSURE

In addition to the confidentiality agreement described in the *Confidentiality Agreements* chapter which the parties signed at the outset of the deal, the duty of confidentiality each party owes to the other should be reinforced by affirming in the letter of intent the continuing application of that agreement to the deal, or setting out any exceptions to that agreement which may have become necessary.

The letter of intent should also provide that the confidentiality agreement and the duties prescribed under it are to survive the failure of the deal to close. Reiterating these duties of non-disclosure and confidentiality also serves to reinforce the duty of exclusivity, discussed below, which is likely to be imposed by the prospective buyer upon the current owner who might otherwise be tempted to "shop" the letter of intent around in the hope of a better offer from other possible buyers.

There will often be a "private and confidential" notice on the top of the first page of the letter of intent to reinforce its confidential nature. Furthermore, the letter of intent may provide that if any disclosure to a third party with respect to the deal is felt desirable or necessary, the parties should agree to cooperate with each other in the preparation of the announcement or disclosure to be made.

ACCESS FOR INSPECTION AND PHASED DISCLOSURE

To facilitate the prospective buyer's due diligence investigations, the letter of intent may give the buyer access to the company's place or places of business during regular business hours upon written notice to look at the company's books and records, and interview certain employees, relating to the business.

Alternatively, in an effort to reduce disruption to the ongoing operations of the business and maintain confidentiality, the letter of intent may specifically provide for the establishment of a "data room", possibly located away from the company's place of business, which contains copies of all of the relevant minute books, accounting and tax records, contracts, and other materials. The prospective buyer's access may be restricted to that room only. Electronic copies of the materials may be accessible instead through a secure server on the Internet and not at any physical location.

The extent and timing of permitted access and due diligence disclosure often depend upon the amount of trust and comfort the parties share with each other. If they are direct competitors in the same market, the current owner may insist that the letter of intent provide for access to and disclosure of sensitive financial and customer information only upon the signing of the purchase and sale agreement. As mentioned in the *Confidentiality Agreements* chapter, the parties may use the letter of intent to set out a phased disclosure schedule, itemizing when particular categories of documents will be made available for inspection, or when certain customers, suppliers or employees may be interviewed.

If it is expected that signing of the purchase and sale agreement and closing will occur at the same time, such access and disclosure may not be given by the current owner until a relatively short time before the expected closing date.

EXPENSES, DEPOSITS AND BREAK FEES

The process for buying and selling a business generally involves considerable time and professional fees being spent by the parties during the due diligence and document preparation stages without any assurance that the deal will actually close. Most letters of intent state that the parties will be responsible for their own fees and expenses. Yet both parties incur not only out-of-pocket expenses but, more significantly, an "opportunity cost" of pursuing the deal instead of using their resources to pursue alternative business opportunities which could prove to be even more financially beneficial.

This notion of opportunity cost may be particularly relevant to the current owner. Depending upon his own finances, health and personal goals, he may feel he is under considerable pressure to select a successor and complete the sale of the business within a relatively short time frame. Facing the possibility of a protracted deal failing to close and then having to start all over again with all of the attendant additional expenses may strongly influence his desire for some cost protection.

But both parties will be making a considerable investment in attempting to close the deal, and will therefore explore the possibility of recovering their investment from the other should the other prevent the deal from closing. The letter of intent will often set out one or more of a number of possible mechanisms to enable a party to recover its investment from the other. Which party receives such a right of recovery in the letter of intent often depends on the bargaining power of the parties and how anxious each party is to close.

For example, the current owner may insist that the prospective buyer advance a fixed amount on signing of the letter of intent which is to be held by the owner or owner's lawyer as a deposit and applied on closing to the purchase price owing, or be forfeited by the buyer should the buyer fail to close.

Alternatively, the prospective buyer may be required to pay the current owner's professional fees and other expenses incurred in respect of the deal, up to a prescribed amount, in the event the buyer fails to close. Or, the current owner may be required to pay the prospective buyer's fees and expenses, again up to a stated maximum amount, should the owner fail to close. These obligations of one party to pay the fees and expenses incurred by the other are sometimes called "break fees", although the party entitled to be reimbursed runs the risk of being unable to collect from the other.

In addition to addressing the fees and expenses directly incurred by one party for his own benefit, there are often fees and expenses incurred by one party for the benefit of the other party, or for the benefit of both parties, such as the cost of environmental audits, property surveys, mechanical inspection reports, or government approvals to the deal. Such costs should be identified and allocated amongst the parties in the letter of intent.

CONSULTING AGREEMENTS

Many of the agreements with third parties which the current owner or prospective buyer may enter into as part of the due diligence process create more than just cost issues which should be addressed in the letter of intent. These agreements, sometimes referred to as consulting agreements, involve the retention by either the owner or buyer of certain consultants to conduct various studies and carry on certain analyses for due diligence and business valuation purposes. They might involve environmental reports, technology audits, insurance adequacy reports, mechanical fitness inspection reports, property surveys, furniture and equipment valuations, and so on.

The letter of intent should address not only who pays for these reports and related services as suggested above, and whether the payment by one party or the other should be contingent on the closing of the deal, but also who owns the work product created by the consultant, or who has the copyright in the delivered report, should the deal close or fail to close.

If completion of the deal is to be conditional upon delivery of satisfactory reports, the letter of intent should try to define what is meant by satisfactory, who decides and how much discretion can be exercised. If satisfactory is to mean that no additional cost is to be incurred in order to achieve a recommended standard, it's preferable to state this in the letter of intent.

CONDUCT OF THE BUSINESS UP TO CLOSING

Depending upon the amount of time expected to elapse between the signing of the letter of intent and the signing of the purchase and sale agreement, the letter of intent may generally require that the current owner operate the business in this interim period in the same manner in which he has operated the business before, but may leave it to the purchase and sale agreement to more comprehensively set out the specific rules for running the business up to closing.

However, if the purchase and sale agreement is likely to be signed at the closing along with all of the other definitive agreements, a practice which occurs more frequently than not, the letter of intent may provide more specific guidance to the current owner for the pre-closing period. A list of "major decisions" requiring the prior consent of the prospective buyer, such as material capital expenditures, long term contracts, the hiring or firing of key officers, a significant raising of compensation levels, the declaration of dividends, or borrowing for more than ordinary operations, might be agreed upon and either set out in the letter of intent or attached as a schedule to it.

NON-SOLICITATION OF EMPLOYEES AND CUSTOMERS

In an effort to deter the prospective buyer from using the access afforded during the due diligence period to become familiar with the company's employees and customers and then subsequently entice them away should the deal fail to proceed, the current owner should insist that the letter of intent prohibit the buyer from soliciting the company's employees and customers.

This non-solicitation provision usually survives the termination of the letter of intent unless it is replaced by a similar provision in the purchase and sale agreement. Sometimes this provision is made reciprocal, thereby preventing a seller from soliciting any of the buyer's employees who may be involved in carrying out some of the due diligence.

EXCLUSIVE DEALING

Often called a "lock-up" or "no-shop" provision, a duty is usually imposed in a letter of intent upon a seller to refrain from talking to any other parties about possibly investing in the seller or buying a significant portion of the seller's assets for a certain period of time after the letter of intent has been signed. This is designed to protect the "opportunity cost" mentioned above of both parties and to motivate them to focus their time and resources on closing the deal. The length of time covered by the exclusivity provision can be hotly debated, but is intended to reflect the amount of time which the parties anticipate is reasonably required in order for the deal to be completed.

However, in his attempts to get the highest possible purchase price, the current owner may want to encourage other parties to submit offers and effectively create an auction. The owner might be able to avoid giving outright exclusivity to the prospective buyer by substituting in the letter of intent a "go-shop" provision with a right of first refusal in favour of the buyer. The owner would then be permitted to solicit other offers, yet the buyer would have the right to buy the business on the same or better terms which may be offered to the owner by a third party.

NEGOTIATION IN GOOD FAITH

Given that the current owner and the prospective buyer may not be under an implied duty to negotiate with each other in good faith[3], the letter of intent should state that they will exercise good faith during the preparation of the purchase and sale agreement. However, the buyer is likely to insist that this duty should terminate in the event that the buyer comes to the conclusion that the due diligence results are unsatisfactory and thereby wishes to terminate the letter of intent, as discussed below.

TERMINATION AND SURVIVAL

The binding provisions of a letter of intent may usually be terminated if the due diligence investigations prove to be unsatisfactory to the buyer, or if the purchase and sale agreement is not executed by the parties by a certain deadline. Some letters of intent also provide for termination if a crucial report or necessary third party consent, or up-to-date financial statements, are not obtained by a prescribed date. These termination dates are often called "drop-dead" dates.

A letter of intent usually provides that termination will not relieve any party from liability for breach of any of the binding provisions prior to termination, and usually provides that at least some of the binding provisions survive termination and continue to be enforceable. The non-disclosure and confidentiality provisions, along with the non-solicitation and expense provisions, are generally stated to survive the termination, but are usually superseded by comparable provisions in the purchase and sale agreement once that agreement is signed.

However, the exclusive dealing and negotiation in good faith provisions are ordinarily applicable for only a specified period of time and do not survive termination.

GOVERNING LAW

Far from being an innocuous "boilerplate" provision, the law chosen to govern a transaction can have substantial cost significance to the party whose own local law is not chosen, and therefore should be addressed early on in the discussions and inserted as a principal term in the letter of intent.

Although the law chosen is often the law of the place where the business is primarily conducted, a buyer located in a different jurisdiction may want to use for the deal the documents (and the law firm) he has used in previous deals in his own home jurisdiction and with which he is already quite comfortable.

Should the current owner accede to a prospective buyer's request to have the law of the buyer's jurisdiction, if different, designated as the governing law, the parties will then have to customize the buyer's forms to reflect the specific laws applicable to the various assets of the purchased business. More significantly, the current owner will then be faced with the cost of retaining counsel in the buyer's jurisdiction to assist with document reviews and rendering of a legal opinion regarding the enforceability of the documents under the laws of that jurisdiction.

Due Diligence

The due diligence process essentially involves the prospective buyer's evaluation of information relating to the current owner and the company, and the verification of such information through independent sources wherever possible. Verification is generally accomplished by searching public registers, examining accounting records and contracts, and interviewing third parties such as customers and suppliers.

However, the current owner may feel it necessary to make comparable investigations of the prospective buyer if the buyer wishes to pay the purchase price in installments, or to pay part or all of the purchase price in shares or other non-cash assets.

It is understandable that the current owner may regard the prospective buyer's due diligence investigations with suspicion and impatience. The owner may feel that the investigations will disrupt the company's day-to-day operations and subject the company to leaks of confidential information and rumours of sale which will adversely affect employee morale and customer loyalty. The buyer's inquiries and requests for documents may well be perceived as time-consuming and difficult to satisfy.

But the current owner should be prepared to co-operate with the prospective buyer's due diligence requests. As mentioned in the *Letters of Intent* chapter, the buyer will likely have the right to terminate the deal if the buyer decides that the results of the due diligence investigations are unsatisfactory.

The current owner should be equally prepared to co-operate with similar requests from any bank or other financier which is expected to provide purchase funding to the buyer. If the financier's due diligence produces satisfactory results, the buyer is more likely to be funded and the current owner more likely to be paid at closing.

The purpose of this chapter is to give the current owner an overview of the due diligence process so that she may be better prepared to deal with it.

REASONS FOR DUE DILIGENCE

It may be helpful for the current owner to appreciate that there are a number of reasons why the prospective buyer will insist on a rigorous due diligence process. While due diligence requires time and money to be conducted properly, and often more time and money than the prospective buyer might expect, there are definite benefits to be gained.

From the buyer's perspective, conducting due diligence helps to ensure that the purchase price is fair and falls within an acceptable range of appropriate values. It allows the buyer to rely on information provided by sources independent of the transaction, not just provided by the current owner. It helps to determine whether any deal killers exist, and allows for their attempted removal or rectification early on in the process, even though in practice some deal killers are revealed only days before the scheduled closing date.

Due diligence also assists the buyer in evaluating the likelihood of future claims being brought against the purchased business or the buyer after closing by lenders, suppliers, partners, licensees and other parties having commercial dealings with the purchased business.

Instead of having to wait for some time after the deal is closed to discover problems and then pursue legal remedies based upon the purchase and sale agreement and other closing documents, the buyer given advance warning of such problems may be in a position to renegotiate the deal's business terms. The buyer may then request an abatement of the proposed purchase price or payment of the purchase price in installments, or perhaps require a guarantee or release from a third party.

From the perspective of the buyer's counsel, the results of the due diligence investigations provide backup for any legal opinions which may be required on closing. Due diligence also provides guidance to those lawyers who are drafting the purchase and sale agreement and various closing documents, and gives support to the many representations and warranties that may be given. The wording in draft documentation is often changed to reflect what has been learned from the investigations being carried out. The less conclusive the investigations, the more comprehensive the documentation tends to get, to cover all the questions and concerns that haven't been satisfactorily disposed of during the due diligence process.

All of these reasons serve the overriding goal to ensure that the buyer's expectations are realistic and can be met once the deal is closed. There are, however, limitations as to what can be accomplished through due diligence.

No matter how thorough the professionals undertaking due diligence tend to be, many interests and encumbrances are simply not registered or documented. Searching various public registries won't disclose possessory and statutory liens and certain kinds of intellectual property. For those property interests that are registered, registration may not necessarily be proof of ownership or ensure priority, but merely give rise to a presumption of validity.

WHAT IS INVESTIGATED

If the deal is structured as a share sale, anything that confirms the status and capacity of the current owner, and anything that confirms the assets and liabilities of the company, should be the subject of a due diligence investigation. If the deal is structured as an asset sale, anything that confirms the status and capacity of the company, and the company's assets and liabilities which are being acquired or assumed by the prospective buyer, should be investigated.

For the purposes of this chapter under either structure, the assets and liabilities to be investigated and confirmed will be referred to as the assets and liabilities of the purchased business.

On-site inspections of the tangible assets of the purchased business may have already been conducted by the prospective buyer to determine their operating condition even before the signing of the letter of intent. But additional physical inspections may be required throughout the due diligence period and extend even beyond closing to a post-closing audit of inventory and other assets. Environmental assessments may necessitate a number of visits to the properties being acquired.

Numerous public records and registries may have to be searched. Records maintained by provincial ministries for provincial corporations and business names, and by Corporations Canada for federal corporations, will usually be searched at the outset to determine the status of the parties involved. Other records maintained by the Superintendent of Bankruptcy, Canada Revenue Agency, the various tax branches of provincial finance ministries, provincial workplace safety and labour relations boards, and the courts may also have to be searched.

Title records and records of liens and other encumbrances concerning the assets of the purchased business which are maintained by provincial land registry offices, personal property security offices, and environment ministries will have to be investigated. Searches of federal title and lien records kept by the Bank of Canada, Canadian Intellectual Property Office, Registrar of Ships, and the Aircraft Registration and Leasing Division of Transport Canada, may also have to be conducted.

An examination of all required licenses, permits and other regulatory consents to operate in all jurisdictions where the purchased business appears to be carrying on business will likely be carried out.

A comprehensive review of the business records of the purchased business, including employment records and benefit plans, its financial records, including financial statements and tax returns, and its corporate records, including minute books and share register, will have to be conducted, along with a review of its marketing and sales materials, insurance policies, environmental reports and many other types of documents.

And numerous kinds of agreements may have to be looked at. They often comprise a very lengthy list. They may include financing agreements, security agreements, equipment leases, premises leases, supply agreements, joint venture agreements, shareholder agreements, partnership agreements, non-competition agreements, customer contracts, trust agreements, sales agency agreements, employment contracts, licensing agreements, distributorship agreements, non-disclosure agreements, collective agreements, and so on.

The prospective buyer may be particularly concerned about detecting within these agreements certain kinds of restrictive covenants. These covenants may prohibit or restrict the agreements from being assigned, or the type of business which may be carried on, the geographical territory of operations, the dealing with certain competitors, or any change in the ownership or voting control of a contracting party.

The buyer may also be on the lookout for any clauses covering early termination, cross-default, rights of first refusal, set-off, extended warranties, indemnities, and many other items imposing unexpected liability.

Ascertaining the existence of any unregistered or undocumented encumbrances, restrictions and other interests affecting the purchased business will be a challenge for the prospective buyer, particularly in respect of intellectual property. Consequently, it may not be possible to eliminate entirely the need to conduct personal interviews with those who may have a potential claim against certain assets, or who manage such assets, in order to discover unrecorded interests.

LOCATION OF INVESTIGATIONS

The inspection of assets and review of records and documents generally take place at the various offices and plants of the purchased business where the assets and records are located. While many of the records and documents to be reviewed may be brought together by the current owner in a centralized data room as mentioned in the *Letters of Intent* chapter, it may be impractical for the owner to assemble all the essential records and documents in just one location. Scanning and placing all of the relevant documents on a secure Internet site for the prospective buyer and others to review may be a preferable alternative.

The various public records and registries mentioned above may have to be searched in those jurisdictions where the current owner resides and where the company is incorporated and where it has its executive offices, as well as where the purchased business has its assets and where it is being carried on. Fortunately searches of most of these records and registries can be conducted without having to arrange for someone to actually attend at a government office, and can be completed either by fax or on-line.

INVESTIGATING TEAM

While many of the searches and document reviews discussed above will be carried out by the lawyers retained by the prospective buyer, the due diligence process often requires a multi-disciplinary team of professionals to work alongside the buyer in conducting many of the inspections and investigations.

The prospective buyer may wish to retain accountants to examine financial records, actuaries to review any pension and benefit arrangements, environmental experts to conduct an environmental assessment of any real property, and technology specialists to investigate any intellectual property. Various other consultants and advisors may be deemed necessary, including those recommended to the buyer by the financial institution, venture capital firm or other party which may be financing the purchase.

The current owner and her own team of advisors will therefore be required to deal directly with the team established by the buyer in responding to various due diligence requests.

TIMING OF INVESTIGATIONS

As reflected in the deal continuum, many purchase and sale transactions have four stages during which due diligence may be conducted, although the length of each stage may vary from a few hours to many months, and some stages may be combined.

The first commences before the signing of the confidentiality agreement, the second runs between the signing of the confidentiality agreement and signing of the letter of intent, the third runs between the signing of the letter of intent and signing of the purchase and sale agreement, and the fourth runs between the signing of the purchase and sale agreement and the closing.

Because carrying out comprehensive due diligence is very time consuming and expensive, the prospective buyer will have to decide when various due diligence matters ought to take place.

Ordinarily the basic status searches on the current owner and company and preliminary title and encumbrance searches on only the most essential assets of the purchased business tend to be conducted before a letter of intent is signed. If some of the records and documents to be reviewed have been assembled by the current owner in a centralized location for examination by a number of potential buyers, they may be accessible for review immediately after a confidentiality agreement is signed.

A larger part of the due diligence investigation may take place once the letter of intent is signed, especially if the letter of intent is legally binding and contains a clause providing for the prospective buyer to be compensated by the current owner in the event the deal doesn't close.

If the letter of intent is non-binding, much of the due diligence may be deferred until the purchase and sale agreement is executed, despite the assistance earlier due diligence can provide to the drafting of representations and warranties in the purchase and sale agreement. The agreement will likely then give the buyer the right to terminate the deal if the due diligence results prove to be unsatisfactory.

INVESTIGATION DIFFERENCES BETWEEN SHARE AND ASSET PURCHASES

While the due diligence process is generally the same for share purchases and asset purchases, certain tasks may be given more emphasis than others depending upon the transaction structure.

Whereas all of the company's assets and liabilities need to be looked at in a share purchase, only the specific assets being acquired and specific liabilities being assumed need to be investigated in an asset purchase. For example, excluding certain inventory or equipment may obviate the need to review lengthy supply agreements and equipment leases or to conduct an on-site inspection around the time of closing.

For a share purchase, the prospective buyer's counsel may spend considerable time conducting a thorough review of the company's minute books and share registers with a view to determining what rectification efforts should be undertaken by the current owner prior to closing.

For an asset purchase, the production on closing of a certificate relating to the company's incumbent signing officers and a certified copy of the company board resolution authorizing the deal may be about as close to the contents of the company's minute book as the buyer's counsel gets.

ORGANIZING THE PROCESS

A comprehensive checklist often serves as the main organizing tool for the due diligence process. Once the principal business terms of the transaction have been agreed upon, the checklist can be tailored to fit the particular assets and liabilities of the purchased business. As mentioned above, the buyer may exercise some influence in determining priorities amongst the various items on the working checklist.

Assigning responsibility for carrying out certain items on the checklist to various members of the buyer's due diligence team can be a frustrating task if the team is comprised of professionals from different disciplines and different firms, engaged at different times throughout the process. Although it may not be necessary to prepare a formal critical path model indicating the various milestones to be met, each item on the working checklist should have a due date and a named individual assigned to its completion.

The prospective buyer may select a team leader through whom the results of all investigations flow and are recorded. That person should also have the unenviable task of ensuring that the named individuals complete their assigned items by the applicable due date. More importantly, that person should be directly involved in negotiating and drafting the applicable documents, or work closely with those who are.

Purchase and Sale Agreements

Unless the various due diligence investigations reveal such serious problems with the purchased business as to cause the potential buyer to avoid proceeding with the transaction, legal counsel may be instructed to prepare a first draft of a legally binding purchase and sale agreement aimed at turning the potential buyer into a real buyer.

This first draft, ordinarily prepared by the buyer's lawyer, may deviate from the principal business terms reflected in the letter of intent. If certain problems were discovered during the due diligence process, they may only be solved by imposing special conditions in the draft which need to be satisfied before the deal can close. Or the draft agreement may simply introduce either a reduction in the purchase price or provision for deferred or escrowed payments.

The main difference between the draft purchase and sale agreement and the letter of intent, and the reason for the agreement's considerable size by comparison, is the presence of numerous representations and warranties which the current owner makes in respect of the purchased business and the provision for the owner's indemnification of the buyer in the event that the representations turn out to be false.

The representations and warranties attempt to address all aspects of the purchased business and the ability of the current owner to transfer the business free and clear from the claims of others. They cover all of the items which the buyer may have attempted to investigate during the due diligence period, plus many more, and serve as a contractual "backstop" to the due diligence by providing the buyer with recourse against the owner for any problems which weren't discovered during the buyer's investigations.

The representations and warranties covered in the draft agreement, whether it is based upon a share sale or an asset sale, address potential undisclosed or undiscovered problems which might arise after closing which the buyer will then be required to deal with. Either form of agreement will usually represent the absolute ownership of the company's assets and the absence of any undisclosed mortgages or liens on such assets, the proper operating condition of the equipment, the saleability of the inventory, the collectability of the receivables, the compliance with all applicable laws, the adequacy of all insurance, the absence of any environmental contamination or intellectual property infringement, plus much more.

If the draft purchase and sale agreement is based upon a share sale, it might also contain more comprehensive representations regarding the disclosure of all material contracts, the payment of all taxes, the completeness of all financial statements, and the absence of any lawsuits.

As a means of permitting the buyer to recover from the current owner any losses and expenses which the buyer may incur in the event that any of the representations turn out to be false after the deal closes, the draft agreement will ordinarily include a number of indemnification provisions. These provisions may require the owner to defend, or pay for the defence of, any claims brought by outside parties against the buyer or the company after the sale which involve the business before the sale, and to pay for any judgments arising out of such claims.

The indemnity provisions also prescribe the process under which the buyer may make a claim directly against the current owner for a false representation. These indemnification provisions are usually the only way the buyer can seek recourse against the owner after the deal closes, and are often limited or "capped" at the amount of the purchase price paid.

To ensure that the buyer will be able to collect from the current owner the amounts claimed under the indemnification provisions, the draft purchase agreement may provide that a certain percentage of the purchase price be paid over time after closing in installments and that the buyer may be able to reduce such installments by the amount the buyer claims as an indemnity.

Alternatively, the draft agreement may provide for a certain percentage of the purchase price to be deposited on closing with a third party, such as a trust company or perhaps one of the law firms acting on the deal, to be held in escrow and applied to any indemnity claims made by the buyer within a prescribed period of time. Often the representations, and the indemnification and escrow provisions supporting them, will be enforceable for a period of two years after the deal closes.

Although the letter of intent will usually specify certain conditions which must be satisfied before the deal can be closed, the draft purchase and sale agreement may contain a number of additional conditions, depending upon the results of the due diligence investigations and any changes to the terms of the deal arising out of the ongoing deal negotiations.

The approval of a specific regulatory body, the preparation of updated financial statements, the completion of an environmental audit, the consent of a certain creditor or landlord, the extension of a major supply agreement, the commitment of a major financial institution, the hiring of key employees, and the approval of the buyer's board of directors, are all examples of closing conditions that may be inserted into the draft agreement.

The remainder of this chapter is designed to help the current owner understand and negotiate many of the complicated terms of the purchase and sale agreement. After all, the agreement will be, once signed, legally binding upon the current owner and form the basis for his residual liability for the deal after closing.

What follows is a discussion of the more contentious details which the owner will have to struggle through when reviewing, negotiating and hopefully finalizing the agreement's contents for signature. However, those issues that have already been discussed in the *Letters of Intent* chapter will not be repeated here even though they are just as applicable to purchase and sale agreements.

Because the following discussion includes provisions found in either share purchase agreements or asset purchase agreements, or both, the current owner and the company will both be referred to as the "seller".

DEFINITIONS

Assumed Liabilities and Excluded Liabilities
If the deal is structured as an asset purchase, the agreement will likely include a definition of "assumed liabilities". This definition often attempts to make the buyer responsible for all of the liabilities incurred by the seller in operating the business which are not itemized in the companion definition of "excluded liabilities". It may make specific mention of prod-

uct or service warranties being assumed by the buyer, along with bank indebtedness, employee benefits, or any other liability which the buyer is prepared to assume but which would ordinarily be excluded in an asset transaction.

Since the breadth of the definition of assumed liabilities often includes many contractual and other liabilities that are not specifically recorded in the financial statements (as discussed below), the buyer will attempt to determine the extent of such liabilities in its due diligence review prior to signing the agreement.

Considering that many buyers prefer to structure their business acquisitions as asset transactions for the sole purpose of avoiding seller liabilities, the list of specifically assumed liabilities is generally shorter than the list of specifically excluded liabilities. However, for those buyers concerned about the possible defection of existing customers or suppliers once the business has changed hands, while recognizing the advantages of maintaining direct contact with them afterwards, the assumption of certain liabilities may be necessary.

For example, since the seller may not be as inclined as the buyer to promptly pay off trade creditors, or as capable as the buyer to effectively deal with warranty claims from disgruntled customers, after closing, the buyer may be prepared to assume all of the payables and warranties in order to ensure that the suppliers and customers remain loyal to the business.

Purchased Assets and Excluded Assets

With an asset purchase, a definition of "purchased assets" is ordinarily inserted into the first draft of the agreement which includes all of the assets used by the seller in carrying on the business, whether or not they are listed in the applicable schedules, unless they are specifically mentioned in the companion definition of "excluded assets". However, such a definition often undergoes a number of revisions as the buyer and seller work through the details of what assets should be included and what assets should be excluded.

For example, considerable time can be spent negotiating whether the accounts receivable should stay with the seller or be transferred to the buyer, and if they are transferred, how much the buyer should have to pay for them. While the seller may insist that the buyer should pay the full face value of the receivables and thereby assume the responsibility of collecting them, the buyer may prefer to take them only on an agency basis and remit to the seller only the amount collected within a certain period of time after closing, less any applicable collection expenses. Any receivables which then remain uncollected can be returned to the seller to deal with. Alternatively, the buyer may acquire the receivables for their full face value, or perhaps at a discount, but on a "recourse" basis, requiring the seller to buy back any uncollectable receivables after a certain period of time.

Although the buyer and seller may agree upon which assets are to be transferred, some assets may not be transferable due to the lack of a required consent from a third party. Most leases and many customer contracts would fall into this category. A landlord may be prepared to consent to the transfer of a leasehold interest by the seller upon being satisfied as to the creditworthiness of the buyer. However, a customer may not be prepared to allow the assignment of a long-term service agreement if the customer has reservations about the buyer's ability to comply with the agreement's performance standards.

For those agreements that cannot be transferred, the seller may be required to retain the buyer to perform them as a "subcontractor" on the seller's behalf, with the seller holding in trust and eventually remitting to the buyer the revenues earned under them.

The definition of "excluded assets" in an asset purchase agreement may attempt to exclude from the purchased assets only cash, possible income tax refunds, and the seller's minute book and other corporate records. Such a definition may reflect the seller's desire to end up merely as a "corporate shell" after the closing with only cash to be distributed to its current owner.

But the parties may decide otherwise. The seller may wish to retain ownership of certain real estate or intellectual property, and lease or license it to the buyer instead. The buyer may wish to avoid acquiring certain machinery and equipment because of excess manufacturing capacity it already has at another facility, or certain inventory because of obsolescence, or certain receivables because of serious doubts over collectability. The buyer may also wish to avoid the "frills" which the seller enjoys in running the business by excluding aircraft, luxury cars, executive condominiums, artwork, etc. All of these items may therefore be mentioned in the excluded assets definition.

Given that cash is often designated as an excluded asset, the seller is often restricted in converting the purchased assets into cash during the interim period between signing the purchase agreement and the closing.

Financial Statements

Many provisions of the agreement refer to the seller's financial statements for the business, but the agreement may provide more than one definition of financial statements. It may specifically define the latest "annual financial statements" delivered by the seller to the buyer for review prior to signing as being audited. However, the buyer may be prepared to base its purchase decision on information acquired through other sources and decide it doesn't need to review a full set of audited annual financial statements for the most recent fiscal year before signing the agreement, especially if it is the seller's normal practice to forego an annual audit.

But while the buyer may agree to rely upon only unaudited annual financial statements before signing, it may be less inclined to accept unaudited financial statements used to facilitate the determination of any post-closing adjustments. The agreement may then provide a definition of "closing date financial statements" which are to be audited.

The definition of closing date financial statements may place on the seller the obligation and expense of producing them. The buyer's auditors will then be given the right to review what the seller's auditors produce. Sometimes, the buyer's auditors perform the audit and produce the statements, with the costs being included as a downward adjustment to the purchase price.

Instead of choosing the closing date as the date of the final financial statements upon which the various adjustments to the purchase price will be determined, the parties and their accountants may prefer to use an effective date that is more convenient or tax effective. They may choose a date which falls at the end of the standard billing cycle for the business or coincides with its regular inventory count, or a date by which beneficial ownership must be transferred for tax purposes. If such a date is chosen, the agreement may instead include a definition of "effective date financial statements".

Depending on the length of time that has elapsed since the date of the most recent audited annual financial statements, the buyer may insist on at least being given an unaudited interim balance sheet and income statement for such period before signing the agreement, which will be defined as "interim financial statements".

Best Knowledge

As described in more detail below later in this chapter under *REPRESEN-TATIONS AND WARRANTIES*, the parties may agree that some of the representations should be qualified by the phrase "to the best knowledge of the seller" or the phrase "to the best knowledge of the buyer". If this is the case, a definition of "best knowledge" should then be inserted.

While there may be little debate amongst the parties that the best of their knowledge should include their actual knowledge, there may be considerable debate over whether a party should be under a duty to diligently inquire into the matters involved. A selling shareholder or any of the other parties may strongly object to this standard of diligence being imposed upon them in connection with any representation they are expected to give if they are not actively involved in the business and if such standard would require them to make inquiries which would be prohibitively time consuming and expensive in what may be a relatively short period before the closing.

For a corporate party, this definition may provide for the insertion of specific officer titles, such as the president or the chief financial officer, or the names of specific individuals, whose knowledge will be deemed to be the knowledge of the corporation involved.

Accounting Terms

The parties may generally agree that all accounting terms used in the purchase agreement and in all of the financial statements should be interpreted or prepared in accordance with generally accepted accounting principles or GAAP, or possibly international financial reporting standards or IFRS. However, they may decide that certain deviations from or exceptions to GAAP or IFRS may be appropriate for the deal. If so, such deviating terms should be defined, and possibly supported by reference to a separate schedule to the agreement setting out which assets and liabilities, or which revenues and expenses, deserve special treatment.

PURCHASE PRICE

Payment of Purchase Price

There are a number of different ways the purchase price can be paid, and a number of different means used to secure its payment if spread out over a number of installments.

Even if a deposit is not provided for in the letter of intent, the agreement may still add a requirement for a deposit to be paid on signing which is to be held in an interest-bearing bank account, usually in the name of the seller's lawyer. The agreement will usually state that the deposit is either to be applied on closing to the purchase price owing, or is to be forfeited by the buyer should the buyer fail to close.

The payments on closing may include one amount to an escrow agent, to be held pursuant to a separate escrow agreement entered into between the parties and the escrow agent, and for another amount to the seller. Further amounts payable to the seller may be made in later installments under a promissory note.

In a share purchase, the payments due from the buyer under the note may be secured by the buyer's pledge of the purchased shares. However, a pledge of the shares may prove to be inadequate security if and when the buyer defaults under the promissory note, given that the shares at that time may have considerably less value than at the date of closing and the seller may step back into the role of running the business which has deteriorated significantly in the meantime.

In an asset purchase, the payments under the note may be secured by a charge over the buyer's assets, including the purchased assets, pursuant to a general security agreement. This security agreement can also be used to provide security for the buyer's performance of any assumed liabilities. As the seller will remain contractually liable to the creditors of the business under any trade payables and other obligations being assumed by the buyer, the seller runs the risk that the buyer may fail to pay such creditors after closing,

As an alternative to, or in addition to, securing payment of the promissory note with a general security agreement or share pledge from the buyer, the seller may request a guarantee from the controlling shareholder of the buyer if the buyer is a corporation (which might in turn be secured by a general security agreement covering that shareholder's assets) or a letter of credit from a financial institution.

If a general security agreement or pledge is taken from the buyer to secure the promissory note, the seller will in all likelihood not only have to subordinate its security position to the security taken by the financial institution which is providing purchase or working capital financing but also postpone its rights to payment under the promissory note if the buyer goes into default with that institution.

While the placing in escrow of a certain portion of the purchase price may be requested by a buyer to provide a dedicated fund against which claims for indemnification may generally be made, some of the purchase price might also be placed in escrow to be used to satisfy a liability which is not quantifiable at the closing date, such as the amount needed to remediate polluted real estate.

As an alternative to placing funds in escrow, the purchase and sale agreement may provide the buyer with a right to set-off any claims for indemnification against any amounts due under the promissory note.

Final Determination of Purchase Price

In addition to what the letter of intent may have, or may not have, stipulated for the adjustment of the purchase price, the parties may use the purchase and sale agreement to comprehensively define how one or more adjustments are to be calculated.

The agreement may provide, for example, an adjustment to the purchase price based upon any differences between the net worth of the business recorded on the financial statements delivered prior to signing the agreement and the net worth recorded on the closing date or effective date financial statements prepared later on. If the net worth goes up, the buyer pays the amount of the increase to the seller, and if the net worth goes down, the seller pays the amount of the decrease to the buyer. The net worth of the business is often defined as the amount by which the value of its assets exceeds the value of its liablities.

Instead of using changes in the net worth of the business, the agreement may refer to changes in something else for determining the adjustments. The parties may prefer to use changes in "working capital", often defined to be the difference between current assets minus current liabilities.

If the deal is structured as a share purchase, the agreement might provide for an adjustment based upon "shareholders equity", often defined to be the company's stated capital, retained earnings or accumulated deficit, and contributed surplus, as indicated on the closing date financial statements when compared with such items on the previously delivered financial statements. Or the agreement may instead use changes in the company's "EBITDA", defined to be the company's earnings before interest, taxes, depreciation and amortization, for the period between the date of the previous financial statements and the closing date when compared with a prescribed threshold.

Depending upon the size of the adjustment expected and the time limits set for its calculation and payment, the agreement may provide that interest accruing from the closing date should also be payable on any adjustment amount. Furthermore, instead of adjustments to the purchase price being paid by draft or cheque, they might be satisfied by using a portion of the escrow amount, or by adjusting the amounts of the promissory note delivered for the remaining installments.

In a share purchase agreement, adjustment of the purchase price may be provided by reference to the company's income statements for one or more fiscal periods following the closing. Such an adjustment is commonly called an "earnout". Earnout provisions typically operate over a three to five year period after the closing, and provide that the purchase price initially agreed upon will be increased, depending upon the future success of the company.

Earnouts can be structured in a number of different ways. The earnout payment, for example, can be a percentage of the amount by which the company's earnings for a year exceed the earnings for a base year, perhaps the year of closing. Alternatively, it can be designed to recognize only the growth in earnings in excess of a benchmark earnings amount that increases yearly during the earnout period. Finally, it can be based on the company's cumulative earnings for the entire earnout period.

In contrast to using an earnout that increases the initial purchase price set, the agreement may instead use a "reverse earnout" which decreases the initial purchase price if the company fails to achieve certain performance conditions after closing. In these circumstances, the buyer ordinarily attempts to defer making full payment of the purchase price until the reverse earnout performance conditions have been satisfied. If they are not, the amount of the purchase price that remains outstanding is reduced. If the purchase price was paid in cash on closing, the buyer would then be entitled to receive an adjusting payment from the seller.

The buyer is much more likely to prefer an earnout over a reverse earnout, since initially paying what the buyer considers to be a high price subject to a contingent reduction is less attractive than paying a low price subject to a contingent increase. The seller, on the other hand, usually prefers a reverse earnout. The form of the earnout and the percentage it represents of the total purchase price will be influenced not only by the relative bargaining power of the parties when negotiating the agreement but also by the extent to which the seller will continue to be involved in the company and have some control over its earnings after the closing.

While amounts paid under an earnout can be fully taxed, it is possible for them to be treated as capital gains.[1]

Allocation of Purchase Price on Asset Sale

In an effort to minimize their respective tax liabilities resulting from an asset deal, the buyer and seller will use the agreement to allocate the purchase price amongst the various asset categories which comprise the purchased assets. However, a high value allocated to a particular category may be advantageous to one party and disadvantageous to the other. While the seller may be concerned about the tax implications of such values for the year of the sale, the buyer may be more concerned about the tax implications for those years following the sale and the extent of various deductions then available.

For example, a high value allocated to depreciable property may provide the buyer with greater deductions for capital cost allowance in subsequent years, but may trigger a recapture of capital cost allowance for the seller in the year of the sale.[2] The buyer may prefer to allocate high values to inventory, whereas the seller may prefer to allocate high values to non-depreciable capital property.[3]

Tax Elections on Asset Sale

The buyer and seller may elect upon the sale of all or substantially all of the assets of a business that goods and services tax, or GST, does not apply to such sale, provided that they are both GST registrants.[4] The election is to be filed by the buyer with his GST return for the period in which the closing takes place, and until the buyer does so, the seller remains liable for collecting and remitting GST on the deal. The seller should therefore require some evidence from the buyer that filing of the election has taken place. In the absence of such an election, the seller is generally required to collect GST on the purchase price paid for the assets supplied.[5]

Also on the sale of all or substantially all of the assets of a business, the buyer and seller may jointly elect what value is to be allocated to the seller's accounts receivable in order to reduce the amount of income tax which might otherwise be paid by the seller if the face amount of the receivables was taken into the seller's income.[6] A purchase price allocation to receivables that is for less than their face value creates a loss for the seller which can be deducted from his income, but which is included in the buyer's income.

If the purchased assets include any real estate, the buyer will have to consider the possible impact of any provincial land transfer taxes that may be payable on the portion of the purchase price allocated to such real estate. Provincial retail sales taxes that generally apply to the transfer of tangible personal property may also have to be considered, although inventory purchased for resale is often exempt.

REPRESENTATIONS AND WARRANTIES

The seller's representations and warranties set out in the agreement constitute a comprehensive description of the seller and the business. They usually appear in most purchase and sale agreements under the heading of "representations and warranties", reflecting a technical distinction between the two terms. Representations are statements of past or existing facts, whereas warranties are promises that existing or future facts are or will be true. For convenience, the remainder of this chapter will refer to them as simply representations.

The seller's representations have three main purposes. First, they disclose to the buyer important information about the seller and the business. The representations, and the exceptions to them which may be expressed in either the representations themselves or in schedules to the agreement, should provide the buyer with enough detailed information about the seller and the business to motivate the buyer to complete the deal and justify the price the buyer has agreed to pay. Second, they provide a means of escape from the deal, since the buyer's obligation to complete the deal is usually subject to a condition in the agreement that the representations are true and accurate at the time of closing. Third, they allocate some or all of the risk in relation to a particular matter or liability between the buyer and the seller. A buyer discovering a breach of a representation after closing will normally have a right to be indemnified for that breach by the seller.

The extent of the seller's representations will depend upon the relative bargaining strengths of the parties. If two or more potential buyers are competing to buy the business, the balance of power may shift to the seller. If the seller is motivated by the desire to sell quickly, perhaps because of personal retirement plans or uncertainty over future profitability of the business, and the buyer is aware of that motivation, the buyer may have the power to insist on more extensive representations.

Who the buyer is will also influence the extent of the seller's representations. As mentioned in earlier chapters describing family, employees and other shareholders as possible successors, some buyers may not want or require the same level of disclosure about the business as others. If a buyer is already quite familiar with the business, perhaps as a current manager of the business or as a direct competitor, the buyer may be willing to accept fewer or more heavily qualified representations.

Representations are generally qualified three ways: the agreement may set out specific exceptions to them, or limit them to the knowledge of the seller, or limit them by reference to materiality.

Qualifying a representation by specific exceptions can be accomplished in the schedules to the agreement or in the text of the representation itself. The buyer will ordinarily insist that any exceptions should be quite specific and avoid general or vague wording. The seller may seek a right in the agreement to update the various disclosure schedules during the interim period between signing and closing and thereby shift the risk associated with any changes during such period to the buyer.

The buyer will also want the agreement to state that the seller's representations are not qualified or affected by the buyer's due diligence. Such a provision ensures that the seller will not escape liability, even if the buyer discovers certain facts during the due diligence process that would make a representation incorrect, subject of course to the applicable limitation periods. The seller should try to negotiate the removal of such a provision on the basis that it would be unfair for the buyer to withhold knowledge of a breach of a representation in order to claim against the seller after the closing.

As mentioned above in connection with the definition of "best knowledge", the seller may also qualify a representation by limiting it to those facts of which the seller is aware. A qualification based upon knowledge attempts to limit the seller's risk and shifts to the buyer the burden of proving that the seller knew of the breach of representation. However, the buyer is likely to resist such a qualification when the seller or the seller's advisors are in a position to confirm the truth of the representation. Even when the seller does not know and is not in a position to discover the facts, the buyer may still take the position that all of the risk relating to things unknown should be borne by the seller.

The seller may also qualify a representation by making it subject to a materiality threshold. For example, a representation regarding the records of the business may be qualified by stating that they are complete and accurate records of all "material" matters relating to the business. Sometimes a purchase and sale agreement will define materiality by using a monetary threshold. A seller may represent, for example, the completeness of a list of all material contracts of the business, with "material" being defined as representing at least $100,000 worth of goods or services.

However, if the indemnification provisions of the agreement, as discussed below, give the buyer a right to indemnity for breaches of representations only if the buyer's damages exceed a specified threshold or "floor" level, the buyer may resist any qualifications based on materiality. Such qualifications, when combined with a floor for indemnities, will permit the seller to avoid liability for non-material breaches even though such breaches in the aggregate exceed the floor amount.

The specific representations discussed below often deserve particular attention from the seller and possible qualification.

Financial Statements

Since a review of the financial statements is an essential part of the buyer's due diligence investigation of the business, the buyer will usually require a representation that the annual financial statements are "complete and accurate". The seller, however, may well object to giving such a representation because it goes beyond the kind of assurance ordinarily given by the accountants who prepared the statements.

The seller may also object to a representation in the agreement that any interim financial statements or closing date financial statements are presented fairly in accordance with GAAP or IFRS because these statements do not include year-end adjustments or notes. If the financial statements are not audited but merely prepared on a "notice to reader" basis which would not entail a GAAP or IFRS analysis or review being undertaken by the accountants involved, such a representation should be restricted to the seller's knowledge or possibly not given at all.

Dividends and Distributions

A draft share purchase agreement will often contain a representation that the seller has not removed cash or other assets from the company by way of dividends or share redemptions since the date of the latest annual financial statements which were given to the buyer to review. If the seller insists that the company should be allowed to distribute cash prior to closing in order repay any outstanding shareholder loans or remove all or part of the company's retained earnings, this representation will need to be qualified accordingly.

Compliance with Laws

A representation will usually be included in the draft agreement that the business has complied with all laws, both current and historical. The seller may attempt to change this representation so that it refers only to compliance since a certain date, arguing that non-compliance before then has long been irrelevant, especially if the seller was not the owner of the business at that time. The seller may also try to restrict this representation to only material violations.

Furthermore, the seller may prefer to make any required disclosure of actual or potential violations outside of the agreement or the schedules as these documents may become available to third parties or regulatory authorities.

Accounts Receivable

There will often be a representation in the draft agreement that the accounts receivable are collectable, subject to a reasonable allowance consistent with past practice for doubtful accounts. Sometimes a buyer will want this representation to state that the accounts receivable will be fully collected, subject to a reserve, by a certain date.

There are other ways in which the buyer can be reassured that the accounts can be collected. As mentioned above in discussing the definition of "purchased assets" in an asset sale, the buyer might require the seller to repurchase any accounts receivable uncollected by a specified date, or have the buyer attempt to collect the accounts on behalf of the seller who would continue to own them. It is perhaps easiest for the buyer to simply have the right to apply the value of any uncollected accounts against any holdback or installment promissory notes.

The seller should be aware that a representation that the receivables are collectable, as opposed to a representation that they are legitimate or bona fide, can operate as a purchase price adjustment similar to the working capital price adjustments discussed earlier in this chapter. Consequently the seller may refuse to give any representation regarding collectability, either to avoid any possible "double counting" for uncollected receivables, or simply because the control over their collection rests with the buyer after closing.

Customers and Suppliers

The draft agreement may contain a representation that all of the major customers and suppliers of the business have been listed on a schedule and that all arrangements with them are in good standing. It may also include a statement that the relationships with them will continue in the same manner after closing as before. Given the difficulty of making this kind of prediction, the seller generally attempts to qualify this representation by reference to the seller's knowledge.

Leased Premises

Often a draft agreement will include comprehensive representations about leased as well as owned real estate. The seller may resist giving such representations about any leased premises, arguing that it's unreasonable to expect the seller occupying only a portion of a building as a tenant to have complete knowledge about such things as whether the building complies with zoning setbacks or whether there are any structural defects in the building. However, such an argument may not be very convincing if the seller is a long-term tenant of all or substantially all of a building.

As a compromise, the parties may agree to separately identify those buildings with substantial leases as "major leased premises". The seller may then agree to provide unqualified representations with respect to those premises, if the buyer then agrees to accept representations regarding all of the other leased premises which would be restricted to the seller's knowledge.

Environmental Matters

Representations that the seller is not responsible for any clean-up or corrective action under any environmental laws and that none of the owned or leased real estate has ever contained any hazardous substances are usually contained in the draft purchase agreement. The seller will often try to qualify these broad representations by restricting them to facts the seller knows about. Given the potential costs associated with environmental remediation, the buyer will likely resist any attempted qualification of these representations.

To remove such an impasse between them, the parties may retain an independent investigator to conduct an environmental assessment of the real estate used in the business and then allocate their respective liabilities based upon the remedial efforts recommended in the assessment report. As mentioned above, a holdback from the purchase price to cover estimated remediation costs may also be used to resolve this issue.

Representations of the Buyer

If the draft agreement sets out any representations by the buyer, they will be much less extensive than those given by the seller. If they are given, they are likely to be similar to those given by the seller, but generally confined to just the status, power and authority of the buyer to enter into the deal.

However, if a significant part of the purchase price is not to be paid at closing, the seller may quite legitimately be entitled to expect additional representations regarding the buyer's financial capability and overall creditworthiness. If the seller is to receive shares of the buyer in full or partial satisfaction of the purchase price, and will therefore become, in effect, an investor in the buyer, the seller may reasonably expect to receive much more comprehensive representations which would more closely parallel those given by the seller to the buyer.

COVENANTS

A draft purchase agreement will ordinarily set out a number of specific covenants or agreements by the parties to take or refrain from taking various actions, primarily during the interim period between signing the agreement and the closing.

Compliance by each of the parties with their respective covenants is usually a condition of closing, although as with any condition, may be waived by the party in whose favour the covenant was made. Alternatively, the failure to satisfy a condition usually allows the innocent party to terminate the agreement and refuse to close the deal. The failure of a party to comply with its covenants may also give rise to a liability to indemnify the innocent party, as discussed later in this chapter.

The standard covenants discussed immediately below often require qualification by the seller.

Prohibited Actions

A covenant is often found in the draft agreement prohibiting the seller from taking certain actions which could adversely affect the value of the business. It is intended to generally maintain the state of the business without any changes in its assets and liabilities or general operations. These prohibited actions might include major capital expenditures, mortgaging real estate, signing joint venture or partnership agreements, entering into long-term leases, and selling material assets.

As well as wanting to exclude from such prohibitions any actions which are taken in the ordinary course of the business, the seller may want to specifically permit the payment of dividends and repayment of shareholder loans during the interim period, at least in a manner consistent with past practices. The seller may also want to ensure that any obligations the business may owe to parties related to the seller can be fully performed without running afoul of the prohibitions.

Regulatory and Contractual Consents

Another covenant likely to be included in the draft agreement is the requirement imposed upon the seller to obtain all consents from any regulatory authorities under applicable laws or third parties under existing contracts which may be needed for the deal to close. The seller should ensure that this obligation is qualified, not absolute, perhaps by requiring only the use of "reasonable commercial efforts" to obtain the consents involved.

If the seller fails to obtain a required consent, and the consent is a condition of closing, the buyer may be able to terminate the agreement and not complete the deal. However, with the seller's obligation qualified and provided that the seller has used reasonable commercial efforts to obtain the consent though unsuccessful, the buyer will at least have no claim against the seller for breach of contract.

Instead of allowing the seller to use only reasonable commercial efforts to obtain a required consent, the buyer may insist that the seller use "best efforts". Since both terms invite debate over their respective meanings, the seller should insist that the agreement provide a definition of whichever term is to be used. While the definition may require the seller to use available internal resources, it should not require the seller to incur any additional expenditure of funds or retain external resources.

To avoid possible disputes over which consents may actually be needed to close the deal, or at least to prevent the seller's inability to obtain a trivial consent being used by the buyer as a means of getting out of the deal, the seller might insist that all of the required consents be specifically listed in the agreement or on a schedule.

Access to Information

Although the buyer's rights of access to the business for due diligence purposes may have already been provided for in the letter of intent, the draft agreement may attempt to expand upon those rights, particularly if the preliminary investigations conducted by the buyer have raised the need for more comprehensive disclosure. While the buyer may insist upon the right to continue due diligence up to closing, the seller should attempt to have such investigations terminate before then by a certain date.

The seller will have to carefully consider whether the buyer should be permitted to contact any regulatory authorities regarding the compliance of the business with applicable laws. Not only may such inquiries prove to be disruptive to the business, they may also jeopardize the ongoing relations with such authorities, especially if the deal fails to close, as well as result in the loss of confidentiality of the deal. As mentioned earlier in the *Letters of Intent* chapter, a similar concern applies to any approaches being made by the buyer to employees, customers and suppliers.

From the seller's perspective, in general, the buyer should be required to inform the seller of all breaches or potential breaches of covenants and representations in the agreement as soon as they are discovered in order to give the seller an opportunity to cure them and avoid having the buyer either terminate the agreement or closing the deal and then seeking indemnity for damages.

SURVIVAL OF COVENANTS AND REPRESENTATIONS

How long the covenants and representations will be enforceable or "survive" after closing is usually prescribed in the draft agreement. Determining survival periods is essentially the allocation of risk between the parties and assigning the length of time a particular risk should be borne by a party. The parties attempt to negotiate the "limitation period" which will apply to their deal in an effort to override any limitation period which might otherwise be imposed upon them by applicable limitation statutes.[7]

While the buyer may prefer to have indefinite recourse to the seller for any breaches of the seller's covenants and representations, the seller will demand certainty over when its liabilities will end.

Often the parties will agree that any representations with respect to fundamental matters, such as corporate existence and authority, as well as the ownership of assets, survive indefinitely. Representations regarding tax matters will often survive until the expiry of any assessment and possible appeal period. The survival period for the covenants and most other representations typically falls within a range of six months to two years. The parties often compromise at 18 months on the basis that most problems with the business are discovered by the completion of the next audit after closing.

CONDITIONS OF CLOSING

The draft agreement will itemize a number of conditions which have to be met for the deal to close. If a particular condition is not, the party for whose benefit it was given will be able to terminate the agreement and walk away from the deal unless the party's right to enforce compliance with that condition has already been waived. Some conditions, such as certain required governmental approvals, may not be waived and may result in automatic termination of the agreement if they cannot be satisfied.[8]

The accuracy of the representations and compliance with the covenants set out in the agreement generally constitute important conditions. Often key representations or covenants will be reinforced by specific corresponding conditions which mirror or supplement their language.

The seller may want to be aware of the implications of certain conditions discussed immediately below.

No Material Adverse Change

The draft agreement may contain a condition for the benefit of the buyer that there has not occurred a "material adverse change" in the business by the time of closing. The buyer may attempt to add that such change will be determined in the buyer's sole discretion or opinion, but such attempts should be resisted by the seller.

Although it may be difficult for the parties to arrive at a mutually satisfactory definition of material adverse change, the seller should a least ensure that the buyer is required to act in a commercially reasonable manner and does not have unfettered discretion.

No Adverse Law or Actions to Restrain

A condition that no law has been passed or legal action taken which adversely affects the business is usually included in the draft agreement. The seller may want to narrow this condition so that it does not apply to laws or legal actions which existed at the time the buyer entered into the agreement but only to those which came into effect afterwards.

The seller should not allow "threatened" litigation to be included in such a condition. Such litigation could be frivolous, without merit, or even orchestrated by the buyer as an excuse to get out of the deal. Furthermore, the seller should oppose any effort by the buyer to expand this condition to include any laws which may merely be "proposed" by the time of closing.

Third Party Consents

A condition will usually be found in the agreement requiring the delivery at closing of all consents from third parties which are necessary or material to the business. These consents will at least include all required regulatory and contractual consents. As mentioned in the above section on *COVENANTS*, it is preferable for the seller to have these consents reduced to a list set out in the agreement or in a schedule so that the buyer cannot back out of the deal just because a trivial consent is not obtained.

The seller should be particularly wary if the condition includes any third party consents which apply only to the buyer and which are completely beyond the influence or control of the seller. For example, the buyer may want to make closing of the deal conditional upon satisfactory financing being made available to the buyer or upon the consent of one of its lenders being received. Such a condition can easily be abused by a buyer intent on escaping from a deal.

Certain Agreements

In order for the deal to close, the buyer may insist that certain individuals agree to provide consulting services or serve the business as employees for a specified period of time after the deal closes, often as a way of ensuring a smooth transition of the business to the new owner. The agreement may include as a closing condition the delivery of executed consulting or employment contracts with these individuals in a form acceptable to the buyer.

However, it is not unusual for a deal to be delayed, or even terminated, because the individuals involved would not sign the contracts presented to them by the buyer. In executing the purchase and sale agreement without having first settled the terms of these consulting and employment contracts, both the buyer and seller are running the risk that these contracts will not be signed and the deal will be terminated.

To avoid such a possibility, the terms of the contracts should be settled with these individuals and attached to the agreement as a schedule before the agreement is executed by the buyer and seller. By leaving the negotiation and settlement of these contracts until after the purchase and sale agreement is executed, the individuals concerned may become extremely difficult or self-interested and use a pending closing as extra leverage to obtain considerably more favourable terms.

The same concern applies to any non-competition or non-solicitation contracts with individuals whom the buyer feels could diminish the value of the business after closing should they go to work for a competitor or solicit customers or employees of the business. The terms of these contracts should also be settled and attached to the purchase and sale agreement before the agreement is executed.

Satisfactory Due Diligence Results

Although often appearing in letters of intent, it is important for the seller to strongly resist the appearance in the purchase and sale agreement of any condition which allows the buyer to terminate the agreement and refuse to close if the results of the due diligence investigations prove to be unsatisfactory. The seller usually wants certainty as early as possible that the buyer is not going to find an excuse to walk from the deal.

However, even in the absence of such a due diligence "out", the buyer may still terminate the agreement and decline to close if it discovers facts about the business which would constitute breaches of covenants or representations which are not remedied by the seller prior to closing.

Conditions for the Benefit of the Seller

Apart from a condition relating to the accuracy of any representations and the performance of any covenants given by the buyer, the draft agreement is unlikely to contain any conditions in favour of the seller. However, the seller should consider the need to include as conditions the release of any guarantees which may have been given to support any financing, leases or other obligations of the business. Perhaps the repayment of a shareholder loan, or the assignment of a life insurance policy to the seller personally if the policy is owned by the business, should also be included as important conditions for the benefit of the seller.

The seller may even require as a condition of closing the delivery of a legal opinion from the buyer's lawyers regarding the good standing of the buyer and the legal enforceability of the buyer's post-closing obligations, particularly those relating to indemnities and any purchase price adjustments and holdbacks.

INDEMNIFICATION

The indemnification provisions are among the most intensely negotiated provisions in a draft purchase and sale agreement. While the buyer wants some protection for the seller's representations and covenants, the seller wants to avoid any residual liability for a business the seller will no longer own. These provisions usually require the seller to indemnify and fully reimburse the buyer for all losses and damages the buyer might suffer as a result of the breach of any of the seller's representations and covenants. The buyer, however, may be required to indemnify the seller for any breaches of the buyer's representations and covenants.

Depending upon the relative bargaining power and level of sophistication of each of the parties, the negotiations can produce a wide variety of outcomes. The seller may reluctantly have to agree to an open-ended indemnity if the business is failing and only one party appears to be interested in buying. More frequently, however, the parties will want to place a maximum on their respective total potential liabilities under the agreement, and may agree to a fixed limit for certain classes of liability.

Since the protection provided by an indemnity is dependent upon the creditworthiness of the party giving it, the other party may demand some collateral to support it. The buyer may request that personal guarantees or substantial holdbacks from the purchase price be included in the agreement. Similarly, if the seller is concerned about the possibility of non-payment of any deferred portions of the purchase price, either as holdbacks or earnouts, the buyer may be asked to give security for those continuing obligations.

If there is more than one seller, the sellers may decide to bear different levels of liability for the indemnity, reflecting perhaps their respective percentage of ownership or the extent of their management involvement with the business. This allocation of liability can be provided for in the purchase agreement, or alternatively, the sellers may agree to be jointly liable in the agreement and then reallocate responsibility amongst themselves in a separate contract.

If the parties have agreed upon the use of escrow amounts, earnout amounts or holdbacks, the buyer may insist that the indemnification provisions in the agreement allow the buyer to set-off against these amounts any indemnity claims, and that any promissory notes and escrow agreement to be delivered at the closing should mirror such rights of set-off. The seller should attempt to limit the buyer's set-off rights to those situations where all disputes over any indemnity claim have been definitively resolved.

Indemnification by the Seller

Depending upon the nature of the business and the results of the due diligence investigations, the buyer may insist that the agreement contain specific indemnities from the seller for specific risk categories. These categories might include unknowable environmental risks, probable changes in the laws affecting the business, the outcome of a disclosed lawsuit, or the loss of a major customer of the business.

Negotiating the terms of a specific environmental indemnification can be a difficult process because the degree of risk is usually unknown, any environmental problem can be hugely disruptive and expensive to the business, and claims can be made by government agencies or third parties which are not bound by the agreement. Furthermore, unlike most other types of liabilities which tend to decrease over time, environmental liabilities tend not to.

If required to provide the buyer with specific indemnification for environmental risks, the seller may prefer to retain control over the handling of environmental claims and over any clean-up efforts. Alternatively, as a way of better quantifying the liability, the seller might avoid giving a separate environmental indemnification and deal with environmental risks by way of a purchase price reduction or an increase in any escrow amount or holdback.

Indemnification by the Buyer

The first draft of a purchase and sale agreement will frequently exclude any indemnification by the buyer of the seller. If the buyer has no material representations or covenants which survive the closing of the deal, this exclusion may be acceptable to the seller. However, a seller with some bargaining power should always insist upon inclusion of such a provision in the agreement, especially if payment of any portion of the purchase price is deferred or the buyer has any significant obligations to be performed after closing.

If the deal is structured as an asset purchase and the buyer is to assume any contracts of the business, the buyer should specifically indemnify the seller for the proper performance of such contracts after closing.

Maximum and Minimum Amounts

The parties may decide that the agreement should include both a minimum or "floor", and a maximum or "ceiling", for indemnification. The floor operates like a deductible in an insurance policy so as to avoid any claims or disputes involving only minor amounts. The buyer may try to recover all damages, not just damages in excess of the floor amount, once the floor is reached. The parties may end up having different floors for different types of liabilities.

The seller will often try to have a ceiling of not more than the total amount of the purchase price, arguing that the potential "burden" or indemnity claim that may be suffered should not exceed the "benefit" or purchase price received. Although the buyer may accept such an argument, certain claims, such as those for tax or environmental matters, may be permitted without a ceiling, or separate ceilings may be established for different heads of liability.

The agreement may provide that neither floors nor ceilings shall limit claims for breaches of representations which were known, or for covenants which were willfully ignored, by the indemnifying party.

Limitation on Remedies

The seller should ensure that the indemnification provisions clearly indicate that the indemnity rights of the parties represent their exclusive remedies in connection with the deal. While the buyer may want to avoid such exclusiveness to preserve possible remedies outside of the agreement relating to breach of contract, fraud and certain statutory rights, the benefits of the indemnity ceiling to the seller may be lost if the buyer is able to seek other legal recourse.

GENERAL PROVISIONS

While the general provisions contained in the draft purchase and sale agreement may appear to be mere "boilerplate" and not particularly contentious when compared with the other provisions of the agreement discussed above, some general provisions deserve special scrutiny by the seller.

The implications to the seller of those general provisions dealing with confidentiality, expenses, exclusive dealing and governing law have already been discussed in the review of legally binding provisions found in the *Letters of Intent* chapter. However, the seller may wish to also consider the implications of the following two provisions.

Public Announcements and Disclosure

The draft agreement may contain a provision that allows for public disclosure of the deal by one of the parties without the consent of the other when such disclosure is required by applicable law or perhaps by a stock exchange. Sometimes the agreement will impose certain limits on this right by requiring the party obligated to disclose to consult with the other prior to making such disclosure.

The parties may wish to expand upon this provision to include how employees, customers and suppliers will generally be informed about the deal at some time between the signing of the agreement and the closing. Disclosure to these groups will usually be subject to the mutual consultation of both the buyer and seller, and the buyer may insist on being present during any such disclosure, especially to employees.

If the seller has serious doubts that the deal may not close despite the agreement being signed, the seller may insist that no announcement may be made until closing regardless of the impact such a delay might have on a smooth transition of the business to the new owner.

Assignment by Buyer

The seller may require a provision in the purchase and sale agreement prohibiting any assignment of the buyer's rights or obligations under the agreement without the seller's prior written consent. Even with such consent, the buyer may have to deliver to the seller a document obligating the permitted assignee to perform all of the buyer's obligations under the agreement.

One of the reasons for such a prohibition is the possibility of the agreement being assigned by the buyer to a "shell" corporation with only nominal assets with which to satisfy its obligations under the agreement. A more important reason may be the seller's desire to leave the business in good hands. If the seller has spent considerable time and expense in sourcing and investigating the buyer as a suitable successor for the business, the seller may be very reluctant to permit the assignment of the agreement to someone else.

Closing the Deal

Once the purchase and sale agreement has been signed, the seller then faces the last stage of the deal continuum, the closing. Getting the deal closed often proves to be more difficult than the seller might expect. While the closing conditions and list of deliverable documents set out in the agreement may provide some guidance on what has to be done for closing, the seller soon realizes that closing and getting paid are not as straightforward as they might appear in the agreement.

This chapter will attempt to provide the seller with some understanding not only of the process leading up to the actual closing but also of the possible delays and obstacles which are likely to arise. The most frustrating of these invariably involve the need to obtain the consent of numerous third parties. Financial institutions, landlords, trade creditors, and government agencies represent just some of the third parties whose consents may not be easily or quickly obtained.

However, this chapter will not attempt to address the delays and obstacles which may be specific to a particular deal even though they can be extremely expensive and time-consuming to resolve. In this category belong outstanding lawsuits and regulatory proceedings, polluted land, damage or destruction of significant assets, labour disruptions, and any material changes to the business that unexpectedly occur just before closing.

Nor will this chapter repeat the discussion on the need for proper documentation found in the chapter on *Putting the Company in Saleable Condition*. However, it is not unusual, for example, for a closing to be delayed because the signature of a former shareholder is missing on a previous share transfer, or an unexpired option to purchase material assets of the business has not been terminated.

CLOSING AGENDA

Well before the expected closing date, the buyer's lawyer generally prepares and circulates a draft closing agenda which identifies the various actions which must be taken and numerous documents which must be drafted in order for the deal to close.

The agenda will ordinarily set out at a minimum the actions and documents itemized as closing conditions in the purchase and sale agreement. It may bear some resemblance to the checklist earlier described in the *Due Diligence* chapter by assigning to the buyer and seller and their respective teams of advisors responsibility for various items needed for closing. The description of each document on the agenda will identify who drafts it, who has to sign and deliver it, and how many copies of it will be required on closing.

Many closing agendas also include items which are to be completed before or after closing so that the agenda will serve as a comprehensive checklist of everything to be done in connection with the transaction. For example, the "pre-closing" section might include all documents relating to the incorporation and organization of a new corporation being established to carry out the deal.

The "post-closing" section might list certain tax election forms or notices of changes in corporate directors which need to be filed with appropriate government authorities. It might also include the filing of articles of amendment to change the name of a corporate party, or the registration of an assignment of intellectual property.

Some closing agendas may be separated into two or more distinct parts, with separate closings for each part, if the deal actually combines two or more transactions which may or may not be conditional on each other. Such separation may occur, for example, when an asset purchase transaction immediately precedes a share purchase transaction, or a purchase transaction is immediately followed by a loan transaction.

Whatever particular form the closing agenda may take, it will likely form the basis for the index or table of contents to appear in the transaction or closing book which will contain all of the documents delivered at the closing and which will be provided to the parties by their legal counsel after the deal closes.

Of the many items ordinarily appearing on a closing agenda, some of the more contentious or aggravating to satisfy are discussed below.

FACILITATING THE BUYER'S FINANCING

The buyer may have obtained the commitment from one or more banks and other lending institutions, venture capital or private equity funds, wealthy individuals or other external sources to provide most of the money the buyer will require in order to complete the purchase.

As discussed in the *Due Diligence* chapter, the seller may therefore have to cooperate with various requests for information from these financing sources when they are investigating the business as part of their assessment of whether or not to provide the buyer with sufficient funds to buy the business.

This need to cooperate continues as the closing approaches, since the buyer's financier may not provide purchase financing unless the seller agrees to let the financier be paid ahead of the purchase price installments which may be owing to the seller after closing. This will often be accomplished by the seller signing a postponement and subordination agreement prepared by the financier's lawyer.

In such an agreement, the seller generally postpones any right to claim payment under the promissory note for an installment if the buyer has failed to repay the financier, and further subordinates any security for the note behind any security given by the buyer to the financier to secure the purchase financing. However, it may also prevent the seller from receiving any installments until the financier has been fully paid off by the buyer.

Although the purchase and sale agreement may provide that the closing is conditional upon the buyer receiving adequate purchase financing and upon the seller delivering a postponement and subordination agreement in favour of the financier, the form of the postponement agreement is rarely attached as a schedule to the purchase agreement. This omission then leaves the seller in the position of having to negotiate the form of the agreement with the financier while knowing that the deal will fail to close if the financier's form is not signed. Depending upon how long the seller is required to postpone receiving any of the installment payments, the negotiations to resolve the specific terms of the agreement with the financier can be difficult, lengthy, and threaten to severely delay the closing.

DISCHARGING MORTGAGES AND LIENS

Besides having to deal with the buyer's financier, the seller will likely have to deal with many of the parties who have financed the business over the years and who may still have various mortgages, liens, security interests and other "encumbrances" against the assets of the business. Whether the transaction is structured for the sale of shares or assets, the seller will often be required to ensure that most or all of the assets of the business are free and clear of all such encumbrances at closing. The purchase and sale agreement will ordinarily contain a representation from the seller to this effect.

Unless the purchase and sale agreement or a schedule to it permits a specific encumbrance to remain outstanding after the deal closes, the seller will therefore be expected to produce on or before closing a discharge or release of that encumbrance. But obtaining such a discharge can involve a time-consuming and sometimes convoluted process, especially when the encumbrance is held by a large, decentralized institution. Not only is a considerable amount of lead-time often required to obtain the required discharges by closing, but requesting such discharges arouses suspicion that a transaction may be imminent and thereby threaten any confidentiality the seller wants to maintain.

The creditors to be approached for discharges may comprise a large and diversified group. They may include leasing companies which provided financing for the motor vehicles, machinery and equipment used in the business, banks which made operating loans, insurance companies which gave long-term mortgages, factoring companies which collected accounts receivable, and suppliers which granted favourable credit terms.

Some of these creditors to be approached may need a written termination of their respective agreements with the business, or payment in full of all amounts they may be owed, before they will be able to provide the required discharges. While repayment may not be a problem for the relatively small amount that may be owed, for example, under a lease for a photocopier, paying off a large bank loan will pose a significant hurdle to the seller who will need the closing proceeds to do so.

This can create a classic "chicken or egg" problem, since the seller cannot close without a discharge, but can't get a discharge without the money payable on closing. A resolution of this problem is often achieved by the willingness of the buyer to close the deal by relying upon a written undertaking of the seller, and possibly the seller's lawyer, to obtain the necessary discharge within a certain period of days or weeks after closing.

Instead of obtaining a discharge from a third party that removes an encumbrance, receiving written confirmation from that party that the encumbrance does not cover the assets being transferred may be acceptable proof to the buyer that the assets are free and clear. Often called an "estoppel" or "acknowledgment" letter, such confirmation is generally used to assure the buyer that an outstanding encumbrance applies only to assets which are being excluded from the deal.

ASSIGNING CONTRACTS

Many closings are delayed because of a failure to obtain the consents necessary to assign specific contracts.

Since many contracts contain a clause which prohibits their assignment and transfer by one party without the written consent of the other party, the seller may face considerable challenges in obtaining the consents of the counterparties to the many contracts which have to be assigned to the buyer on an asset deal. The amount of time required to obtain such consents may depend upon the preparedness of the counterparties to release the seller of any further liabilities under the contracts being assigned.

Some counterparties may only be concerned about the buyer's creditworthiness and ability to pay under the assigned contract after the deal closes. For example, the consent from a lessor under an equipment financing lease or the supplier under a master purchase agreement may be easily obtained if the buyer has a good credit history.

However, other counterparties may be concerned about the buyer's ability to perform quite specific duties which they feel can only be properly performed by the seller. For example, consent to the assignment of a construction contract by a seller who is a builder may not be readily given if the buyer has a reputation for shoddy work within the construction industry and the customer questions the ability of the buyer to complete the building satisfactorily. If the seller is unable to assign that contract, the buyer may still be able to get the benefits under it by acting as subcontractor in its performance and having the seller remit to the buyer any monies received from the customer.

A related problem can arise on a share deal if the contracts of the business can be terminated should there be any change in the ownership of the business. If the counterparties are not concerned about the creditworthiness or business reputation of the buyer, they should be prepared to waive their rights to terminate and allow the contracts to subsist after closing.

OBTAINING GOVERNMENT APPROVALS

Of the many third parties to be approached when attempting to satisfy the closing requirements identified on the closing agenda, certain government agencies may appear to require more time than other parties to produce a particular document. While some documents may consist of licenses, permits or consents which necessitate a comprehensive investigation of the seller or buyer to be carried out by the agency involved, other documents may simply require the written confirmation of information recorded in a government database.

It is often difficult to predict how long it will take to obtain a required government approval. While some approvals may be discretionary so that their receipt cannot be presumed, other approvals can be expected in the ordinary course. If a government approval is expected within a reasonable period of time, the buyer and seller may decide to close the deal in escrow while receipt of the approval is pending.

For those government approvals of a monetary nature which may be delayed, such as those relating to taxes which may be outstanding or arise upon completion of the deal, the parties may agree to close the deal with a portion of the purchase price being held in escrow equal to an estimate of the amount which will be payable to the government when known. Some government agencies may provide their interim consent to such an arrangement by suggesting an appropriate escrow amount to be used to pay the taxes when finally determined.[1]

ORGANIZING THE CLOSING

Once the actions identified on the closing agenda have been taken and the terms of the necessary documents have been settled, the signing and exchanging of the final form of the documents and delivery or transfer of the purchase monies can take place at the closing of the deal. While some deals may be closed with the parties meeting at a common location "face-to-face", other deals may be closed "remotely" with the parties participating from a number of separate locations, and may even be closed through a "virtual deal room" on the Internet.

The more traditional face-to-face closing involves the parties to the transaction sitting around a large boardroom table and signing the various documents identified in the closing agenda one after another, following which certified cheques or bank drafts are delivered, the parties shake hands, and their lawyers then divide up the signed documents for eventual inclusion in the closing or transaction books. The boardroom may be exclusively used for the transaction over a number of days to allow for last minute negotiations and document amendments, and perhaps accommodate a "pre-closing" during which legal counsel for the parties finalize all of the documentation and oversee the execution of a number of documents in advance of the designated closing date.

Instead of meeting face-to-face to close the transaction, the parties may sign the documents in separate locations at their own offices, and then copies of those document pages bearing their signatures are either faxed to the others, or scanned and converted into electronic format and sent to the others by way of e-mail attachment. Funds are delivered by wire transfer or direct deposit, not by certified cheque or bank draft. While these remote closings may be more convenient to the signing parties and easier to schedule than face-to-face closings, they nonetheless entail some risk that the signature pages being transmitted may be mistakenly switched or relate to earlier draft documents, or even worse, bear fraudulent signatures.

As a further alternative, the closing may take place in a virtual deal room, which may be an extension of the secure website which the parties may have used for document reviews during the due diligence stage of the transaction. The documents identified in the closing agenda are made available for review, revision, and eventually, execution, and the completed signature pages can be uploaded to close the deal.

Whether the closing is face-to-face, remote or carried out in a virtual deal room, the parties conduct themselves on the basis that unless otherwise agreed, all documents and funds are to be held in escrow. The escrow is not terminated and the closing is not made final until all of the parties have agreed that the documents are in satisfactory form, and that all acts to be performed at the closing have been properly performed, including the completion of any searches and registration of any transfers of title or security interests.

Although the funds required for closing may have already been wired by bank transfer or delivered by certified cheque to the seller's lawyer before the signed documents have been exchanged, they will continue to be held and not released until everything else has been done to terminate the escrow.

Even though the escrow may be terminated, and the deal regarded as closed, there will probably be a number of post–closing items which will need to be dealt with, as described above. The documents resulting from these post-closing items are often included in the transaction books which are prepared and distributed after the closing. The transaction books, however, are as likely to appear in electronic form as paper form.

Conclusion

This book has attempted to identify some of the steps which a current owner might take when planning to transfer her ownership of a private company, along with the process that she might follow and the documentation that she might use. It has tried to give the owner some idea of what she'll be getting into, so that she'll be better prepared to manage the process.

However, this book has not identified how the owner will actually decide who her successor should be. While it has suggested that the owner may start with her family members first when considering possible successors, preferably on a collaborative basis with them, she may not necessarily consider the various groups discussed in this book in any particular order. Employees, other shareholders, outside parties and family may all have to be considered at the same time, depending upon a number of factors.

The current owner's financial circumstances, health, and desire for some continuing involvement with the business are just a few of the many factors which may favour one possible successor over another. The amount of the purchase price may not be as important a factor as the time it may take to receive the purchase price in full.

If the current owner is prepared to select her successor on the basis of price alone, a business broker as discussed in the *Transfers to Outside Parties* chapter might be retained to generate an auction among a number of interested buyers. Employees, other shareholders, outside parties, even family members, could all be included in a controlled bidding process. While such a process may not be appropriate for many businesses, its relative objectivity and finality may be necessary in certain circumstances.

Whatever criteria the current owner may wish to use in assessing possible candidates as her successor, she may in all likelihood be heavily influenced by her assessment of which candidate is most likely to ensure that the company will grow and prosper so that her hard efforts over, in many cases, a lifetime will continue to be felt by her community. Leaving the company in "good hands" may be just as important a goal to the current owner as closing the sale and relying upon the sale proceeds to provide for her financial security in retirement.

Whichever path the owner follows in pursuing these goals, and with the proper amount of planning, the owner should be able to avoid being forced to sell the company at a discount or, worse still, to lay off all of the employees and liquidate the company's assets in the absence of any of the other preferred alternatives discussed in this book.

Endnotes

Chapter 1 — Introduction

1   R.S.C. 1985, c. C-44.

2   Section 2(1) of the CBCA Regulations defines a "distributing corporation" as a "reporting issuer" under certain provincial securities legislation, or if not a "reporting issuer", a corporation which has filed a prospectus or registration statement, or which has securities listed on a stock exchange, or which has amalgamated or been reorganized with a corporation which has done so.

3   See the definition of "private issuer" in section 2.4(1) of National Instrument 45-106 *Prospectus and Registration Exemption*. The number of shareholders is limited to 50, excluding employees and former employees.

4   See subsections 125(7) and 248(1) of the *Income Tax Act*, R.S.C. 1985, c. 1 (5th Supp.) (the "ITA").

Chapter 2 – Creating a Business Succession Plan

1   See, for example, section 7 of the Ontario *Substitute Decisions Act, 1992*, S.O. 1992, c. 30, which provides for a continuing power of attorney.

2   See, for example, section 22 of the Ontario *Substitute Decisions Act, 1992*.

3   See, for example, section 46 of the Ontario *Substitute Decisions Act, 1992*.

Chapter 3 – Implementing a Business Succession Plan

1   For example, see subsections 34(2) and 36(2) relating to the repurchase and redemption of shares, respectively, and section 42 relating to the payment of dividends, under the CBCA.

2   For example, see the 2004 Literature Survey conducted by Derek Picard at http://cfib.org.

3   For example, see Deans, Thomas William, *Every Family's Business*, 2nd ed. (Orangeville: Détente Financial Press, 2009).

Chapter 5 – Valuation

1   In the context of the ITA, since fair market value is not defined in the ITA, the judicial definition often accepted by the courts in Canada is that of Cattanach J. in *Henderson v. Minister of National Revenue*, 73 D.T.C. 5471, 1973 CarswellNat 189 (Fed. T.D.), affirmed 1975 CarswellNat 189 (Fed. C.A.), which states at page 5476 as follows: "The statute does not define the expression "fair market value", but the expression has been defined in many different ways depending generally on the subject matter which the person seeking to define it had in mind. I do not think it necessary to attempt an exact definition of the expression as used in the statute other than to say that the words must be construed in accordance with the common understanding of them. That common understanding I take to mean the highest price an asset might reasonably be expected to bring if sold by the owner in the normal method applicable to the asset in question in the ordinary course of business in a market not exposed to any undue stresses and composed of willing buyers and sellers dealing at arm's length and under no compulsion to buy or sell. I would add that the foregoing understanding as I have expressed it in a general way includes what I conceive to be the essential element which is an open and unrestricted market in which the price is hammered out between willing and informed buyers and sellers on the anvil of supply and demand.".

2   Subsection 69(1) of the ITA applies to gifts and transfers of property between persons who are not dealing with each other at arm's length. For a gift or sale below fair market value, the current owner is deemed to have disposed of the shares for fair market value regardless of the stipulated purchase price. For a gift or transfer above fair market value, the recipient is deemed to have acquired the shares at fair market value.

3   The owner may have decided to pay less compensation to himself and greater compensation to certain members of his immediate family who pay tax at a lower marginal rate than the owner's own marginal tax rate, thereby allowing the family to collectively pay a lower amount of personal taxes than would be paid by the owner alone.

4   Discretionary cash flows are normally calculated before payments of interest and principal on the company's debt are made, on the assumption that the costs and benefits of financing are incorporated into the discount rate which is applied to the discretionary cash flows.

5   For example, subsection 173(1) of the CBCA provides that an amendment to
     a company's articles requires authorization by a "special resolution", which
     is defined in subsection 2(1) as a resolution passed at a meeting of sharehold-
     ers by at least two-thirds of the votes cast.

Chapter 6 – Reorganization

1   The specific rules for calculating the capital gains deduction for qualified
     small business corporation shares can be found in subsection 110.6(2.1) of
     the ITA.

2   Subsections 70(5) and 70(6) of the ITA deem the owner to have disposed of
     her property immediately prior to her death for proceeds equal to its fair
     market value, subject to possible tax-free rollover treatment for bequests to
     her spouse or common–law partner or a trust established for her spouse or
     common-law partner. The owner's estate therefore becomes liable for any
     unrealized capital gains which have accrued on such property up to the date
     of her death.

3   If the owner has already used her $100,000 ordinary capital gains exemption
     (before it was eliminated in 1994), she will only have a $650,000 capital gains
     exemption available. Her maximum entitlement in any one year can also be
     limited if she has a cumulative net investment loss balance or has previously
     deducted allowable business investment losses.

4   These tests are described in the definition of qualified small business corpo-
     ration shares found in subsection 110.6(1) of the ITA.

5   Subsection 248(1) of the ITA.

6   A specified investment business will include a holding company earning
     rents, interest, royalties and other types of passive property income. The
     exception for personal services businesses prevents "incorporated employ-
     ees" from earning what might otherwise be active business income and then
     claiming a capital gains exemption on the sale of their corporation's shares.

7   A reorganization often relies upon the rollover provisions of section 85 of
     the ITA and upon tax-free inter-corporate dividends permitted under subsec-
     tion 112(1) of the ITA to avoid incurring capital gains on the purification.

8   Subsection 84(3) of the ITA provides that upon a share redemption, the
     shareholder is deemed to have received a dividend equal to the amount by
     which the redemption price exceeds the paid-up capital of the shares re-
     deemed.

9   Although subsection 112(1) of the ITA would ordinarily allow such deemed
     dividends to be received free of tax as intercorporate dividends, the anti

surplus-stripping rules found in subsection 55(2) of the ITA recharacterizes certain receipts as taxable capital gains. Subsection 55(2) can apply where a dividend is received as part of a transaction or series of transactions which result in a significant reduction in the capital gain that would have been realized on the disposition of any share in the absence of the dividend.

10 Section 86 of the ITA allows the owner to exchange all of her shares in the company for new shares and to elect as her adjusted cost base for her shares $750,000 or the amount still available to her under her lifetime capital gains exemption.

11 Section 85 of the ITA allows the owner to transfer her company shares to a holding corporation and elect as her proceeds of disposition an amount which is between her adjusted cost base for the shares and their fair market value.

12 The individual family members need not hold the shares for the required two-year period mentioned above to qualify for the exemption so long as they and the owner have held the shares for a total of at least two years or more. See the definition of "qualified small business corporation share" in paragraph 110.6(1)(b) of the ITA.

13 An alternative to the butterfly reorganization as a means of separating business assets from non-business assets involves the transfer by the company of its business assets to a newly incorporated subsidiary of the company in exchange for fixed value preferred shares of the new subsidiary. New common shares of the subsidiary could then be issued to the owner (or a trust for the benefit of his family). Since the subsidiary has only business assets, its common shares would qualify for the lifetime capital gains exemption once they have been held for the required two-year period. However, this alternative is less than ideal because the transfer of business assets often necessitates the consent of various third parties, such as banks and landlords, and may trigger the application of bulk sales legislation, such as the Ontario *Bulk Sales Act*, R.S.O. 1990, c. B.14, which requires that provision be made for the creditors of the company upon a sale in bulk.

14 The shares may be transferred to the holding corporation without incurring immediate tax by using subsection 85(1) of the ITA.

15 While this approach may reduce the sale price of the company and result in lower capital gains tax payable by the owner, it does not allow the owner to sell her company shares directly and use her capital gains exemption since the shares are owned by the holding corporation.

16 Subsection 83(2) of the ITA allows the company to elect the full amount of a dividend to be a capital dividend to the extent of the company's capital dividend account immediately before the payment of the dividend. The dividends can be in cash or in kind.

Chapter 7 — Transfers to Family — Part I

1 See subsections 70(5) and 70(6) of the ITA which deem the owner to have disposed of his property immediately prior to his death for proceeds equal to its fair market value, thereby making his estate liable for any unrealized capital gains which have accrued on such property up to the date of his death. These gains are subject to possible tax-free rollover treatment for bequests to his spouse or common–law partner or a trust established for his spouse or common-law partner.

2 See subsection 69(1) the ITA which applies to gifts and transfers of property between persons who are not dealing with each other at arm's length. The current owner is deemed to have disposed of the shares for fair market value where there is a gift or sale below fair market value. Where there is a gift or transfer above fair market value, the recipient is deemed to have acquired the shares at fair market value.

3 See note 2 immediately above. To avoid this imbalance between the amount deemed to be received by the owner and the amount paid by the children, the transfer documentation may contain a "price adjustment clause" which states that if the Canada Revenue Agency decides that the fair market value of the shares is greater than the price paid by the children, the price will be retroactively adjusted to the greater value if the parties agree.

4 See subparagraph 40(1)(a)(iii) of the ITA for a definition of an eligible reserve. The 10-year reserve is available under subsection 40(1.1) of the ITA when shares of a small business corporation are sold to a child who is resident in Canada.

5 Outright gifts or transfers below fair market value may also trigger the attribution rules found in subsections 74.1(1) and 74.1(2) and sections 74.2 and 74.3 of the ITA which apply to gifts and transfers of property between family members if the consideration is less than fair market value. They are intended to prevent income and capital gains splitting between spouses and income splitting with related minors. If common shares under the freeze are issued to the owner's spouse, common-law partner or the owner's children who are less than 18 years of age, any distributions made to them under such

shares may be attributed back to the owner and taxed in his hands at his own marginal tax rate.

6   In addition to reducing the amount of tax payable on unrealized capital gains described in note 1, an estate freeze may reduce the amount of estate duties and probate fees by capping the size of the owner's estate.

7   This exchange of common shares for preferred shares is ordinarily accomplished on a tax-free rollover basis under section 51 or 86 of the ITA, which provide that the proceeds of disposition received by a person exchanging shares will be deemed to be equal to the adjusted cost base of the shares so that no capital gain or loss should arise on the share exchange transaction. The preferred shares usually have the following characteristics: (i) they are redeemable at the option of the holder; (ii) they carry voting rights on matters pertaining to such class of shares; (iii) they have a first preference in any distributions of assets on a liquidation, winding-up or dissolution; (iv) they have no restrictions on transferability other than required under corporate law; and (v) they restrict the company from paying dividends on other classes of shares if the company would end up with insufficient assets to redeem the preferred shares. The preferred shares may contain a "price adjustment clause" similar to the clause described in note 3 above in order to address the possibility that the Canada Revenue Agency determines that the fair market value of the company is different from the redemption amount of the preferred shares, so that the redemption amount is retroactively adjusted to avoid any capital gain arising on the freeze.

8   The owner might file an election under section 85 of the ITA designating specific proceeds of disposition and thereby crystallizing all or a portion of the accrued gain on his shares. The amount designated also becomes his cost of the preferred shares received in exchange, so that the "bump" in his cost will result in a smaller taxable capital gain being realized when he later disposes of the preferred shares or when they are deemed to be disposed when he dies.

9   The transfer would be made by special election under section 85 of the ITA.

10 The owner's transfer of his common shares to the holding corporation would likely be accomplished pursuant to section 85 of the ITA on a tax-free rollover basis. So long as the holding corporation is a QSBC, the attribution rules described in note 5 may not apply.

11 See subsection 84(3) of the ITA, which provides for the taxation of the redemption proceeds as a dividend to the extent they exceed the paid-up capital of the shares.

12   See subsection 104(2) of the ITA.

13   However, before distributing any trust property (as opposed to income) to a beneficiary, the trustee should obtain a tax clearance certificate from the Canada Revenue Agency since the trustee is personally liable under subsection 159(3) of the ITA for any unpaid taxes, interest or penalties owing by the trust. However, the trustee's liability is limited to the value of the property distributed to the beneficiaries.

14   If the trust chooses to retain income in the trust for tax purposes and designates an amount for retention under subsection 104(13.1) of the ITA, such amount is not deductible by the trust and is not taxable to the beneficiary.

15   See subsection 69(1) of the ITA.

16   See subsection 75(2) of the ITA.

17   See subsection 73(1) of the ITA.

18   See section 69 of the ITA.

19   See section 104 of the ITA.

20   The distribution to beneficiaries can be accomplished on a tax-deferred basis if the trust qualifies as a "personal trust" as defined in subsection 248(1) of the ITA.

21   See subsection 107(2) of the ITA.

22   There are other ways the owner's children can be provided for differently using a family trust. For example, if the owner is unsure about whether a particular child deserves to have any entitlement as a beneficiary at the time the trust is being set up, that decision may be deferred to a later time by giving the owner a power of appointment to alter the trust's beneficiaries by deed or in his will. A power of appointment can also be used to give the owner the right to alter the proportionate share of each beneficiary under the trust.

23   The comments made in this chapter relating to the application of provincial family law are based upon the Ontario *Family Law Act*, R.S.O. 1990, c. F.3, but similar, though not identical, legislation exists in the other provinces.

24   See subsection 4(2) of the Ontario *Family Law Act*.

Chapter 8 — Transfers to Family — Part II

1   Should the owner decide not to have a will and she dies "intestate" or without a will, her shares in the company and the rest of her property will be dealt with in accordance with applicable provincial law. For example, in Ontario, the *Succession Law Reform Act*, R.S.O. 1990, c. S.26 (the "SLRA") will govern her estate and the disposition of her assets. In the absence of her will, her

immediate next-of-kin will ordinarily initiate legal proceedings upon her death to appoint an administrator of her estate, although the appointment may be challenged by others. Upon the court's appointment of the administrator, sections 44 to 47 of the SLRA provide that all of the owner's estate will be transferred to her spouse if still alive, provided there are no surviving children. If the owner dies with a spouse and one or more children surviving, the spouse will receive the first $200,000 of the estate and the balance will be divided up equally between the spouse and child, where there is just one child, and one-third to the spouse and the remainder equally to the children if there is more than one child.

2   The owner may prefer to prepare the will herself without the assistance of a lawyer, using various "self-help" guides or "will kits" which are generally available, although her will still has to meet the general legal requirements described in this chapter for a valid will.

3   R.S.O. 1990, c. F.3.

4   See note 1 above.

5   See section 58 of the SLRA.

6   See section 62 of the SLRA.

7   Under the Ontario *Family Law Act*, a spouse's "equalization" entitlement is determined by first calculating each spouse's "net family property", which is essentially a measure of the increase in a spouse's net worth during the marital relationship, and then calculating one-half of the amount by which the deceased spouse's net family property exceeds the surviving spouse's net family property. However, a court is given the discretion, under subsection 5(6) of that Act, to order an equalization payment which is less or more than one-half the difference between the spouses' respective net family properties if an equal division of net family properties would be unconscionable. The surviving spouse's equalization claim is calculated based upon the asset values on the date of death.

8   Ordinarily inheritances received by a spouse during marriage are excluded from the calculation of net family property of the recipient spouse. Even income derived from such property may be excluded if the deceased provided in her will for such exclusion. However, if the property is inherited by a child prior to marriage, and in the absence of a marriage contract to the contrary, it will be included in the calculation of the child's net family property although its value at the date of the child's marriage will be deducted. In order to avoid such an equalization claim by a child's spouse, the owner may prefer to establish a discretionary trust in her will for the child instead of

making an outright bequest of the property. Even though property inherited during a marriage is excluded from the child's net family property, it may still be vulnerable to an equalization claim because its value may have to be used to satisfy the claim if the child's other assets are insufficient to do so.

9 In Ontario, estate administration tax is payable under the *Estate Administration Tax Act, 1998*, S.O. 1998, c. 34, Sched. The tax payable by the estate trustee is calculated at a rate of $5 per $1000 for the first $50,000 of estate value, and $15 per $1,000 for the value of the estate in excess of $50,000.

10 As with other transfers to family members discussed in the previous chapter, the half-interest in her shares transferred to her child as a joint owner will be deemed to be disposed at fair market value and taxed accordingly.

11 See *Pecore v. Pecore*, [2007] 1 S.C.R.795 and *Saylor v. Madsen Estate*, [2007] 1 S.C.R. 838, decisions of the Supreme Court of Canada which considered a bank account opened by an elderly father jointly with his adult daughter with a right of survivorship, and questioned whether each daughter should be presumed to either have received a gift from the father or was holding the account in trust for the father. In *Pecore*, the daughter was allowed to keep the joint account proceeds upon her father's death, but in *Saylor*, the daughter was required to divide the joint account proceeds in accordance with her deceased's father's will. These decisions confirm that the "presumption of resulting trust" will be favoured over the "presumption of advancement" or gift, and that the onus of proving a gratuitous transfer of money, shares or other property was a gift will be on the family member receiving the property. A gift may be presumed, however, in dependency-based relationships, as may exist between a parent and minor child.

12 See subsections 73(1.01) and (1.02) of the ITA.

13 An alternative to an alter ego trust is a self-benefit trust, which is similar to an alter ego trust but the individual creating it does not have to be 65. However, no other person may have an absolute or contingent right to any of the trust property, and probate fees can only be avoided in relatively narrow circumstances, where for example the creator of the trust is the sole income and capital beneficiary of the trust while alive but upon death, the capital is to be transferred under a general power of appointment exercised by someone named in the creator's will. A self-benefit trust is often established as a "blind" trust used by politicians and others to avoid potential conflicts of interest.

14 Because alter-ego and joint partner trusts are inter vivos trusts, they are taxed at the top rate of tax and not at the graduated rates available to testamentary trusts.

15 See subsections 70(5) and 70(6) of the ITA. The "rollover" to the surviving spouse under which the surviving spouse acquires the transferred capital property at the deceased's tax cost can eventually result in a capital gain covering the period of ownership of both the deceased and the surviving spouse, which is taken into income when the surviving spouse either disposes of the property by sale or is deemed to have disposed of it by death. A qualifying spousal trust is similarly deemed to have disposed of the property upon the death of the spouse. In order to achieve a rollover to a spousal trust, the spouse must be entitled to receive all of the income of the trust that arises before the spouse's death, and no one other than the spouse may receive any of the income or capital of the trust during the spouse's lifetime. This latter requirement is not met, and the rollover cannot be achieved, if the terms of the spousal trust provide for the payment of the trust property to a third party in the event that the surviving spouse remarries. An exception to this latter requirement is provided in subsection 108(4) of the ITA which allows for the payment of estate or income taxes with respect to the trust property. A further exception allows for the payment of debts using part of the spousal trust property provided that such property is disposed of at fair market value, with the remaining assets being eligible for the rollover.

16 Subsection 164(6) of the ITA provides an exception to this principle by allowing the estate to transfer its capital losses and terminal losses incurred by it during its first taxation year against the deceased's income in the year of death.

17 See subsection 150(3) of the ITA.

18 A trust's residence may not always be determined by the residence of its trustees, as held by the Supreme Court of Canada in *Fundy Settlement v. Canada*, 2012 SCC 14, [2002] 1 S.C.R. which decided that a trust is resident in the country where the central management and control is exercised.

19 See subsection 20(2) of the SLRA.

20 See section 23 of the SLRA.

21 See section 31 of the SLRA.

22 Absent any specific investment authority in the will, the authority provided in the *Trustee Act*, R.S.O. 1990, c. T. 23 will cover a will governed by Ontario law.

23 Reinvestment of excess income of a trust may be restricted. For example, under section 1 of the Ontario *Accumulations Act*, R.S.O. 1990, c. A.5, the trustees under a will may not be directed to reinvest income for a period extending beyond the 21st anniversary of the testator's death. To avoid the

possible application of this restriction, the will may direct the trustees to pay out to the beneficiary, in each year following the maximum period allowed by law for accumulation, all of the net income derived in that year.

24 For example, the traditional common law rule against perpetuities which prohibited the "remote" vesting of property interests beyond a "perpetuity period" continues in modified form. Section 4 of the Ontario *Perpetuities Act*, R.S.O. 1990, c.P.9 adopts a "wait and see" approach by making a gift in a will "presumptively valid" until actual events determine that the gift is incapable of vesting. The perpetuity period applicable to a will commences on the death of the testator and ends on the 21st anniversary of the date of death of the last "life in being" at the beginning of the period. This rule is likely to be inadvertently breached when the will provides for successive interests, such as to children and grandchildren, with the vesting of each being postponed for more than 21 years.

25 The common law rule contained in *Saunders v. Vautier* [1841] EWHC Ch J82 provides that when all of the beneficiaries of a trust have reached the age of majority, they may collectively demand that the trust property be distributed to them, even though the trustees have been directed to hold the property in trust until a specified later date or event. Furthermore, in addition to property being held in trust for a class of beneficiaries, an absolute gift to one beneficiary which is to be held in trust until a later time can be demanded by that beneficiary upon reaching the age of majority. To avoid this possibility, the will may subject the gift to a condition, thereby making it a conditional as opposed to absolute gift.

26 See section 54 of the ITA.

27 See section 4 of the SLRA.

28 See section 12 of the SLRA.

29 See section 6 of the SLRA.

30 When the shares are purchased or redeemed from the estate, the estate will be deemed to have received a dividend pursuant to subsection 84(3) of the ITA equal to the redemption proceeds less the paid up capital of the shares. However, because the death benefit received by the company under the policy will be added to the capital dividend account of the company, and because the company may elect to have the deemed dividend treated as a capital dividend under subsection 83(2) of the ITA, the proceeds are received by the estate without any tax.

Chapter 9 — Transfers to Employees

1   If an employee acquires his shares by exercising stock options granted by the company, subsection 7(3) of the ITA provides that no taxable benefit is recognized when a stock option is granted. A benefit is recognized under paragraph 7(1)(a) of the ITA when the option is exercised, unless the company is a Canadian-controlled private corporation, or CCPC, dealing at arm's length from the employee, in which case the taxable benefit will be included in the employee's income only when the employee disposes of the shares. On disposing of the shares, the difference between the exercise price of the options and the fair market value of the shares at the date the options are exercised will be taxed as employment income. Any increase in the value of the shares from the date they are acquired will be taxed as a capital gain when they are disposed of. If the shares are held for two years, the employee benefit will be reduced by half, and the shares will then qualify for the $750,000 lifetime capital gains exemption. If the company is not a CCPC, upon the exercise of the option, the employee is taxed on the difference between the fair market value of the shares at that time and the exercise price of the option, whether or not the employee sells the shares, although a deferral of the benefit may be possible under subsections 7(8) to 7(16) of the ITA. Furthermore, under paragraphs 110(d) or (d.1) of the ITA, an offsetting deduction of one-half of the benefit may be available. The benefit will usually be added to the employee's cost base of the shares under paragraph 53(1)(j) of the ITA. Because of subsection 143.3(2) of the ITA, stock options are not deductible by the company. If the company lends money to the employee to buy the shares, subsection 15(2.4) of the ITA will exclude the loan from being a taxable benefit if, among other things, the employee pays interest at prevailing market rates.

2   Subsections 7(2) and 7(6) of the ITA set out the specific rules for employee trusts.

3   If the owner transfers his shares to a corporation owned by the employees, but the employees are also members of the owner's family, the capital gain may be treated instead as a dividend under section 84.1 of the ITA which will not be sheltered from tax using his lifetime capital gains exemption.

4   Subsection 84(3) of the ITA provides that a share repurchase by a corporation entails a deemed dividend to the seller of the shares for the amount paid in excess of the paid up capital on those shares. Because the amount is treated as a dividend and not as a capital gain, the amount cannot be included in the

taxpayer's lifetime capital gains exemption. Section 54 of the ITA in defining "proceeds of disposition" excludes in subparagraph (j) "any amount that would otherwise be proceeds of disposition of a share to the extent that the amount is deemed by subsection 84(2) or (3) to be a dividend received and is not deemed by paragraph 55(2)(a) or subparagraph 88(2)(b)(ii) not to be a dividend".

5   Subparagraph 40(1)(a)(iii) of the ITA defines an eligible reserve.

Chapter 10 — Transfers to Other Shareholders

1   Subsection 84(3) of the ITA provides that a share repurchase by a corporation entails a deemed dividend to the seller of the shares for the amount paid in excess of the paid up capital on those shares. Because the amount is treated as a dividend and not as a capital gain, the amount cannot be included in the taxpayer's lifetime capital gains exemption. Section 54 of the ITA in defining "proceeds of disposition" excludes in subparagraph (j) "any amount that would otherwise be proceeds of disposition of a share to the extent that the amount is deemed by subsection 84(2) or (3) to be a dividend received and is not deemed by paragraph 55(2)(a) or subparagraph 88(2)(b)(ii) not to be a dividend".

2   For example, subsection 34(2) of the CBCA prohibits the payment by a corporation to purchase any of its shares if the corporation would after the payment be unable to pay its liabilities after they become due, or the realizable value of its assets would after the payment be less than the aggregate of its liabilities and the stated capital of all classes. Subsection 36(2) of the CBCA prohibits the payment by a corporation to purchase or redeem any of its redeemable shares if the corporation would after the payment be unable to pay its liabilities after they become due, or the realizable value of its assets would after the payment be less than the aggregate of its liabilities and the amount that would be required to pay the holders of its shares that have a right to be paid, on a redemption or in a liquidation, rateably with or before the holders of the shares to be purchased or redeemed, to the extent that the amount has not been included in its liabilities.

3   The definition of an eligible reserve is found at subparagraph 40(1)(a)(iii) of the ITA.

4   Section 84.1 of the ITA may apply if the owner disposes of her shares to another corporation with which she does not deal at arm's length. She will realize a deemed dividend to the extent that the non-share consideration paid

(such as cash or a promissory note) exceeds the greater of the paid-up capital or adjusted cost base of her shares. Her capital gain will therefore be converted into a dividend which cannot be sheltered under her lifetime capital gains exemption. Under subsection 251(1) of the ITA, related persons are deemed not to deal at arm's length.

Chapter 11 — Transfers to Outside Parties

1   Section 68 of the ITA allows the buyer and seller to elect what amount of the overall purchase price is to be allocated to specific classes of the assets being purchased. In an effort to minimize their respective tax liabilities resulting from the deal, the buyer and seller will attempt to allocate the purchase price amongst the various asset categories, while recognizing that a high value allocated to a particular category may be advantageous to one party and disadvantageous to the other. While the seller may be concerned about the tax implications of such values for the year of the sale, the buyer may be more concerned about the tax implications for those years following the sale and the extent of various deductions then available. For example, a high value allocated to depreciable property may provide the buyer with greater deductions for capital cost allowance in subsequent years, but may trigger a recapture of capital cost allowance for the seller in the year of the sale. The buyer may prefer to allocate high values to inventory, whereas the seller may prefer to allocate high values to non-depreciable capital property. Although the Canada Revenue Agency may be entitled to reallocate the purchase price among all of the purchased assets pursuant to section 68 if it deems the allocations made by the parties to be unreasonable, the allocations negotiated between arm's length parties are generally upheld. A special election is available to the buyer and seller under section 22 of the ITA regarding accounts receivable. They may jointly elect what value is to be allocated to the seller's accounts receivable in order to reduce the amount of tax which might otherwise be paid by the seller if the face amount of the receivables was taken into the seller's income. A purchase price allocation to receivables which is for less than their face value creates a loss for the seller which can be deducted from the seller's income, but which is included in the buyer's income.

2   Subsections 13(1) and 39(1) of the ITA.

3   Subsection 111(1) of the ITA.

Chapter 12 — Family Trust Agreements

1   The transfer of property to a trust constitutes a "disposition" as defined in subsection 248(1) of the ITA and, as described earlier, the "proceeds of disposition" arising from the transfer are deemed to be equal to the fair market value of the property regardless of whether the disposition is by way of a gift, a transfer for no proceeds, or a transfer for less than fair market value.

2   See generally sections 74.1 to 74.4, and subsections 75(2) and 107(4.1) of the ITA.

3   Under subsection 74.3(1) of the ITA, where an individual has transferred property to a trust in which a "designated person" is a beneficiary, any income or loss from the property, as well as any capital gains arising from the property if the designated person is a spouse of the individual, which would be included in computing the income of the beneficiary upon a distribution from the trust to the beneficiary, will be included in the income of the individual who transferred the property. A designated person includes a spouse or common-law partner, minor nieces and nephews, and any minor (under 18 years of age) who does not deal at arm's length with that individual.

4   See subsection 75(2) of the ITA, an attribution rule which applies when a person exercises some control over the property transferred to a trust or retains a certain type of interest. This subsection will apply when property is held by the trust on the condition that it will revert to the person who transferred it to the trust or to another party later designated by that person, or that it will not be disposed of unless that person consents. In order to avoid the possible application of this attribution rule, any person who contributes property to a trust, whether or not the settlor, should not be a capital beneficiary of the trust.

5   Although subsection 75(2) of the ITA may appear to have little practical impact on the choice of a settlor if the initial settled property such as a single coin will not generate any income, its impact can be increased by the application of subsection 107(4.1) of the ITA. Ordinarily a distribution of trust capital to a capital beneficiary is accomplished under subsection 107(2) of the ITA on a tax-deferred basis, with no resulting income or capital gain to the trust. However, subsection 107(4.1) provides that when subsection 75(2) applies to any trust property, the trust will not be able to distribute any of the trust property to a beneficiary on a tax-deferred basis other than to the person from whom the property was received (or her spouse). The trust is then deemed to have disposed of the property at fair market value. Consequently, if the settlor contributes just a nominal amount to the trust yet

reserves some of the powers described in subsection 75(2) as a trustee, subsection 107(4.1) could apply to every asset of the trust. Therefore, having the settlor as a trustee or beneficiary of the trust can have negative tax implications regardless of the item or amount initially contributed by the settlor.to the trust.

6   See, for example, the Ontario *Trustee Act.*

7   See subsection 2(1) of the ITA and Interpretation Bulletin IT-447 regarding the determination of the residence of a trust, and subsection 128.1(4) of the ITA regarding the deemed disposition of a trust's property upon ceasing to be resident in Canada. However, a trust's residence may not always be determined by the residence of its trustees. The Supreme Court of Canada in *Fund Settlement v. Canada*, referenced in note 18 of Chapter 8, held that a trust is resident in the country where the central management and control is exercised.

8   To avoid the application of subsections 75(2) and 107(4.1) of the ITA discussed above, neither the settlor nor any other person who has transferred property to the trust should be a capital beneficiary, although they may be an income beneficiary.

9   See Mark Gillen, Lionel Smith and Donovan W. M. Waters, *Waters Law of Trusts in Ca*nada, 3ʳᵈ ed. (Toronto: Carswell, 2005), at pages 966 – 967.

10   See note 9, at page 788.

11   Payments by the trustees to minor beneficiaries of certain types of income may give rise to what is commonly referred to as "kiddie tax". Under section 120.4 of the ITA, where a trust receives dividends from a private company, or rent or business income earned from a property or business carried on by a person related to the minor beneficiaries, and an attempt is made to have that income taxed in the hands of the minor beneficiaries, the kiddie tax rules require the minors to pay tax on that income at the highest marginal tax rate. However, the kiddie tax does not apply to "second generation" income, or income on income, and the trust may receive income subject to the tax and reinvest it instead.

12   For example, subsection 27(1) of the Ontario *Trustee Act* requires the trustees to exercise the care, skill, diligence and judgment that a prudent investor would exercise in making investments, thereby enabling them to view the trust fund as an entire portfolio rather than as a number of individual, permitted investments. They must, however, consider the seven criteria set out in subsection 27(5) when making investment decisions, and must, under subsection 27(6), diversify the investment of the trust property to the extent

it is appropriate to the needs of the trust and to the general economic and investment market conditions.

13   For example, sections 67 and 68 of the Ontario *Trustee Act* allow the terms of the trust agreement to override any provision of the *Trustee Act.*

14   The duty of trustees to diversify trust investments has been made a statutory obligation. For example, under the Ontario *Trustee Act*, subsection 27(6) requires a trustee to act as a prudent investor.

15   The power of the trustees to delegate the investment of the trust fund to an "agent" is subject to certain restrictions under section 27.1 of the Ontario *Trustee Act.*

16   The implications of having the settlor serve as a trustee and the possible application of subsection 75(2) of the ITA are discussed in notes 4 and 5 above.

17   See *Gisborne v. Gisborne* (1877), (1876-77) L.R. 2 App. Cas. 300 (U.K. H.L.).

18   See *Fox v. Fox Estate*, 28 O.R. (3d) 496, 1996 CarswellOnt 317 (Ont. C.A.), leave to appeal refused (1996), 207 N.R. 80 (note) (S.C.C.).

19   See *Smith, Re*, [1971] 2 O.R. 541, 1971 CarswellOnt 629 (Ont. C.A.).

20   See *Sayers v. Philip*, 38 D.L.R. (3d) 602, 1973 CarswellSask 198 (Sask. C.A.).

21   See section 104 of the ITA.

22   See, for example, the Ontario *Perpetuities Act*, R.S.O. 1990, c. P.9, which prescribes a perpetuity period of 21 years from the death of the last relevant life in being.

23   For example, Ontario trusts are governed by the Ontario *Trustee Act.*

24   See note 9, at page 852.

25   See subsection 122(1) of the CBCA.

26   Agreements to fetter the discretion of company directors have traditionally not been permitted under common law. See for example *Motherwell v. Schoof*, [1949] 4 D.L.R. 812, 1949 CarswellAlta 50 (Alta. T.D.) and *Ringuet v. Bergeron*, [1960] S.C.R. 672, 24 D.L.R. (2d) 449, 1960 CarswellQue 46 (S.C.C.). For those individuals who are both trustees and directors, exercising their discretion as fully as corporate law permits may make them liable for breach of trust under trust law. Fortunately for them, the courts have held that the beneficiaries do not have a right to call on the directors to use their powers as directors as if they hold them in trust for the beneficiaries. See the leading English case of *Butt v. Kelson* (1951), [1952] 1 Ch. 197 (Eng. C.A.).

27   See *Lindholm v. Lindholm*, 2000 CarswellBC 322, 76 B.C.L.R. (3d) 167, 4 R.F.L. (5th) 356, [2000] B.C.J. No. 312 (B.C. S.C.).

28   See section 42 and paragraph 115(3)(d) of the CBCA.

29 The form rule was set out by the Privy Council in *Hill v. Permanent Trustee Co. of New South Wales*, [1930] All E.R. Rep. 87 (New South Wales P.C.), and has been applied by the Supreme Court of Canada in *Hardy Trusts, Re*, 4 D.L.R. (2d) 721, 1956 CarswellOnt 50 (S.C.C.) and *Waters, Re*, 4 D.L.R. (2d) 673, 1956 CarswellOnt 49 (S.C.C.).

30 See subsection 189(1) of the CBCA.

31 The amount of the bonuses to be paid in a closely-held company is often made equal to the amount needed to reduce the company's income to the "business limit" which allows the company to qualify for the small business deduction under section 125 of the ITA.

32 This duty to account to the trust for director fees was addressed in *Re Macadam* (1945), [1945] 2 All ER 664, [1946] Ch. 73 (Eng. Ch. Div.).

33 See the definition of "beneficial ownership" in subsection 2(1) of the CBCA which includes ownership through a trustee, legal representative, agent or other intermediary, and the definition of "complainant" in section 238 of the CBCA which includes a registered or beneficial owner of the security of a corporation.

34 Section 241 of the CBCA.

35 See *The Canadian Oppression Remedy Judicially Considered: 1995-2001* (2004) 30 Queen's L.J., a survey of the oppression remedy conducted by Professors Ben-Ishai and Puri which includes the results of a second study for the period December 2001 to February 2004. Of the 71 cases considered in their first study, 92% dealt with private, closely-held companies. The authors observed, at page 89, that the majority of the successful oppression actions in the period of the first study involved the diversion of corporate profits, personal use of corporate profits by those controlling the corporation, the exclusion of the applicant from the operations of the corporation, or the alteration of proportional shareholdings. The remedy most often granted was a share purchase, usually in the context of a closely-held corporation where the shareholders lost confidence in each other and could not continue to work together.

36 See *Sutherland v. Birks*, 65 O.R. (3d) 812, 2003 CarswellOnt 2733 (Ont. C.A.), additional reasons 2003 CarswellOnt 3524 (Ont. C.A.), leave to appeal refused 2004 CarswellOnt 1317, 2004 CarswellOnt 1318 (S.C.C.) and *Cohen v. Jonco Holdings Ltd.*, 2005 MBCA 48, 2005 CarswellMan 131 (Man. C.A.).

Chapter 13 — Shareholder Agreements

1   Subsection 146(10) of the CBCA.

2   See for example *Motherwell v. Schoof*, [1949] 4 D.L.R. 812 (Alta. T.D.) and *Ringuet v. Bergeron*, [1960] S.C.R. 672, 24 D.L.R. (2d) 449 (S.C.C.).

3   Subsection 102(1) of the CBCA.

4   See *Duha Printers (Western) Ltd. v. R.*, [1998] 1 S.C.R. 795 (S.C.C.) .

5   Subsection 146(1) of the CBCA.

6   Subsection 6(3) of the CBCA.

7   Paragraph 49(8)(c) of the CBCA.

8   Subsection 146(2) of the CBCA.

9   Subsection 146(5) of the CBCA.

10 Section 119 of the CBCA.

11 Paragraph 122(1)(a) of the CBCA.

12 Subsection 84(3) of the ITA provides that a share repurchase by a corporation entails a deemed dividend to the seller of the shares for the amount paid in excess of the paid up capital on those shares. Because the amount is treated as a dividend and not as a capital gain, the amount cannot be included in the taxpayer's lifetime capital gains exemption. Section 54 of the ITA in defining "proceeds of disposition" excludes in subparagraph (j) "any amount that would otherwise be proceeds of disposition of a share to the extent that the amount is deemed by subsection 84(2) or (3) to be a dividend received and is not deemed by paragraph 55(2)(a) or subparagraph 88(2)(b)(ii) not to be a dividend".

13 See subsections 34(2) and 36(2) of the CBCA.

14 See *Elsley v. J.G. Collins Insurance Agencies Ltd.*, [1978] 2 S.C.R. 916, *H.L. Staebler Company Ltd. v. Allan* (2008), 92 O.R. (3d) 107 (C.A.), and *Shafron v. KRG Insurance Brokers (Western) Inc.*, 2009 SCC 6.

Chapter 14 — Confidentiality Agreements

1   For example, the decision in *Martel Building Ltd. v. Canada* [2000], 2 S.C.R. 860, 2000 SCC 20.

Chapter 15 — Letters of Intent

1   For example, subsection 4 (1) of the Ontario *Bulk Sales Act*, R.S.O. 1990, c. B 14, requires a seller in a bulk sale to provide the buyer with a sworn statement listing the amount of the seller's debts to each of the seller's secured and unsecured creditors. Upon delivery of the sworn statement, the buyer

may then elect under subsection 8 (1) to pay the sale proceeds to the seller if the seller has also sworn that all of the creditors have been paid in full or if the seller has made provision for payment of all of the creditors immediately after the closing except for those creditors waiving their rights to immediate payment.

2   For example, subsection 9(1) of the Ontario *Employment Standards Act, 2000*, S.O. 2000, c.41 and subsection 69(2) of the Ontario *Labour Relations Act*, S.O. 1995, c. 1, Sched. A., impose certain obligations of the seller towards employees upon the purchaser of a business as a successor employer.

3   See, for example, the decision in *Peel Condominium Corp. No. 505 v. Cam-Valley Homes Ltd.*, (2001) 53 O.R. (3d) (C.A.).

Chapter 17 — Purchase and Sale Agreements

1   Amounts paid under an earnout can be fully taxed as amounts "dependent on the use of or production from property" pursuant to paragraph 12(1)(g) of the ITA. However, the Canada Revenue Agency pursuant to IT-426R permits use of the cost recovery method to treat such amounts as capital gains. If the seller is a Canadian resident and the earnout doesn't last longer than 5 years, the seller's adjusted cost base of the purchased shares can be reduced when the amounts payable under the earnout are determinable, and once the cost base is reduced to zero, any amounts subsequently determinable are then treated as capital gains.

2   See subsections 13(1) and 39(1) of the ITA.

3   See section 68 of the ITA and note 1 under the *Transfers to Outside Parties* chapter.

4   See subsection 167(1) of the *Excise Tax Act*, R.S.C. 1985, c. E-15. "Substantially all" is defined to be 90%. The election may be filed using form GST 44.

5   Since it is important that the parties be GST registrants, the asset purchase agreement should contain warranties of both the seller and buyer regarding their respective GST registration numbers. An Internet-based GST registry operated by the Canada Revenue Agency allows each party to confirm that the other party is registered for GST and whether the GST number provided by that party is valid. Should a seller fail to collect and remit any GST payable while relying on the buyer to do so, only to learn after closing that the buyer was not registered despite the buyer's warranty to the contrary, the seller will not be able to escape liability for the GST despite the buyer's misrepresentation. This was the result of the decision of the Tax Court of Canada in

Lee Hutton Kaye Maloff & Paul Henriksen v. Canada [2004] T.C.J. No. 429 (QL).

6   See section 22 of the ITA. The election may be filed using form T2022.

7   For example, if the agreement is governed by Ontario law, the parties will consider Ontario's *Limitations Act, 2002*, S.O. 2002, c. 24, Sched. B, which provides that business agreements between parties who are not "consumers" (as defined in Ontario's *Consumer Protection Act, 2002*, S.O. 2002, c. 30, Sched. A) may vary or exclude a basic limitation period, and may vary an ultimate limitation period provided that it may be suspended or extended only if the relevant claim has been discovered.

8   For example, approval to proceed may be required for larger transactions under the *Investment Canada Act* , R.S.C. 1985, c. 28 (1st Supp.) or *Competition Act*, R.S.C. 1985, c. C-34 and any waiver by the parties of conditions for obtaining such approvals would not ordinarily be permitted.

Chapter 18 — Closing the Deal

1   For example, section 6 of the Ontario *Retail Sales Tax Act*, R.S.O. 1990, c. R.31 requires that a certificate be obtained from the Ontario Minister of Finance before a "sale in bulk" can be completed. A practice has developed that such a certificate will be issued on the undertaking of the seller's lawyer to retain a specified amount in escrow from the purchase monies received.

Index